ROBERT ALLERTON

The Private Man and the Public Gifts

By

Martha Burgin and Maureen Holtz

With new photography by Michael Holtz

Adaptation of Robert Allerton's logo for The Farms,
possibly designed by John Wyatt Gregg Allerton.

EDITOR AND PUBLISHER John Foreman
PROJECT EDITOR Amy George
ART DIRECTOR Joan Millis

Cover design and book layout: Joan Millis, The News-Gazette
Soft cover ISBN: 978-0-9798420-7-8

First edition originally published in softcover by The News-Gazette, Inc., 2009

Printed in the United States of America

The News-Gazette, Inc.
15 Main Street
Champaign, IL 61820
Phone: (217) 351-5252
Fax: (217) 351-5245
www.news-gazette.com

CONTENTS

ABOUT THE AUTHORS

Martha (Marty) Burgin, like Robert Allerton, realized after completing her formal art studies that she was not destined to become a painter. Allerton chose farming as an official profession; Marty launched a thirty-year career as a biomedical graphic designer. Having illustrated several textbooks, in 2002 she retired from the University of Texas Southwestern Medical Center at Dallas and returned to her hometown of Monticello, Illinois. Coauthoring this book brings her full circle. Her childhood explorations of Allerton Park inspired her to become an artist, and exploring the life and times of Robert Allerton helped her translate those skills to writing.

Maureen Holtz and her husband Michael moved to Monticello in 1991 and have spent many happy hours exploring and enjoying Allerton Park. She retired from the computer industry in 2004 and since then, has focused on her first love—writing. After penning a lighthearted novel (about the computer industry) that is still seeking a publisher, she turned her attention to Robert Allerton. The love of words and reading, history, and travel rule her life. She thanks her parents for insisting that the family visit the library every Friday evening to get a week's worth of books.

Preface and Acknowledgements

One sculpture was never enough for Robert Allerton, if he could find a matched pair. And true to that requirement, it took two of us to write his biography. We hope our two viewpoints, like stereoscopic lenses, have focused to create the illusion of a three-dimensional Robert Allerton. Our partnership put words on the pages, but our reconstruction of Robert is composed of myriad glimpses through the eyes of those who knew him and studied what he left behind. We thank each of those people, and those who helped in other ways to bring Robert Allerton back to life.

First, we thank our publisher, Champaign, Illinois' *The News-Gazette*. Marketing Director Amy George and Publisher and Editor John Foreman appreciated the merit of our proposal and took a risk on two new writers. To our even greater fortune, they teamed us with their skilled designer Joan Millis.

University of Illinois Director of Allerton Park and Retreat Center Jim Gortner and Director of Marketing and Communications Jessica Hampson championed our work from the start. We thank Jessica, along with Chris Hermann and Hilary Holbrook, for their assistance and contributions to our Epilogue. Former Allerton Park directors David Bowman and Jerrold Soesbe shared their insights, and archive volunteer Connie Fairchild's diligent work over the years provided us a well-organized starting point for our research. Delphine M. Kranz, Associate Director of the Office of Technology Management, helped smooth the way for publication.

Elaine Palencia-Fowler offered welcomed editing suggestions, and The Red Herring Writers Workshop critique group provided willing ears as the writing progressed.

Monticello residents with first-hand accounts of Robert Allerton shared their stories. We thank Ecus Vaughn, the late Myrlin Buckingham, the late Pauline Shonkwiler, Juanita Gale, and the late Donn Piatt.

William Tyre, of Glessner House Museum in Chicago, completed the landscape of Robert's early life on Prairie Avenue. Rick Hanna, librarian of the National Tropical Botanical Garden in Hawaii, shared his knowledge about Robert's and John's later years at Lawai-Kai.

Descendants of the Allerton and Gregg families, Sean Johnstone and Jane Schowalter, filled many gaps in our understanding of Robert's sister, Kate Allerton Johnstone, and John Wyatt Gregg Allerton. Elisabeth Bartlett Sturges, J. Kent Planck, and the staff at Bonnet House in Fort Lauderdale provided background information about Robert's lifelong friend, Frederic Clay Bartlett. We are especially grateful for the generosity of Brooklyn artist Ellen E. Rand (granddaughter of the artist who was Robert's dear friend) for sharing recently discovered correspondence between Robert Allerton and her grandmother.

We thank the staff of the University of Illinois Library archives, and the staff of Monticello's Allerton Public Library for capably and cheerfully handling our many requests.

Several biographers and historians graciously answered our specific questions: Valerie Langfield (on Roger Quilter), Paul Delaney (on Glyn Warren Philpot), and David Levesque (on St. Paul's School). We also owe much to the scholarship of previous Allerton researchers: Dr. Muriel Scheinman, Anthony Rubano, Scott Mehaffey, Dr. Lachlan F. Blair, Georgia Soruika Evans, Nancy Becker Hahn and the late Dr. Etta Arntzen.

We thank Maureen's husband, Michael Holtz, for his beautiful new photographs, and Marty's parents for words of wisdom. Our families and friends have shared our dreams and discoveries. Most of all, the authors thank each other for her patience and persistence. It was worth every rewritten word.

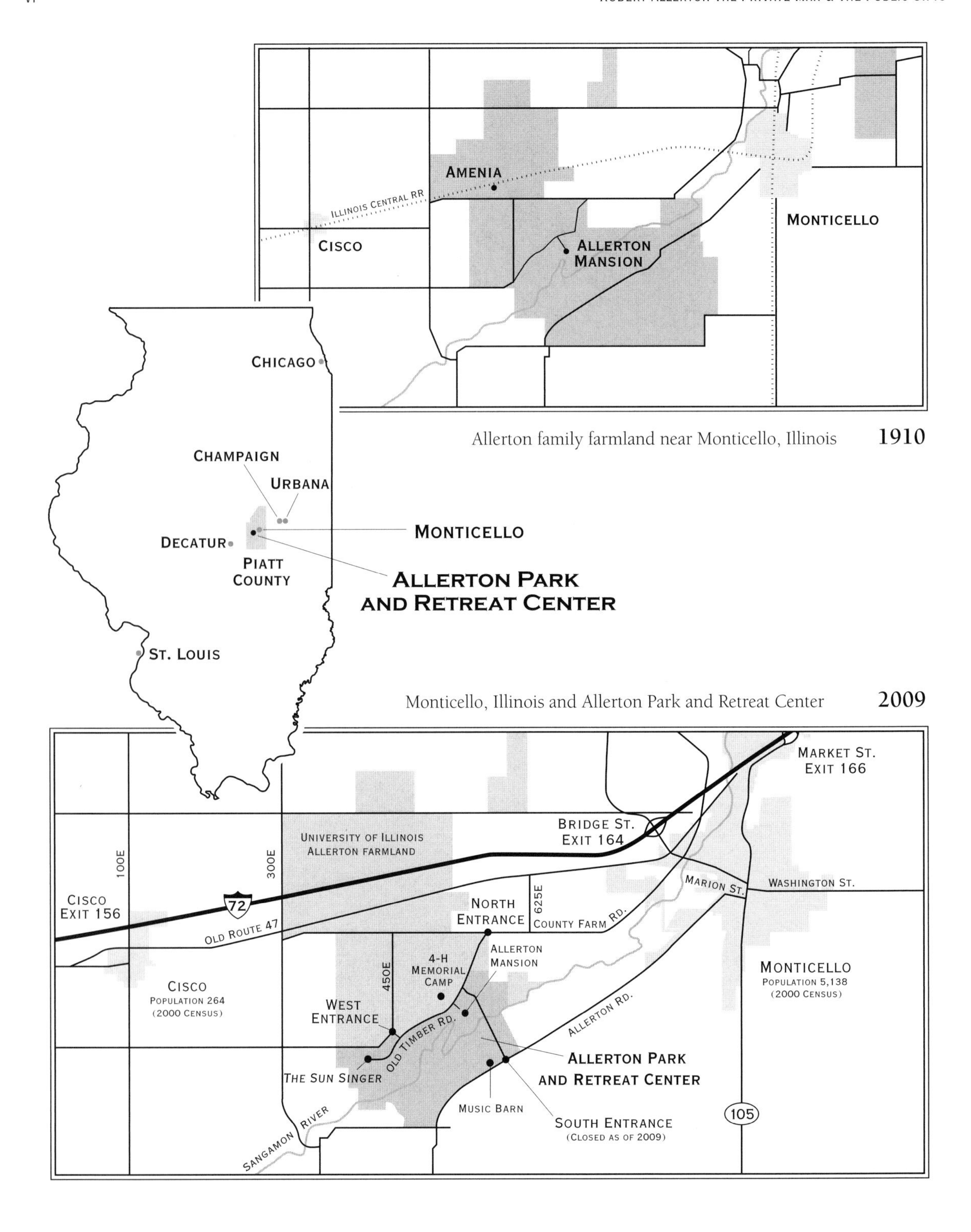

Allerton family farmland near Monticello, Illinois **1910**

Monticello, Illinois and Allerton Park and Retreat Center **2009**

ROBERT ALLERTON

The Private Man and the Public Gifts

INTRODUCTION

Robert Henry Allerton (March 20, 1873 – December 22, 1964)
John Wyatt Gregg Allerton (November 7, 1899 – May 1, 1986)

For the last sixty years, residents of the small farm town of Monticello, Illinois have spent lazy hours wandering through formal, walled gardens of clipped hedges, punctuated with sculptures from around the world. Allerton Park and Retreat Center could be their private backyard, if only for an afternoon, where each could imagine being master of the forty-room mansion, its image perfectly doubled in the calm Reflecting Pond. More visitors than ever join them these days, especially since 2007, when the Illinois Bureau of Tourism designated the site as one of the "Seven Wonders of Illinois." Allerton Park is reinventing itself with an enhanced list of conferences, weddings, private bookings, and the conversion of one of the barns to a spectacular music venue. Still, it manages to maintain the enigmatic, intimate quality created by Robert Allerton's designs. Who was this man who decided to create a wonderland in the middle of the prairie?

By 1946, when Robert Allerton donated his 5,500-acre estate to the University of Illinois, the family's name had long resonated throughout the area. "Allerton" is carved in stone above the door to Monticello's public library, identifies several farms tended by local families, and designates a town forty-two miles east of Monticello. In spite of the ubiquitous family name, Robert Allerton himself was as much legend as substance to the local citizenry. To some, he was more the representation of an abstract idea, frozen in time, than he was flesh and blood—not unlike the statues of mythical figures one might encounter in his gardens. To others, he was simply a rich man from Chicago who liked to keep to himself.

Few knew that the Allerton ancestors were one of the wealthiest families on the *Mayflower* and among the most influential founders of Plymouth Plantation. Closer inspection reveals a less sanitized account. The fortune was repeatedly lost and won again, with hands getting dirty in the process. But it was "dirt" of the honest kind that allowed Robert's father, Samuel Waters Allerton, to reclaim the family wealth. After speculating and working in the hog market during the Civil War, as well as helping found the Chicago stockyards, he earned the nickname of "Hog Allerton." With those achievements and his role in starting the First National Bank of Chicago, by the late 1890s Sam Allerton was the third richest man in Chicago. His land holdings stretched from Ohio to Nebraska.

His son, Robert, enjoyed a privileged childhood on Chicago's fashionable Prairie Avenue, growing up with the children of the other millionaires. Inspired by the art exhibits at The World's Columbian Exposition of 1893, he chose to study art in Europe but returned home in 1896 after realizing he didn't have the talent to succeed.

Having no better plan for his future, Robert

accepted Sam's offer to become manager of "The Farms" in Piatt County, prime farmland Sam had purchased after his entrepreneurial successes in the Civil War. Sam sweetened the deal with funds for Robert to build a suitable house for himself. After visiting estates and homes throughout Europe with his friend and architect, John J. Borie III, Robert selected Ham House in Surrey, England as a model for his mansion. By 1900 Robert was ready to move in.

Especially in Robert's life, but even in his father's, there was much to reconcile between the trappings of wealth and the growing of corn and livestock. Sam had risen to riches, but Robert worked his way back, literally, to his prairie roots. Robert's life at The Farms was more than an experiment in architecture; farming was the estate's lifeblood. He finessed the management of the agricultural concerns by hiring expert help, trusting their judgment, and treating his employees with respect.

He seemed to have found the connection to the land that Sam had hoped for—but Robert's temperament was much more refined than that of the plain-spoken Sam, a Chicago man of Sandburg's big-shouldered stature. Where Sam saw corn and beans only as commodities, the prairie lay before Robert like a blank canvas. He would continue his family's agricultural heritage and add his own unique twist, discovering his counterbalance in the art of landscape architecture. His masterpiece, the acres of gardens surrounding the mansion, would evolve over the next four decades.

During those years, Robert entertained his Chicago friends at The Farms, filling summer weekends with revolving combinations of guests. The *Chicago Tribune's* "Madame X" featured the coming and goings of Chicago socialites to The Farms, following their visits with the same tenacity as modern-day paparazzi. Monticello residents gossiped among themselves about huge parties held at the mansion and guests prancing about on the lawn dressed in exotic costumes. Tales of trainloads of theater people and artists arriving at the depot were exaggerated, but only in terms of quantity. Robert hosted not only performers and artists, but also the leaders of business and politics—names still well-known today.

He entertained a select few Monticello families at The Farms, but separately from his out-of-town guests. At the time of his arrival in 1898 the town was already dotted with gracious homes of the founding fathers, business leaders, and landed gentry, and a booming patent medicine business attracted even more wealth. Robert's mansion inspired a new trend in building among these citizens, raising expectations and standards for their residences. By the 1920s, Monticello's State Street had sprouted a dozen or more new homes of grand scale and style. "Millionaires' Row" is anchored near the courthouse square by Allerton Public Library and stretches a half-mile north. Robert's relatives were among those early State Street homeowners.

Through his Monticello family connections, Robert met a young architecture student at the University of Illinois, John Wyatt Gregg, with whom he would eventually forge a lifelong partnership. They spent their years together traveling the globe to collect art, spending only the warmer months of the year in Monticello. Their relationship culminated with Allerton being allowed in 1960, by virtue of a new Illinois law, to legally adopt John Gregg as his son.

When a perfect property became available on the Hawaiian island of Kauai in 1937, they could not resist purchasing it. John Gregg designed a home for them on the island, and their interest in traveling and living in Illinois declined. John and Robert developed this final home, named Lawai-Kai, with as much enthusiasm as they had for the Monticello estate. After donating the Monticello estate to the University of Illinois, Robert and John only visited their Illinois home for a month each spring, staying in a white farmhouse on the premises. When John Gregg Allerton died in 1986, twenty-two years after Robert's death, the Kauai

Allerton Gardens were placed in a trust now managed by the National Tropical Botanical Garden of Hawaii.

Robert's donations to the University of Illinois and to Hawaii represent only a fraction of his philanthropies. Throughout his life, he gave generously to numerous hospitals, schools, and orphanages. He helped countless people individually, with no wish for public recognition.

Despite their annual travels around the world and their years at Lawai-Kai, John Gregg Allerton preferred to remember Robert at their Monticello home. Almost every brochure describes Allerton Park as a beautiful anomaly, hidden in an otherwise uninspiring prairie. The same question inevitably follows. "Why here?" After all, the Allerton family owned other homes in Chicago, Lake Geneva, and Pasadena, and at the turn of the century many people chose east coast locations for their retreats. Why would a man so fond of world travel choose the cornfields of Illinois as a backdrop for his masterpiece? Was it only a concession to his father, or was he consciously inspired by the juxtaposition of the rustic and the refined?

Robert left barely enough words on the subject, or on his life in general, to fill a page. Reports from the society pages allow us to piece together a mosaic from which the man emerges. In addition to several letters he left behind, the words of his friends and employees help complete that picture.

As for what Robert intended us to see at his home, his most pure artistic statement was to simply allow his work to speak for itself. His most notable pieces were donated to the Art Institute of Chicago. Later, to honor him as one of its most generous donors and officers, the Art Institute named their main building after him.

At The Farms, you will find pieces by artists Carl Milles, Émile-Antoine Bourdelle, and Lili Auer mixed in among antiques, replicas, and works commissioned from a variety of local and international artisans. The genius of the collection is in its presentation. Each garden gate and each turn of a wooded path reveals a surprise.

Many of the sculptures are of Asian origin, and Allerton's interest was not unique to his era. The fashion of Japonisme had reached its height during his student years, and his wealth allowed him the indulgence of travel and acquisition. However, his sensibility to Eastern concepts presents itself in more subtle ways in his design of the estate. The mysterious energy of the Park is a delicate and deliberate balance between yin and yang—the contrast of the primordial with the civilized, the quaint with the majestic, the geometric with the wild, and the ancient with the modern.

The creation that Robert left us seems to be built for show, but was actually modest and restrained by the standards of his contemporaries, hidden away from sightseers, designed for the pleasure of intimate friends. After repeated visits, the elegant simplicity of his presentation becomes clear. The care with which he leads us from scene to scene in the gardens is a humble offering. Even today, with Robert long gone, one walks his paths as his honored guest, discovering secret after secret.

Up close, we see that each brilliant blue ceramic *Fu Dog* is slightly different, each made by a different hand. We learn that two of the *Chinese Musicians* were created by a Monticello tombstone carver, replacing ones of soft stone that weathered beyond repair. We are glad to see *The Sun Singer* back on its pedestal after restoration, and notice a brick wall being rebuilt. The Park changes with each season, and each season takes its toll. Through it all, Allerton Park and Retreat Center has earned its patina, but is reborn again each day—a dynamic microcosm where timelines converge and new experience begins.

CHAPTER ONE
The Allertons Help Build America

There is no taint upon the money of Chicago's
foremost unmarried millionaire.
The man who bears this distinction is an American to the marrow.

Chicago Tribune, on Robert Allerton[1]

RICHEST BACHELOR IN CHICAGO

"RICHEST BACHELOR in CHICAGO." So announced a *Chicago Sunday Tribune* headline in 1906. The title hovered over drawings of ten women dressed in their Gibson Girl best, tossing kisses, waves, and longing glances at thirty-three-year-old Robert Allerton. Robert, as a candidate for husband, was flawless in every respect. Within the first paragraphs of the article, we learn:

> *He never goes to a manicure shop to have a rosy polish put on his finger nails; he never leads a cotillion; he never smokes monogram cigarets [sic]; he does not wear corsets. He is a plain American citizen; he leads a wholesome life; he measures up to the highest standards of vigorous, rugged manhood; he has not allowed wealth to crucify his ideals nor permitted luxury to dissipate him.*[2]

In his photograph, he stared straight ahead, his expression holding back anything akin to a smile, but his eyes show boyish amusement. He was handsome as any of today's movie stars; only his dapper moustache and high, starched collar define him as a man of another era.

> *His features are cleanly cut and his head is set firmly above muscular shoulders. He is a man of medium height, active, robust, well proportioned. The qualities that combine in the makeup of his personality are qualities that go to*

> *make a man lovable—a strong character, personal fearlessness, the gentleness of strength, optimism, and just enough ideality to guide impulse, a strong sense of justice, humanity, generosity almost to a fault. He is democratic and reserved.*[3]

All that, and he loved dogs.

The article mentioned Robert's annual income of $100,000 accurately enough—equivalent to $2.5 million in 2007. His total net worth, estimated at over $2 million, equaled today's purchasing power of $47.5 million. But the reporter's claim that Robert made the money by simply "tilling the soil"[4] and making "the land fruitful and reaping its harvest"[5] was false—as was the denial that his fortune derived from speculation. Robert invested his money wisely, but his wildly successful father, Samuel Waters Allerton,* whose speculation during the Civil War had established his fortune, handed the capital to him.

Chicago Tribune/University of Illinois

Illustration from a 1906 *Chicago Tribune* special feature naming Robert Allerton the "Richest Bachelor in Chicago."

Sam's vast agricultural holdings, some seventy farms, sprawled throughout the Midwest. The family's Prairie Avenue mansion and their summer home in the enclave of other Chicago millionaires at Lake Geneva, Wisconsin offered conspicuous proof of the family's wealth. Robert could have settled anywhere. But he chose to build his mansion on the family's 12,000-acre[6] Piatt County spread, 150 miles south of Chicago, near the small town of Monticello.

Hopeful young ladies probably lined up shoulder-to-shoulder to meet and flirt with Robert. They must have daydreamed that becoming this particular farmer's wife would present no hardship, beyond brief separations from the opera and society soirees in Chicago. A coterie of friends would surely accompany the couple on dusty train rides down to the farm, all anxious for weekends of bucolic bliss. Robert could have had his pick of any of these young women.

The author of the article remained anonymous, but dozens more about Robert followed, most from the desk of society columnist Caroline Kirkland*—known to faithful readers as Madame X. Was she simply filling column space, or were deeper machinations at work? The Allertons counted the McCormicks,* owners of the *Chicago Tribune,* among their circle of friends. Perhaps Sam worried about Robert not finding a spouse and producing an heir with the Allerton surname. Whether Sam or Madame X instigated the campaign, the "bachelor" part of Robert's title threatened to become permanent. It would only add to the mystique that surrounded his name throughout his life and for decades after his death.

* *Names marked with an asterisk appear in Family and Friends appendix.*

ALLERTONS IN THE NEW WORLD

While the east coast Gilded Age had its Carnegies and Vanderbilts, Illinois had its McCormicks and Armours... and its Allertons. Perhaps not as recognizable as some of the other names attached to great wealth, the Allerton name was important well before Robert Allerton's birth.

The Allerton family fortune resulted from a remarkable confluence of economic opportunity, shrewd risk-taking, and availability of vast acreage as the young nation pushed westward. Robert Allerton's father, Samuel Waters Allerton, was very much in the right place at the right time.

The family descended from Isaac Allerton,* one of the wealthiest of the *Mayflower* pilgrims. Only he and William Brewster (his second father-in-law) were honored with the prefix of "Mr." The fifth signer of the Mayflower Compact, Isaac worked with Miles Standish to conclude the first peace treaty with the Indians. He later rose to the rank of Assistant Governor under Governor William Bradford, but 1633 he left Plymouth under a cloud of suspicion for monetary misdeeds. He died a poor man in Salem in 1659.[7] Isaac's descendants would exert great influence as the colonies forged themselves into a nation, but none would achieve immense wealth. None that is, until Sam.

University of Illinois

Samuel W. Allerton (1828-1914), father of Robert Allerton, circa 1907. From Samuel Allerton's book, *Practical Farming.*

Samuel Waters Allerton was born in Amenia, New York on May 26, 1828, the youngest of nine children of Samuel and Hannah Hurd Allerton.[8] At the time of Sam's birth, his parents were so poor that "they all cried when I was born, so many to feed."[9] His parents continued to struggle, and in 1835 when he was seven, his industrious father's woolen factory failed because of destructive tariff measures during President Andrew Jackson's administration. As young Sam stood by, watching his parents' property being liquidated, his mother wept when her favorite horses were sold. Sam embraced her, promising to provide for her.[10] He greatly admired both parents, but felt "had she been the man, and Father the woman, they would have made better headway in the world."[11] He vowed to make something of himself and worked hard on the farm that his father rented.

In his early twenties, Sam and his oldest brother, Henry, began renting and purchasing farms and trading livestock. After a few years, Sam netted $3,000 from their efforts. Henry, impressed with his brother, told him, "If you continue as you are, in a few years you will own the best farm in this country... You will run across smart and tricky men, but they always die poor—make a name and character for yourself, and you are sure to win."[12]

Sam lost money on his first sale of cattle, but his next opportunity yielded another $3,000. Indulging the Allerton wanderlust, he drifted west to Illinois. In 1855 Sam tried to purchase ten corn-fed cattle from Benjamin Franklin Harris of Piatt County. Harris refused, but sold him 200 hogs instead.[13] Sam then purchased an additional 200 hogs during his drive to the Illinois Central Railroad (ICRR) railhead in West Urbana (now Champaign).

Negotiating one of the first livestock shipments on the ICRR, Sam shipped the hogs north to Chicago and made a good profit. Sam always later claimed that his wealth derived from that first deal with Mr. Harris.[14]

Around that time, Sam lost $300 because a young telegraph operator—Andrew Carnegie—incorrectly quoted a rate. Decades later when the two played golf together at Lake Geneva, Sam joked to Carnegie that he should return the money with compound interest.[15]

Sam continued his central Illinois livestock-trading from Bloomington, working with partner John B. Cheney for two more years until the economic panic of 1858. He returned to New York, ill with typhoid fever and in danger of losing his left leg.[16] After recovering, he purchased an interest in a store with Henry, but Sam's desires and ambitions extended beyond the confines of a sales counter.

Two years earlier, on a journey to Canton, Illinois, he had met and fallen in love with sixteen-year-old Pamilla Wigdon Thompson,* the third of eleven children born to wealthy Asler C. and Berintha Eggleston Thompson. Twelve years older than Pamilla, Sam was still scrimping and saving. After his stint running the store with his brother, he returned again to Illinois, this time determined to earn enough from trading cattle to win her hand in marriage.

Courtesy of Sean Johnstone

Pamilla Wigdon Thompson Allerton (1840-1880), the first wife of Samuel W. Allerton and the mother of Robert Allerton, circa 1875.

Of average height and already showing signs of his later baldness, Sam was worth $3,500 when he married Pamilla in Peoria on July 2, 1860. But according to him, what he had "was better than money—the courage and the knowledge of how to trade." With the girl he loved "better than life,"[17] Sam headed for Chicago, where he felt "the world turned around every twenty-four hours."[18]

THE STOCKYARD KING

South of Sam's home base in Chicago, on the Central Illinois prairie, lay some of the world's most fertile soil for farming. John Deere and Cyrus McCormick had already made their fortunes in Illinois by mass-producing agricultural equipment in the 1830s and 1840s. Factories multiplied during the Civil War, and Illinois soon became a leading source for weapons, iron products, coal, grain, and meat to supply the Union troops. Everyone scrambled to profit, and Sam Allerton aimed to be become the major meat supplier.

Since 1861 Sam had been managing a stockyard for the Chicago, Burlington and Quincy Railroad, where he had increased livestock marketing and enlarged the yard's capacity. In May 1863 his uncle tipped him off that the Union Army was paying such a high price for pork—and much of it infested—that Sam stood to make a huge profit if he could secure and fill a large contract to supply the troops. Sam obtained a pledge for monetary backing from

George Smith's private Chicago bank, and for a day and a half, he and his runners bought every hog entering the city's stockyards—$80,000 worth. According to Sam, for almost two weeks, he "owned every hog in the city of Chicago and nearly all that went on the New York market."[19]

When Sam returned to the bank to get the money, the astonished bank officer, Mr. Williard, balked on the loan—having mistakenly expected to pay out $8,000, not $80,000. Eventually, Sam negotiated financing from Aiken and Norton's bank at one percent interest. Even with this expense, Sam's profit from the hog contract with the Union Army provided financial leverage for his future endeavors.

When Congress passed the National Bank Act in 1863,[20] Sam—still smarting from the earlier $8,000 credit confusion—joined Edmund Aiken and other Chicago investors, pooling $250,000 to establish the First National Bank of Chicago. With Aiken as its President, the bank opened on LaSalle Street on July 1, 1863, the same day as the Battle of Gettysburg.

That same year, on June 10, Pamilla gave birth to their daughter Katharine ("Kate") Reinette Allerton.* As Sam thrilled in his fatherhood, he made his first foray into land ownership. His purchase of 1,280 Piatt County acres, at the cost of ten dollars each, launched the Allerton empire.[21]

Trading livestock in markets located throughout Chicago prompted Sam to write the first letter ever published in the *Chicago Tribune* advocating a consolidated stockyard to bring buyers and sellers together.[22] In 1864 he and others joined together to found the Chicago Union Stock Yards, which opened for business on Christmas day, 1865.

Taking strategic advantage of this new facility, in 1871 he organized the Allerton Packing Company on Halsted Street near the stockyards where they slaughtered "2,000 hogs daily during the season, employ[ed] some 200 men, and pack[ed] principally for the home markets."[23] The stockyards encompassed an area of 280 acres, with 1,200 cattle pens, and 1,600 hog and sheep pens—and produced a stench proportionate to the operation.

In 1871 he became president of the newly formed St. Louis National Stockyards. In his honor, a hotel near the stockyards was named Allerton House. Some years later the name changed to the National Hotel.[24]

Back in Chicago, on the afternoon of September 30, 1871, a fire broke out in Burlington Warehouse "A," a building Sam leased on 16th Street. The fire originated on the second floor, where a massive quantity of broomcorn was stored.[25] The basement held large quantities of flammable spirits and empty barrels. Machinery, food, and household items were stockpiled on the main and third floors. One man died in the fire, and insurance covered only $350,000 of the estimated at $638,000 loss.[26]

Over the next eight days, fires—many suspected to be the work of arsonists—erupted throughout the city. The firemen were already exhausted from more than a week of infernos when the Great Chicago Fire broke out on October 8.

P.B. Greene/University of Illinois

The First National Bank of Chicago after the Great Chicago Fire of 1871.

Fortunately, the Allerton family home at 644 Michigan Avenue[27] was situated well outside the area of most significant damage. The First National Bank suffered severely from the flames, but the contents of the safe survived intact. Operating in temporary facilities for three months, the staff returned to the reconditioned building on January 1, 1872.[28]

While Chicago rebuilt itself, Sam added stockyards in Pittsburgh and New Jersey to his holdings. He purchased acreage throughout Illinois, Ohio, Iowa, Wisconsin, and Nebraska—eventually accumulating over 78,000 acres. Sam obtained railroad access to his Piatt County land in 1872. Six years later, upon the retirement of his farm manager, John Mintun, Sam's brothers-in-law took over managing his 3,200 acres near Monticello.[29]

Within ten years of his entrance into the Chicago livestock business, Sam was shipping his fattened herds from the Midwest, onward to New York and as far away as England. David Rotenstein's article, "Hudson River Cowboys: The Origins of Modern Livestock Shipping," in *The Hudson Valley Regional Review*, stated:

> *With control of the Pennsylvania Railroad's stockyards at Pittsburgh, Philadelphia and Jersey City, Samuel W. Allerton profited from every animal shipped on the nation's largest nineteenth-century railroad.... Allerton may be considered as the 'father of the stockyards' in the United States.*[30]

By 1873 Sam was forty-five and a multimillionaire. On March 20 he became a father for a second time. After a ten-year gap since Kate's birth, Pamilla presented him with a son—Robert Henry. They chose the baby's middle name in honor of Sam's brother.[31]

Cattle prices, in decline for a decade, rose dramatically in 1884 and then plummeted the following year. Local butchers were unable to compete against the major "Big Four" meatpackers: Philip Armour, Gustav Swift, George Hammond, and Edward Morris. Small slaughterhouses claimed that the larger meatpackers used diseased cattle. In 1888, with the market in a precarious state and distrust against the Big Four at an all-time high, the Senate commenced the first federal meat inspection. Two years later, the resulting *Vest Report*[32] charged that the Big Four fixed beef prices and territories, divided the public contracts, and compelled retailers to buy from the Allerton Pool,[33] referring to an 1886 agreement between Sam and the Big Four. Although the *Vest Report* initiated no action, the Sherman Antitrust Act followed in 1890, primarily targeting the Rockefellers.

Sam's name may not have been as well-known to the general public as it was throughout the business world, but to the Muckrackers, Allerton was a king of industry, subject to no less scrutiny.

ROBERT'S EARLY CHALLENGES

On May 25, 1878, the eve of his fiftieth birthday, Sam wrote a letter to his children (aged five and fifteen) giving them a short personal history and advising them how to get by in life. "You must live for less each year than your income... You must act on your own judgment or your money will soon be gone, friends will be scarce…" He signed the letter, "Your devoted father."[34]

He specifically advised his daughter Kate, "should you marry, keep the principal in your own hands—you can let your husband know the income."[35] And the letter counseled Robert, "above all things let rum alone—do not touch it… many smart men have weak stomachs… You must be a leader, and search out your own fortune. Be honest, but not too damn honest so that you let another cheat you." Sam urged him to get the best lawyer but study well his own case, be manly and have pluck. To both, he wrote, "To marry and raise a family is the true course. Try to marry healthy persons."[36]

University of Illinois

Robert Henry Allerton and Kate Reinette Allerton, circa 1875.

The last phrase was undoubtedly prompted by Pamilla's sickliness, which was exacerbated by her giving birth to Robert. Too ill to attend Robert's baptism, Pamilla requested that the child's nurse carry the baby down the aisle of the church. A family friend, Mrs. Anna Rathbone,* thought it dreadful that a paid servant would be holding the child during the ceremony.[37] She stepped in to replace the nurse and later became Robert's godmother.

The same year that Sam wrote his letter of advice, both children were stricken with typhoid fever. They recovered, but in 1880 Pamilla and the children all contracted scarlet fever. Pamilla died, and the hearing of both children was damaged. Treatment at the Politzer Clinic in Vienna[38] yielded some success for Kate, but little could be done for Robert. Both remained impaired.[39] Robert's hearing loss, an ever-present challenge in his childhood development, affected him throughout adulthood as he adapted to society's demands.

The 1880 census lists Pamilla's younger sister, Agnes Catharine Thompson,* as a member of the Allerton household. Apparently she had come to assist during the family's tragedy. On March 15, 1882, two years after Pamilla's death, Sam married Agnes, who was thirty years younger than he. Robert referred to her as "Mother" after Pamilla died, but sister Kate, by now almost nineteen and three years away from her own marriage, would always call her "Aunt Agnes."[40] Robert was very fond of Agnes, and she would also become his mentor in the arts.

ALLERTON INFLUENCE

By 1883 the Allerton family was Piatt County's largest landowner with 11,655 acres, and since 1872, had obtained railroad access.[41] But Sam still saw more opportunities nearby. He purchased farmland in Vermilion County in 1881, and by 1897 deeded the land for the village of Allerton, Illinois.

He and Joseph Sidell convinced the C&EI Railroad to cut through the town of Allerton, conveniently across their property. Sam would travel by train to the town and sidetrack his private Pullman car by the grain company during his business visits. He typically visited every property annually for a week.[42] He and Sidell also established a grain company and developed the town near the company's elevator.

To stimulate growth, Sam established the town's first private bank in 1892, donated funds a year later to construct a schoolhouse, installed a water system, and donated materials for sidewalks. Agnes Allerton equipped the high school's domestic science room and employed the first teacher. In 1903 Sam deeded land to the village for a park and hired a landscape gardener from Chicago to design it.

University of Illinois

Photograph of a bank established by Samuel Allerton in the town of Allerton, Illinois. (Panel Studio, Danville, Illinois 1906.)

So large were his holdings in Vermilion County that he proposed forming a new county around the town of Allerton, with the town reigning as the county seat. He anticipated an expenditure of $1.5 million to achieve his goal. But a nearby newspaper, the *Newman Record,* suspected it was merely a maneuver to sell more lots in the town of Allerton.[43]

Although he gained fame, money, and property, along with occasional negative publicity, he didn't lose sight of his humble beginnings. When Sam was a boy in New York, a nearby Quaker farmer had allowed him to pick fruit from the man's orchard as long as he didn't damage the tree branches. Wanting to extend that same friendship to others, Sam set out 5,000 fruit trees along the road near his land for townspeople who had no fruit.[44] The trees are long gone, but his generosity was remembered for years.

The *Chicago Tribune* wrote that Sam worked "on the credo that nobody can succeed unless he can build up character and credit."[45] By the time of the 1896 Klondike Gold Rush, the newspaper declared Sam, following Marshall Field and Philip Armour, the third richest man in Chicago.

Sam selected talented managers who could run local operations with limited guidance. A skilled farmer himself, as his business enterprises grew successful and self-sufficient, he shifted his attention to developing and implementing innovative agricultural practices: tiled field drainage, crop rotation, and supplemental fertilization. To stimulate competition, he once gave a $1,000 prize for the best fifty ears of corn at the National Corn Expo at Chicago's Coliseum.[46]

During the 1880s and 1890s Sam helped promote the Farmer's Institute, a forerunner of today's Farm Bureau. At the close of these meetings, Sam always gave the same talk, "How to Grow Rich and Be Happy on 40 Acres of Land." At Robert's urging, Sam eventually wrote a book entitled *Practical Farming.*

In 1895 Monticello needed a town hall and a library. Sam proposed to the Township "that if they would erect a suitable building in which to house it, Mrs. Allerton would donate a library."[47] By 1897 the town had constructed such a building and the Allertons donated 2,500 volumes, including 300 reference books.[48] Receipts from an opera house in the building supported the Agnes Allerton Library until 1919, when Monticello Township citizens voted to support it through taxation. When the opera house ceased operation, the Library expanded within the building.

Sam and his family continued to involve themselves in civic affairs and charities. Besides ensuring that ready-made tenant houses and schools were constructed for his farmers, Sam helped establish the St. Charles Home for Boys, west of Chicago.

He also served on the Board of Directors of the Chicago City Railway for more than twenty years. Inspired by a visit to San Francisco, Sam proposed replacing cable cars with electric trolleys. Doing so, the Railway operated profitably from 1860 through the end of the nineteenth century.[49]

Sam served as Vice President of the Chicago Citizens Law and Order League in 1885, and in 1889 was included in a group of one hundred people appointed by the mayor of Chicago to promote the World's Columbian Exposition of 1893. As a director for the Exposition, he chaired the National and State Exhibit Committee.[50]

Allerton Public Library, Monticello, Illinois

The Monticello, Illinois Community Building, housing the Agnes Allerton Public Library.

The race for mayor of Chicago commenced during the planning for the Exposition. Carter Henry Harrison, a Democrat, and previous four-term mayor of Chicago, wanted badly to become the first five-term mayor of Chicago. Presiding over the Exposition would be the crowning achievement of his career. When Philip Armour declined to run against Harrison, Chicago Republicans nominated Sam Allerton. Backed by Chicago newspapers, Sam vowed to operate on business principles and help rid the city of crime and seediness that his opponent enabled. Harrison didn't care how Chicagoans spent their hard-earned money: on prostitution, gambling houses, or saloons. Illinois citizens, incensed at the crime and corruption, claimed that Harrison, in his previous terms, had already turned Chicago into the "Gomorrah of the West."[51]

The campaign proved to be one of the nastiest Chicago had ever seen. With newspapers backing Sam, Harrison was forced to buy his own newspaper, *The Chicago Times*.[52] Sam lost the election, with 93,148 votes to Harrison's 114,237. *The Piatt County Republican* stated that the position of mayor had been "bestowed upon a man so unworthy as Carter Harrison, the chief of thugs and gamblers."[53]

Three years later, in 1896, President-elect William McKinley offered Sam the post of Secretary of Agriculture. Sam, by then sixty-eight years old, declined the offer, believing the job required the energies of younger candidates.

Family Life

In 1879 Sam sold the Michigan Avenue home[54] and moved his family to a mansion at 1936 Prairie Avenue, built in 1869 for Sam's banking associate, Daniel M. Thompson. It was the first $100,000 house on the South Side and the house that spurred more millionaires to move to Prairie Avenue. Boasting a frontage of 193 feet, it was the largest lot on the avenue. The seventy-foot tower of the Italianate house provided the Allertons a spectacular view of Lake Michigan, and the two-story barn and stable sported a second tower.[55]

Emulating Oliver Wendell Holmes' reference to Boston's Beacon Hill, Prairie Avenue

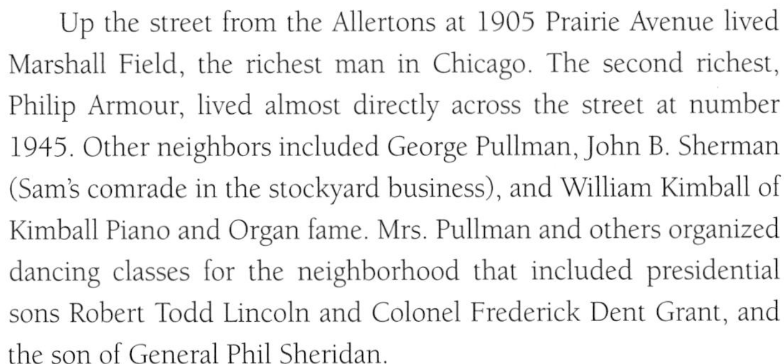

was sometimes referred to as "The Sunny Street that Held the Sifted Few." Other names such as "Fifth Avenue of the Midwest," "Palace Row," and "Millionaires' Row" described the principal street in the six-block area where nearly twenty millionaires lived. According to the *Chicago Tribune,* "beginning at 16th Street, you could hardly throw a stone… without hitting a millionaire."[56]

University of Illinois

The Allerton home at 1936 Prairie Avenue, Chicago, purchased from Daniel Thompson in 1879.

Up the street from the Allertons at 1905 Prairie Avenue lived Marshall Field, the richest man in Chicago. The second richest, Philip Armour, lived almost directly across the street at number 1945. Other neighbors included George Pullman, John B. Sherman (Sam's comrade in the stockyard business), and William Kimball of Kimball Piano and Organ fame. Mrs. Pullman and others organized dancing classes for the neighborhood that included presidential sons Robert Todd Lincoln and Colonel Frederick Dent Grant, and the son of General Phil Sheridan.

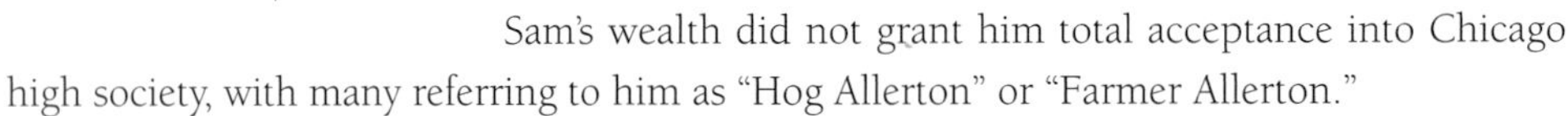

Sam's wealth did not grant him total acceptance into Chicago high society, with many referring to him as "Hog Allerton" or "Farmer Allerton."

In August 1883, shortly after his marriage to Agnes, Sam was determined to have a summer home on the shores of Lake Geneva, Wisconsin, yet another enclave of the super-rich. A twenty-six acre octagonal forest lodge cost him $15,000. When Sam informed Agnes of the new homestead, she is said to have exclaimed, "A fishing lodge? Heavens Samuel, that is sheer folly." The name, "The Folly," stuck.[57]

Sam hired Henry Lord Gay,[58] the original architect, to draw up plans for moving the lodge out of the way of a tree he liked and enlarging the home in the process. Inside, the Allertons enjoyed the use of their Melodeon,[59] a musical device that used disks, not unlike an early jukebox, arrayed with pipes reaching the ceiling.

He purchased a steam launch, *The Time,* said to be the finest on the lake. He would race it against his neighbors to the railroad station. But in late July 1885 a tornado swooped in from the northwest, tearing away the launch's upper deck and capsizing the boat.

University of Illinois

The Allerton's summer home, The Folly, in Lake Geneva, Wisconsin, photographed in 1885, one year after it was completed.

From their additional eighty acres near The Folly, they shipped produce back to the Prairie Avenue home. Agnes loved gardening and became famous for her greenhouses full of roses. She and her gardener, Robert Blackwood, won prizes for chrysanthemums in 1914 and for peonies in 1917.[60]

No matter how grand his houses, Sam was never very polished. He kept a spittoon beside him at the dining room table and a napkin tucked under his chin, even at formal dinners. Though an impressive bear of a man, he was sensitive about his bald head. At times he wore a toupee, but didn't always part the hair the same way. Monticello boys were known to place bets on the outcome, left or right, for a given day.[61]

To help his summer community of Lake Geneva, Sam donated land and money to the trustees of the Yerkes telescope, ensuring that it was placed near the Lakeside club grounds.[62]

University of Illinois

Kate, Robert, Samuel, and Agnes Allerton on the porch at the Folly in Lake Geneva, Wisconsin. Photographed in 1895 by Leo D. Weil, a leading Chicago photographer.

KATE'S MARRIAGE

In a simple ceremony at home on November 11, 1885, two years after the Allertons bought the Folly, twenty-two year-old Kate married Dr. Francis Sidney Papin, a well-known Chicago physician.[63] Four years later, he contracted tuberculosis and journeyed to Mexico in hopes of a cure. The Chicago newspaper speculated that the air, combined with a common cold, actually hastened his death. Papin's body was sent to Keokuk, Iowa for burial. As the *Chicago Tribune* noted:

> *He died suddenly and quickly at the Lacienda [sic] of Carralitos... in the night of the 1st of January... His remains were carried across the State of Chihuahua to the Mexican Central Station of San José and then shipped to Paso Del Norte. Serious impediment and extortion met the friends of the deceased while trying to reach the friendly haven of El Paso with the corpse.*[64]

A young widow, Kate did not remarry for nearly a decade.

A WARMER CLIMATE

By 1903, with Chicago's red light district taking hold near 22nd and State Street and rail traffic and industry blossoming around them, Sam grew tired of the dirt and noise. They had moved into the neighborhood when the elms arched overhead and plants thrived. But over the years, cinders and ashes from the expanded rail services seeped through windows and heat registers, covering everything inside. The pollution severely affected growth of the trees and other vegetation.

He and Agnes wanted someplace warm to live. For $10,000 he bought an unimproved plot of ground in South Pasadena, California at 1025 Highland. Bounded by Fair View Avenue and Buena Vista Street, the 273 x 352 foot property overlooked the bluff below Columbia Street. Plans for the mission style home included a main entrance with mosaic tiles; paneled wainscoting and beamed ceilings; an oak staircase with a raised platform and recessed seats; a den finished in Oregon pine and stained Flemish oak with heavy beams overhead; and a flagstone mantel. The parlor, library, dining room, and kitchen would be on the lower floor, with bedrooms above. The attic housed a billiard room, next to a rooftop garden where Agnes grew avocados and nectarines.[65] As reported, the house would include "gas and electric lights, sanitary plumbing and modern conveniences... and... will cost about $15,000."[66]

Sam and Agnes wintered in California for the next eleven years but kept the Chicago and

Lake Geneva homes, retaining a maid and a cook in Chicago.[67] They returned to the Midwest in the summers to better manage the properties. In June 1912 they returned to Chicago to discover that burglars had helped themselves to the contents of the wine cellar.[68] Agnes had intended to return earlier and "left unpacked a number of coats lined with the finest of furs, many of which had been collected abroad."[69] But as the newspaper surmised, the "thieves were obviously of the male sex, because they did not care to be burdened with coats.... They cut the linings from them, having a particular care not to mutilate the fur."[70]

Agnes' collection of antique laces and embroidery from around the world also disappeared, along with some of the silver and the house's oriental hangings. When the authorities apprehended the "society burglar and forger,"[71] Jacob F. Guthrie, in August, the newspapers published a three-column listing of his immense cache of stolen goods. Guthrie and his gang had also grabbed Sam's silk underwear, handkerchiefs, a gold souvenir cane and spoon, a gold-embossed ring box, Kate's "ivory toilet outfit," engravings, a kimono, Sam's meerschaum pipe, a silver flask, napkin rings, and Sam's director's badge from the World's Columbian Exposition. Later in court, Agnes testified that sixty yards of white silk fabric belonged to her.

Only two items engraved with Robert's initials or name[72] appeared in the pile—a gold pencil and chain, and a napkin ring reading "Robert from May."[73] (May was the nickname for his step-cousin, Mary Lester.)

Strong to the End

For fifty years Sam served as a director of the First National Bank of Chicago, still participating after his relocation to California. His correspondence shows that he also kept an iron hand on management of the farms. He died in his sleep on February 22, 1914, at age eighty-six. At the time of his death, Samuel W. Allerton, the ninth child in a poor family, had accumulated a $4 million[74] estate—equal in 2007 funds to over $85 million. He had witnessed the administrations of twenty-three United States presidents, from John Quincy Adams to Woodrow Wilson, and had been invited to serve in McKinley's cabinet. He left behind a legacy of hard work and tenacity, making a name for himself and his family throughout the country. With his lack of interest in the limelight and his focus on business and the soil, Chicago and Central Illinois were the ultimate beneficiaries.

Most men would have a tough time trying to live up to the example set by Sam—a successful business man and philanthropist, husband and father. Robert may well have struggled in his youth trying to match Sam's accomplishments. But by the time Sam died, Robert had had his own successes. And setbacks.

CHAPTER TWO
Robert, Growing Up on Prairie Avenue

The sunny street that held the sifted few...

An old Chicago saying, about Prairie Avenue

A PRAIRIE AVENUE CHILDHOOD

Shortly after his wife Pamilla's death in 1880, Sam put a parcel of his downstate Illinois property—280 acres of choice farmland along the Sangamon River in Piatt County, near Monticello—in seven-year-old Robert's name. Twenty years later, Robert would build his magnificent mansion there, but even as a child he was master of his own private home. About the same time as Sam's gift of land, young Robert played in a child-sized, backyard replica of the family home. The Lilliputian house even contained a tiny stove on which Robert made pancakes for his friends, Franky Hibbard and Freddy Bartlett, using batter whipped up by the family cook.[1] Franky and Freddy were sons of hardware tycoons William Gold Hibbard and Adolphus Bartlett* from the firm of Hibbard, Spencer, Bartlett & Co., known today as True Value Hardware.

Freddy (Frederic Clay Bartlett)* proclaimed his lifelong friendship with Robert decades later in his memoir:

> *Friendship, ah: what a wonderful English word so seldom carried to the end of its meaning—perfect understanding, perfect loyalty never needing to say, 'Now not a word of this to a soul'—utter confidence that in all things the beloved friend would be trusted, defended, protected, fought for, and forgiven. The friend of a perfect friendship can do no wrong.*[2]

Robert was also very fond of another playmate from across the street, Marshall Field's daughter, Ethel.* On Friday evening, January 1, 1886, Mrs. Marshall Field hosted an extravagant entertainment for her children, twelve-year-old Ethel and seventeen-year-old

Marshall, Jr. Robert and Frederic almost certainly attended the party. The guest list included four hundred neighborhood friends and acquaintances, some coming from as far away as Boston, New York, Philadelphia, Baltimore, and Cincinnati.[3]

Instead of a traditional Christmas-tree party for the children, Mrs. Field modeled the more mature theme of Gilbert and Sullivan's comic opera, *The Mikado,* which had recently debuted in Chicago. The decorations (or more accurately, the complete transformation of the mansion's first floor) included a miniature pagoda for Johnny Hand's orchestra, silk lanterns to soften electric lights, and swinging bead curtains of wood, ivory and glass to replace the doors. Satin fabric, black and gold Japanese tapestries, bamboo screens, and Asian foliage completed the scenery. Some of the food and silver arrived from New York in two private railroad cars. Party favors ranged from toy animals, lanterns, parasols, and Japanese slippers to the more exclusive custom designs of artist James McNeill Whistler—one version created with peacock feathers and a satin sash, the other with a flower and a lantern.[4] Many of the guests arrived at the "Mikado Ball" in full Japanese costume, including wig and makeup. Society photographer Mathew J. Steffens snapped group shots throughout the evening. For weeks afterward, many of the attendees called at his studio to be individually photographed in their costumes.[5]

Photograph of Ethel Field, Alice Keith, and Florence Otis dressed for the Mikado Ball, held January 1, 1886 at the Field mansion, 1905 S. Prairie Avenue.

While Mrs. Field reportedly spent $75,000 (equal to today's buying power of over $1.6 million) on the party, not all gatherings were that lavish. Other neighbors simply invited celebrities such as Oscar Wilde, Enrico Caruso, and Ignace Paderewski to exclusive soirees. Nonetheless, on Prairie Avenue a thirty-foot tablecloth was a requirement. Formal dinners there could include up to fifteen courses. When the Glessners up the street served dinner to ninety-six members of the Chicago Symphony Orchestra, their normal contingent of eight servants was insufficient. They hired twenty-six more servants for the occasion; one man's duty was simply to serve ice cream.

Some, like the Allertons, preferred to host parties on a more modest scale, such as ladies' teas or intimate dinners for friends and family. On one occasion they invited twenty-six friends to celebrate the birthday of Franz Schubert. The Hibbards entertained the Fields and others with dinner, followed by bowling in their own tenpin alley.

Robert Expands His Knowledge

Life on Prairie Avenue was more than a social whirlwind. Sam, attentive to Robert's future, gave stocks and bonds to his twelve-year-old son, teaching him the art of investing. He inscribed a black leather ledger in longhand: "This book presented to my dear son Robert H. Allerton, January 1st, 1886. To be kept by him for life as a remembrance of his father's love and affection."[6]

He listed some of the portfolio he handed over to Robert: twenty-six shares in Chicago City Railway stock; five shares each of First National Bank of Chicago stock and Merchants Loan and Trust stock; and bonds issued by North Chicago City Railway and Chicago City

Railway. Robert duly added the dividends, cash on hand, and current values through his early years, learning from Sam.

Agnes served Robert as a nurturing mentor in the arts. One of her prized books, *The Standard Operas* by George P. Upton, listed operas of all origins, their composers, and languages. She used the book as a journal, noting in the margins her preferences, the dates she attended, and who had attended with her. Robert's Aunt Lois (Sam's sister) accompanied her to many of the operas. Agnes also tucked newspaper announcements for operas into the book. In spite of Robert's hearing loss, she encouraged what would become his lifelong love of music. He never became a master musician himself, but studied the violin.[7]

Robert didn't excel at sports, but he attempted to teach himself how to play golf, using Sam's golf clubs, practicing in the attic.[8] His impairment would have made team sports more challenging. He was lucky to have genuine childhood friends like Freddy, Franky, and Ethel as he was learning to read lips.

Robert didn't particularly care for school.[9] Private tutors helped him keep up with his classmates. He attended two private schools—the Allen Academy, and The Harvard School, a college prep school for boys. Any lack of interest in schooling was not reflected in his January 1885 report card[10] from The Harvard School, signed by Agnes. His scores vacillated between nines and tens (one assumes a possible ten-point scale) in Arithmetic, Composition, Geography, German, Map-drawing, Penmanship, Reading, Speaking, and Spelling. He achieved a perfect score in Deportment, and had no reported tardiness or half-days absent. The teacher, E.W. Brown, wrote in his remarks, "I think Robert is doing very well."

A Budding Artist

Robert also studied painting and drawing in courses conducted by a Miss Webb at the Art Institute.[11] The classes he attended were considered a higher level of instruction for advanced students, with studies of heads and figures cast in full light and shade and still life in colors.[12]

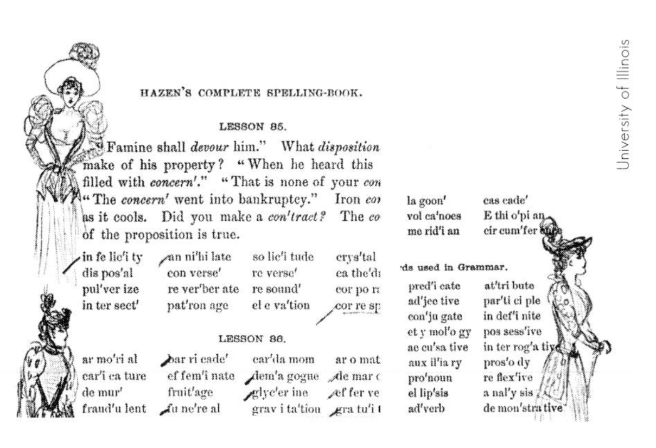

HAZEN'S COMPLETE SPELLING-BOOK.

LESSON 85.

"Famine shall *devour* him." What *disposition* make of his property? "When he heard this filled with *concern'*." "That is none of your *con* "The *concern'* went into bankruptcy." Iron *co* as it cools. Did you make a *con'tract?* The *co* of the proposition is true.

in fe lic'i ty — an ni'hi late — so lic'i tude — crys'tal
dis pos'al — con verse' — re verse' — ca the'd
pul'ver ize — re ver'ber ate — re sound' — cor po ra
in ter sect' — pat'ron age — el e va'tion — cor re sp

LESSON 86.

ar mo'ri al — bar ri cade' — car'da mom — ar o mat
car'i ca ture — ef fem'i nate — dem'a gogue — de mar
de mur' — fruit'age — glyc'er ine — ef fer ve
fraud'u lent — fu ne're al — grav i ta'tion — gra tu'i t

la goon' — cas cade'
vol ca'noes — E thi o'pi an
me rid'i an — cir cum'fer

ds used in Grammar.

pred'i cate — at'tri bute
ad'jec tive — par'ti ci ple
con'ju gate — in def'i nite
et y mol'o gy — pos sess'ive
ac cu'sa tive — in ter rog'a tive
aux il'ia ry — pros'o dy
pro'noun — re flex'ive
el lip'sis — a nal'y sis
ad'verb — de mon'stra tive

University of Illinois

Young Robert Allerton's sketches in the margins of *Hazen's Complete Spelling Book.*

Robert's skill at sketching as a sixteen-year-old can be seen in the margins of his copy of *Hazen's Complete Spelling Book.* There are his quick pencil studies of young girls with ribbons in their hair, and women—some in elegant ball gowns, others in their high-necked dresses, complete with muffs, hats and curved-handled umbrellas or walking sticks. Other drawings pay homage to classical antiquity and to the exotic: one woman is dressed as a Greek goddess, another as a harem girl with a turban-like headscarf and Egyptian eye makeup. All of them, contemporary or romanticized, show Robert's captivation with beauty.

Robert may have copied the following verse (undated) titled "The Lonely Mother," or perhaps he wrote it himself. The last few lines are unreadable because of corrections, but the first few lines are:

The lonely mother listening whilst
Hopelessly she waits to hear
Some understood familiar sound
Some childish sound but for her ear

Did he pine for Pamilla, or was this simply a lovely gesture to Agnes?

ST. PAUL'S SCHOOL

Frederic Bartlett began attending St. Paul's School in Concord, New Hampshire in 1888, and Robert joined him there the following year when he was sixteen. The Episcopal boys' school was founded in 1855 by a physician, Dr. George Shattuck, making it the oldest church school for boys in the country. From its rather austere beginnings, it had blossomed into a prominent institution by the late 1800s; among its students of that era were Cornelius Vanderbilt III, William H. Vanderbilt II, William Randolph Hearst, and John Jacob Astor IV. In 1892 tuition jumped from $500 to $600 per year,[13] the new price rivaling a year's tuition and expenses at an Ivy League university.[14]

Courtesy of St. Paul's School Archives

The "St. Paul's Special," a chartered train from Concord, New Hampshire to New York City. The unidentified boy in the lower left corner bears a striking resemblance to young Robert Allerton.

In Robert's first year at St. Paul's, the school began chartering a special train to shuttle students to New York City where they could conveniently meet their families for their three annual breaks.[15] The train represented a rare extravagance at St. Paul's. The general atmosphere was definitely no-frills, dedicated to rigorous academics and simple, healthy living.

Situated on fifty-five acres of rural land, the school reflected Dr. Shattuck's love of nature. In his own words, "Green fields and trees, streams and ponds, beautiful scenery, flowers, and minerals are educators."[16] Arthur Stanwood Pier,[17] Robert's classmate who later joined St. Paul's faculty, described Dr. Shattuck's vision as being down-to-earth in the most literal sense:

> *... the boys would have hills around... pine woods to ramble in, water to swim in; the wild creatures of the wood and lake would be almost at their door, and almost at their door too would be the picturesque old grist mill, with farmers driving up with sacks of meal. The "side influences" of a school set in so pleasant a place might easily be "the best part of it."*[18]

The accommodations would have required adjustment for the wealthier students. A "bedroom" consisted of a small cubicle with only a bed, clothes trunk, and toiletry shelf. A flimsy white curtain provided the only privacy. In one of Pier's many stories based on life at St. Paul's, he recounts a boy being teased mercilessly for having brought monogrammed towels, rose water, and perfumed soap.[19]

Courtesy of St. Paul's School Archives

Cubicles were standard sleeping accommodations for students at St. Paul's School.

Waking hours were scheduled to allow only small amounts of free time, spent outdoors whenever possible. Sports were highly encouraged, as was exploring on foot and via canoes on Turkey Pond, which stretched over a mile and a half through the campus. The boys translated its many small bays and inlets to global scale, nicknaming specific features the "Gulf of Mexico," "Isthmus of Panama," and the "Everglades."[20]

Most boys would catch a few muskrats or turtles, but Robert and Frederic apparently took broader liberties. They managed to acquire enough material to build a small house in the woods—or at least a hut of some sort—where they could "hide from their teachers."[21] It would be their first humble venture into the world of architecture, a passion each would develop in adulthood.

During their time at St. Paul's, two secret societies established footholds: the "Hoi" (or *hoi aretoi,* meaning "The Best") and the "Bogi." Among other initiation rites, the Hoi used pennies heated over gas jets to brand new members on their stomachs. The Bogi eventually held their meetings in the woods, away from snitches and school authorities. The two rival clubs conducted general mischief such as dirty tricks during school elections, and collecting "dues" to purchase contraband beer, which was consumed in an abandoned hunting lodge at the south end of Turkey Pond.[22] We can only wonder how long Robert and Frederic's woodland retreat remained undiscovered, or whether in fact they entertained guests, invited or otherwise.

Studies at St. Paul's included (as of 1877): Sacred Studies, Latin, Greek, French, German, Mathematics, Physics, Geography, History, English Studies, Writing, Spelling, Elocution, and Music (instrumental). Students were also marked for Punctuality, Industry, and Decorum. Instruction in instrumental music was offered, but there is no record of art classes.

Courtesy of St. Paul's School Archives

Canoeing on the Lower School Pond at St. Paul's School in Concord, New Hampshire.

The most demanding of the classes, according to Arthur Stanwood Pier, was Sacred Studies. Taught by Dr. Henry Augustus Coit, Rector of St. Paul's from 1856 to 1895, the weekly lessons required an oppressive amount of rote recitation. Semi-annual oral examinations for all subjects were held during one week, but those for Dr. Coit's Sacred Studies classes were the most dreaded of all. As Pier recalled:

> *The setting intensified the severity of the ordeal—the dim religious light, the boys huddling together on benches like cowed creatures before a storm, the Bishop sitting in front of the organ, trustees, masters, and the wives of trustees and of masters present as spectators, and the figure of the rector, sternly inquisitorial, as*

> *he stood robed in his surplice on the floor of the chapel and waited for complete stillness before putting the first question.... Between complete success and failure no compromise was admitted.... Many a boy who had recited glibly to himself the ten commandments, his duty to God, and his duty to his neighbor, became hopelessly confused when he rose to answer some comparatively simple question.*[23]

The setting could have been doubly intimidating to Robert, considering his hearing loss. And if Dr. Coit's generally rigorous teaching methodology were not discouraging enough, the Anglican Dr. Coit may have singled out the Universalist Robert for an extra dose of his techniques.

The Allerton *Mayflower* Pilgrims were separatists from their Anglican roots, and hence from the Episcopal Church. But Samuel Waters Allerton, like his father before him, had become a Universalist. The Universalist Church had been strongly affiliated with the Unitarian Church since the mid-nineteenth century; the two churches officially merged in 1961.[24] Coit "abominated Unitarianism,"[25] and likely disapproved equally of Universalism. Little existed in Robert's religious background to endear him to the notoriously uncompromising rector.

Whether due to a specific clash with Dr. Coit, general teen-age rebellion, or some other factor, Robert did not complete his Sacred Studies. He and Frederic both left St. Paul's without graduating.

ON THE CUSP OF ADULTHOOD

Robert and Frederic returned home during holidays and in summer. The society pages already noted Robert's presence, mentioning him in an 1890 article as one of many well-known men who knew how to use a camera.[26]

Eighteen-year-old Robert attended a New Year's Eve party in 1891 at the home of Mrs. Samuel M. Nickerson, in the company of several other Prairie Avenue young adults. Frederic may or may not have joined him in the festivities. Weeks earlier, on December 19, his mother, Mary Pitkin Bartlett, had died at their Prairie Avenue home.[27] Ten years had passed since Robert's own mother had died, but undoubtedly this loss affected both friends.

Years earlier, in 1883 Sam had participated in organizing the Washington Park Race Track. Every June, the track sponsored Derby Day. The South Side elite would jam the boulevards with carriages, buggies, and harness horses for the opening day parade, competing for attention with their finery. As usual, in 1891 the family participated, this time showing off Sam's new four-in-hand coach built to his specifications—primrose yellow body with black panels and moldings, vermilion running-gear, and black irons.[28] As reported by the June 21 *Chicago Daily Tribune,* "all the mountings are of steel and brass, and it is furnished with a full complement of horns, baskets, and robes. Robert Allerton handled the ribbons over four handsome, high-stepping bays."[29]

On July 19 Robert joined his family in Lake Geneva, Wisconsin, where he, W. S. McCrea, and C. L. Withrow judged the Regatta. A month later, as one of twenty-five participants in the Regatta's fifteen-mile race for the Sheridan Cup, he captained his yacht, *White Wings*, losing that race to Julian Rumsey, Jr., son of a former Chicago Mayor. Robert finished the summer by attending his cousin Berintha Thompson's September 24th wedding in Monticello.

Home life the next year (1892) would have been bustling. With Sam busy on committees planning the World's Columbian Exposition and Agnes assisting in raising money for it, what young man wouldn't be excited over the upcoming event? But the Exposition was still a year away—a year in which dropouts Robert and Frederic would have mulled over their futures.

THE WORLD COMES TO ROBERT

In 1893 Robert Allerton and Frederic Clay Bartlett were ready to see the world on their own terms—but when the World's Columbian Exposition finally opened its gates on May 1, the world came to them, just a few miles from their Prairie Avenue homes. The *New York Times* reported the next day:

> *OPENED BY THE PRESIDENT*
> *MR. CLEVELAND PRESSES THE MAGIC BUTTON AT CHICAGO.*
> *THE MACHINERY OF THE BIG FAIR STARTED*
> *Almost a Panic in the Great Crowd Present at the Exercises.*
> *WOMEN FAINTED IN THE CRUSH…*
>
> *Grover Cleveland, calm and dignified, in a few eloquent words delivered in a clear, ringing voice, which was heard by the great multitude gathered before him, declared the World's Columbian Exposition open a few minutes after noon to-day and touched the ivory-and-gold key which started the machinery, gave play to the fountains, and unfurled the flags and banners of the "White City."*[30]

Courtesy of ChicagoPostcardMuseum.org

Postcard of President Grover Cleveland and the Government Building of the World's Columbian Exposition. (Charles Goldsmith, 1893. American Lithographic Company.)

By the end of the event, more than twenty-five million visitors would have come to marvel at the sights.

Opening day had been three years in the making. The 1890 battle in Congress between Chicago and New York City to host the enormous event had been so zealously fought that *New York Sun* editor Charles A. Dana coined the nickname "Windy City" to describe Chicago's vociferous politicians. The new moniker did not entirely eradicate the old one, "The Red City," used by east coast journalists since the 1880s in reference to the years of bloody labor disputes.[31] To rectify the "Red City" reputation, the sparkling white buildings created for the Columbian Exposition were successfully branded as the "White City." Sam Allerton was one of the directors chosen to bring that vision to life.

The Director of Works, Daniel H. Burnham (of Chicago's successful Burnham and Root architectural firm) selected a cadre of major architects to design the White City.[32] The team overshot the target of the 400th anniversary of Columbus arriving in America, but compensated in scale, splendor, and ingenuity. The new city arose seemingly overnight on what was previously a swampy wasteland located seven miles south of downtown, called Jackson Park.

Now visitors could ascend 250 feet on the world's first Ferris Wheel to view the completed 630-acre site—twice the size of today's Epcot Center. The centerpiece, Jackson Park, featured fourteen neoclassical buildings called the "Court of Honor," encircling a shimmering lagoon. Extending west, the eighty-acre Midway Plaisance offered additional amusements and concessions with a more carnival-like atmosphere, for the most part organized in "villages" of international theme. In total, 200 buildings were constructed for the event, housing over 250,000 displays from 46 participating nations, each anxious to share its cultural traditions, historical achievements, and newest technology.

Because the buildings needed to stand for only six months, Burnham resorted to the art of illusion to create the appearance of white marble facades. Workers slathered a mixture of Plaster of Paris and fiber called "staff" over massive frameworks of steel and wood. Only two of those buildings remain standing today. Coincidentally, those two particular buildings each represent a turning point in Robert Allerton's life.

The first of these buildings, north of the main grounds at Michigan and Adams, was designed with dual purpose. It would house the delegates to the scholarly World's Congresses during the Exposition, and afterward it would become a new home for the Art Institute of Chicago.[33] Seventy-five years later, it would be renamed in Robert Allerton's honor.[34]

In the summer of 1893, it was the second of the permanent buildings that thoroughly enraptured Robert and Frederic. The Palace of Fine Arts (today known as the Museum of Science and Industry) still stands by virtue of its more durable masonry understructure, an insurance requirement for the valuable collections of artwork it housed. Each participating country was allotted separate gallery space within the five-acre building, with additional areas devoted to sculpture, water color, and oil painting. Berthe and Potter Palmer, friends of the Allertons, lent some of their prized pieces for the exhibition of "Foreign Masterpieces Owned by Americans." Artists included Manet, Pissaro, Sisley, Delacroix, Corot, Degas, and many others. Paintings were hung floor to ceiling, covering every available square inch of wall space in the building. The effect must have been dizzying.

Paul V. Galvin Library, Illinois Institute of Technology

Interior of one exhibit at the Palace of Fine Arts Building at the 1893 World's Columbian Exposition in Chicago. (From Hubert Howe Bancroft, *The Book of the Fair*, 1893.)

As Frederic Bartlett described in his memoir, he and Robert were overwhelmed not only by the scale of the art exhibition, but by the quality of the creative work.

> *Tired as we were, for as was our custom, we had walked past miles and miles of pictures, a never-ending wild excitement for us. To think that men could conceive such things, and actually bring them into being on a flat bare canvas: Could create illusions of space, perspective, sunlight or storm, all on a piece of cloth with colors taken from dark mines or pungent earth, applied by means of bristles taken from a pig's back fastened to a little stick. All glorious fake, of course, but how exciting.*[35]

Whether to recover from the sensory overload or perhaps to sustain the euphoria, Robert and Frederic sat down at a restaurant to servings of Hungarian goulash and glasses of Rhine wine. If Robert's father had won his 1893 mayoral campaign against Carter Henry Harrison, there might only have been the goulash. Sam was vice president of the Citizens League and a member of the Law and Order League, an organization dedicated to temperance. As a member of the World's Fair committee, he and others directors warned about the possible intrusion of criminal elements.[36]

Paul V. Galvin Library, Illinois Institute of Technology

The German Village on the Midway Plaisance at the 1893 World's Columbian Exposition in Chicago. (From Hubert Howe Bancroft, *The Book of the Fair*, 1893.)

The less dignified amusements were mainly confined to the Midway Plaisance, where Exposition visitors enjoyed beer halls and burlesque houses. At the "Street of Cairo," one could witness the talents of the famous exotic dancer, Little Egypt, or any of her many "stomach dancing" imitators. Frederic and Robert were among the passers-by, as Frederic recalled at the day's end. They did not, however, bypass more libations, which may have prompted the following epiphany:

> *To the strains of "The Beautiful Blue Danube" we pledged our lives to the creation of beauty and forthwith determined to leave the security and luxury of home, and at nineteen to forge out into the world, to learn the techniques, secrets, and methods of artists.*
>
> *To make sure we were serious and making no mistake, we ordered more wine and then to be certain beyond all doubt, we dashed on to the German Village, passing without temptation, the streets of Cairo, where the tom-toms without, announced the stomach dances within.*
>
> *There at a more solid table accompanied by a famous German military band, we drank great steins of Munich's priceless gift to the world, and with all the passion and ardor of youth, we again sold our birthright, and swore eternal friendship.*[37]

Paul V. Galvin Library, Illinois Institute of Technology

A Persian dancing girl from the Street of Cairo on the Midway Plaisance at the 1893 World's Columbian Exposition in Chicago. (From N. D. Thompson Publishing Co., *The Dream City*, 1893-94.)

We don't know how long their plan had been in the works, but now the decision was made. Would the study of art really be, as Frederic put it, a matter of "selling their birthright?" If he meant they would be giving up their Prairie Avenue luxuries for a Bohemian lifestyle, they would not have been unique among privileged young adults of that era. And assuming they did nothing disgraceful enough to risk their inheritances, each had the safety net of a home (actually, a choice of several). Even so, Robert and Frederic each surely took a long, deep breath before announcing their plans to the families.

CHAPTER THREE
The Artist's Life

On the road to nowhere
What wild oats did you sow
When you left your father's house
With your cheeks aglow?

From "On the Road to Nowhere"
by Vachel Lindsay (1879-1931)

STUDYING ART IN EUROPE

Robert's decision to study art in Europe with Frederic represented a major turning point in his personal life—but as a growing historic trend in the late 1800s, studying art was not such a radical idea. Since the end of the Civil War, art was quickly becoming a legitimate business in America, nurtured by new industrial wealth and the doting attention of the press. A *New York Times* article from 1883 entitled "A Crowded Profession" declared, "Chicago, San Francisco, Cincinnati, ay, Boston and New-York, are as full of artists as of lawyers."[1]

Chicago's Academy of Fine Arts (later to become the Art Institute of Chicago) was one of many American art schools to blossom in the Gilded Age. Philadelphia's Pennsylvania Academy of the Fine Arts and New York City's National Academy of Design and Art Students League were schools of choice for serious American artists. More accurately, they served as stepping-stones for those preparing to study abroad. In 1900 *The New York Times* estimated there were "as many as 20,000 American students scattered through the great cities of Europe, studying music in every branch, and likewise painting, sketching, and all the fine arts akin thereto."[2]

The Philadelphia and New York schools had long before opened their classes to women. Young ladies, many having proved themselves in those arenas, flocked to the academies and studios of Europe and lobbied to be taken seriously as professionals alongside their male counterparts. Ironically, many of the young men faced a different challenge: convincing their elders that the profession itself was worthy of their efforts. General public attitudes toward the business of art may have evolved, but on a personal level the decision to enter the field has always been a hard sell to parents. Even those (and sometimes, especially those) from artistic families are still warned of potential heartbreak, financial instability, and the capricious lifestyles with which artists have long been associated.

Robert and Frederic probably hoped their fathers would respond to their proposal in the progressive spirit offered by the author of the *New York Times* "Crowded Profession" article:

> *There was a time when the worthy merchant or manufacturer who had a son with a passion for painting felt himself a martyr to the whims of Providence. He reasoned with that son sternly and as likely as not considered that to put him in a 'store' where it was his duty to sweep the place out at cock-crow was the soundest and surest step toward reformation. Now, the fathers who think so narrowly and believe in measures so Draconian are few and far between. They perceive that at least there is a chance for a boy who shows artistic talent to seize one of the great prizes and become a popular artist.*[3]

But Sam Allerton and Adolphus Bartlett, businessmen to the core, required a much more rigorous sales pitch. They were "horrified" that their only sons would consider doing such a "silly thing" as studying to become painters.[4]

The Chicago Tribune

Caricature of Samuel Allerton by G. Viafora, 1907.

To Sam's credit, he may have had a valid and specific reason to disapprove of Robert's plan; he may have been more realistic about his son's talent. The only remaining examples of Robert's early artwork are the sketches in the margins of his childhood spelling book. His formal training appears to have consisted only of his five days of Art Institute classes during the two years prior to his career decision.[5]

Robert could have studied first in America before taking on the more competitive European art scene—but living in Europe may have been the true dream, and studying art his rationale. In any case, Sam granted Robert $1,000 per year for expenses and sent him on his way.[6] Guidebooks of that era recommended a minimum of $800 to $1,000 for a year's art study abroad.[7]

Robert's artistic skill merited the tutelage of the instructor with whom Frederic Bartlett had begun his studies in Munich. Frederic had previously studied with this man, indicating that his skills may have been more advanced than Robert's. In his 1932 memoir, Frederic only referred to their teacher as the (artfully italicized) *Master.*[8] For equally mysterious reasons, he never once referred to Robert by name. Robert's identity is unmistakable. The *Master* was likely Herr Rudolph Kuppelmayr.[9]

Robert and Frederic rented a sitting room and bedroom in what was once the home of the American-born Count Rumford. Their apartment overlooked the English Gardens and was only a ten-minute walk from the instructor's home and studio. Frederic's memoir reveals more about their evenings at the Carnival and the memorable food and drink than it does about their study, but it does say that their work was diligent to the point of competition with one another.[10]

Sometime during that winter of 1893-94, the *Master* announced that he had submitted their names for the entrance examinations to Munich's Royal Academy of Fine Arts *(Akademie der Bildenden Künste München),* warning them not to be too optimistic, since foreign students comprised only ten percent of the student body. Adhering to the heightened emphasis of that era on figure drawing and painting, the examination required submission of a finished drawing of a head (by which Frederic emphasized "finished, leaving nothing to the imagination"[11]), a nude, anatomy study, and a composition—all in just one week. Exhausted, they returned to their routine studies. Within a few days, to the astonishment of the young men and the *Master,* Robert and Frederic were both accepted.

Munich's Royal Academy of Fine Arts, founded in 1808, remains one of Germany's most prestigious art schools. In the nineteenth century, it ranked second only to the schools of Paris and offered the rigorous classical training prescribed at that time. Today the Academy can boast attendance by some of the twentieth century's most influential artists: Giorgio de Chirico, Paul Klee, Franz Marc, Josef Albers, and Wassily Kandinsky. Kandinsky was rejected on his first try and was admitted to classes of Anton Azbe only with his second portfolio in 1896. Robert's and Frederic's acceptance to the Royal Academy surely made for a more pleasant summer vacation back home in America with their families.

University of Illinois

Robert Allerton, from an 1895 portrait made at The Folly by Leo D. Weil.

That autumn Robert and Frederic returned to Munich and took an apartment together, a five-minute walk from the Academy. Their delight in furnishing it with bargain antiques revealed signs of the notable collectors each would become in later life. Rummaging for furnishings seemed to have interested Frederic more than painting, or at least he remembered it more fondly at the time of his writing in 1932. In fact, he didn't write a single word about their actual studies at the Royal Academy.

Only through the writing of other artists can we get a first-hand look at classes at the Academy and other studios that followed similar curricula. Wassily Kandinsky recalled his 1896 life drawing class with Azbe as follows:

> *Students of both sexes and different nationalities gathered around these ill-smelling, indifferent, inexpressive, mostly characterless phenomena of nature... and tried to copy precisely these people who meant nothing to them, anatomically, constructionally, and characteristically.*

The students, he said, were so focused on the academic exercises that they "never thought for a moment, it seemed, about art." His revulsion to the classes was so intense that, "Only out on the street could I breathe freely again."[12]

By the end of the year's study, Frederic had fallen in love with fifteen-year-old Dora Tripp,* who was also studying at the Royal Academy and traveling in Europe with her mother, Mrs. Ernest Schmid of White Plains, New York.[13] The romance lasted through the summer vacation that Robert and Frederic spent in America. In the autumn, all three met again in Paris. This time Robert and Frederic each found a separate apartment.[14]

Robert and Frederic continued their studies, enrolling at the Ecole Collin for morning drawing classes, the Aman-Jean School of Painting for the afternoons, and the Académie Colarossi in the Rue Grande-Chaumière for nude figure classes in the evenings.[15] Their eyes opened to new sensibilities at a radical turning point in art history: the Impressionist show at Durand-Ruel's gallery caused such uproar that it was heavily guarded by police, and students battled in the streets over Rodin's controversial sculpture of Balzac.

According to Frederic's memoir, Robert remained in Paris the second year, 1897. Dora had returned to America, where Frederic visited her in the summer. Meanwhile, he and Robert traveled throughout Italy and continued their studies.

Also in 1897, Robert's childhood friend, Ethel Field, gave birth to a son, Ronald Tree.* She had married English real estate developer Arthur Tree in 1891.[16] Robert's meeting with Ethel's son many years later shed some light on the nature of his adolescent feelings for her. Sometime after 1937, Ronald Tree asked to tour Robert Allerton's Hawaiian estate, unaware of any connection between his mother and the owner. Robert agreed and met Ronald at the airport, announcing, "I haven't seen you since you were in your cradle."

Ronald, quite surprised, asked, "And what were you doing by my cradle?"

Robert replied, "I was in love with your mother."[17]

Robert's feelings for Ethel may have been no more than a schoolboy crush; we will never know the nature of his "love" for her. When John Gregg Allerton was asked whether a marriage between the two had been desired by their parents, he said the Fields were more interested in obtaining a title of nobility for their daughter.[18] Many of Europe's aristocrats had fallen on hard times, enhancing their appeal to young American heiresses. Ethel eventually obliged in that regard, divorcing Arthur Tree on May 12, 1901. Ten days later, she married the flamboyant David Beatty, First Earl of Beatty[19] with whom she had conducted a clandestine affair since 1898.[20] Ethel suffered from severe depression until her death in 1932 at age fifty-nine.[21]

John Gregg Allerton revealed more about Robert's relationships with women, saying, "You have to remember he was deaf. That's one of the reasons he more or less withdrew, or didn't court any girl, because he didn't want to burden any girl with a person who was handicapped."[22] His inability to follow conversations, especially in crowds, left him ill at ease in social situations. He was embarrassed when people had to "yell at him."[23] Throughout his life, he preferred socializing in very small groups and was content to spend time alone. Frederic was one of the few people with whom he could communicate easily and freely, but Fredric's new preoccupation with Dora would have required Robert to share his friend's attention.

Frederic made no further mention in his memoir of Robert either leaving Europe or staying. Although they remained lifelong friends, Robert must have missed Frederic's full-time companionship. Perhaps he had received unfavorable critiques of his paintings, or simply lost interest in what had become Frederic's game to win. Also, his visit with Ethel and her young son likely did little to raise his spirits.

Whatever factors shaped his state of mind, they were potent enough to lead Robert, around 1898, to burn his paintings and then return to America.

CHAPTER FOUR
Getting in Touch with a Farm Somewhere

See here, Bob, what're you going to do to make a living?

Samuel W. Allerton, to Robert[1]

DOWN TO BUSINESS

Robert's climactic decision in Paris to destroy his artwork, according to John Gregg Allerton, was simply a result of his realization "that he didn't have the natural talent for painting."[2] Nothing more is documented about what must have been an emotionally turbulent time for him. Upon his return, most of his old friends were making new lives for themselves, lives that did not necessarily include him.[3] Now in his late twenties, with his dream of becoming an artist literally in ashes, he had prospects for neither marriage nor career.

He rented a house for a season in New York City's Washington Square.[4] There he could soul-search his future while hobnobbing with friends, several of whom had either relocated there from Europe or passed through on their travels. After returning to Chicago, exactly how he decided to claim the Illinois cornfields as a permanent address and "farmer" as his official job title is a story told with variations. *The Chicago Tribune* reported his father's recollection in a 1907 interview:

> *Robert had completed school and had spent two or three years in Chicago. Coming into the old gentleman's office one morning the old man turned suddenly on the Allerton heir:*
>
> *"See here, Bob, what're you going to do to make a living?"*
>
> *Perhaps "Bob" had considered the question before—possibly he hadn't—but he rose to the occasion and said he believed he'd like to be a farmer.*
>
> *"Alright," said the father. "Get ready for a European trip. Take young Boree [John J. Borie] with you—he's a friend of yours and an architect—and you two*

make a study of country houses over there. Come back in a year with the plans for the house."[5]

John Gregg Allerton claimed, however, that Robert took the initiative of asking his father for a job. Sam Allerton suggested that Robert manage the downstate acreage that had been given to him years earlier. Robert then bargained with his father for the funding to build a house of his own choosing.

Robert had the creative challenge he craved, and it fulfilled Sam's long-held philosophy. His public advice to city boys (Robert being no exception) had always been to:

get in touch with a farm somewhere; while you work it, your good returns will not only be coming in, but you will be laying up health, vitality and character, which are always welcomed by metropolitan enterprises.[6]

University of Illinois

Robert Allerton (left) and architect John J. Borie, III on the porch of the Stallcup house prior to or during construction of the Piatt County mansion.

Robert had already formulated his own philosophy as a gentleman farmer. Although Sam was content to visit his farms only periodically, Robert "disapproved of absentee landlordism."[7] His intention to make the Piatt County property (known to the family as "The Farms") his primary home added to the rationale—if he needed one—for a suitable abode.

His maternal cousin, Jessie Thompson Dighton,* and Jessie's husband, Will Dighton, lived in Monticello. They would give Robert a sense of belonging and provide Sam with extra sets of watchful eyes.

Robert set up housekeeping in May 1898 in "the old Stallcup house,"[8] a three-room cottage previously used by one of the tenant farmers. It lacked running water, so he had it moved to the edge of a grove of trees near a spring where he could bathe. He installed an outdoor privy and proceeded to decorate the interior with posters of Toulouse-Lautrec paintings he had purchased in Paris.

Within a few months he knew he wanted his new home to sit on the knoll opposite his cottage. Damming up the small valley between the two would create a pond between the mansion site and the meadow. The rest of the design decisions would wait for the participation of his friend and architect, John J. "Dickey" Borie III.*

The grandson of one of Philadelphia's founders, John Borie was well established not only in East Coast society, but also in the Midwest. His sister, Emily Borie,* had married steel tycoon Arthur Larned Ryerson of Chicago. Borie attended the University of Pennsylvania and the École des Beaux-Arts in Paris[9] and worked for a few years with Chicago architect James Gamble Rogers.[10]* He was also employed by the Philadelphia firm of Cope and Stewardson[11] and had many connections to New York City artists, as did both of his employers.

Because Robert's presence was required in New York in October, he delayed his European odyssey with John Borie until later that month. On October 5, 1898, after a seven-year engagement, Frederic Bartlett married his sweetheart, Dora Tripp, in White Plains, New

Courtesy of Elisabeth Bartlett Sturges

Tintype of Robert, Dora, and Frederic (top) and two unidentified women (below), possibly Agnes Allerton and Dora's mother.

York.[12] Robert served as best man. The young couple spent two weeks at the Bartlett winter home in Asheville, North Carolina. They planned to return to Paris,[13] where Frederic would continue his studies, influenced by his teacher, muralist Puvis de Chavannes,[14] and L'Academie Carmen master, James McNeill Whistler.

On October 19, Robert's sister Kate, a widow since 1889, married Hugo Richards Johnstone,* a Boston naval officer and attorney. The wedding took place in her New York home at 121 Madison Avenue. Sam and Agnes attended, and one can only assume that Robert was there as well. Kate and Hugo sailed the next day on the SS *Fürst Bismarck* for a three-month European journey.[15] With the Bartletts also planning to sail to Paris, and John Borie and Robert heading for Europe, all three parties may have made the week-long crossing together.

John Borie and Robert arrived in England to study Tudor homes, but Robert soon lost interest in that style. After considering Queen Anne and Georgian designs, they eventually discovered a model for Robert's home in Ham House, a Stuart mansion, overlooking the Thames River in Surrey.

The largest seventeenth-century house in England, Ham House was built in 1610 and extensively remodeled in the 1670s by the Duke and Duchess of Lauderdale. Each room of Robert's new home, like Ham House, would include a view of water—either the Sangamon River or the pond. In some respects, Ham House and Robert's mansion have shared the same destiny, with both now open to the public. And legend has it that both are haunted—Ham House by the Duchess of Lauderdale, and the Allerton mansion by a lady in white who stands at the base of the stairs, putting on her gloves.

A Mansion Rises From The Prairie

John Borie and Robert arrived back in Piatt County by mid-April, 1899 with plans in hand.[16] Groundbreaking would start soon after accomplishing one more vital task.[17] Borie was not licensed in Illinois, so his drawings were stamped, as required, by a licensed architect—James Gamble Rogers.

The *Chicago Tribune* noted Rogers' collaboration on Robert Allerton's $50,000 "summer home" and commented on the 96-x-70-foot main section of the house, and the 75-foot-long servants' wing. The entire house, servants' wing, and stable would encompass 32,229 square feet. Modern features would include steam-heating and electric lighting.[18]

Despite the impressive dimensions, the manor included only four guest bedrooms. Because of Robert's hearing disability, he did not foresee entertaining large groups. But, as his wealth and stature demanded, his design reflected a necessary grandeur.

Construction commenced in earnest on June 13, 1899, supervised by William Mavor* of Chicago, who had been a contractor for buildings at the 1893 World's Columbian Exposition. Many of Mavor's 150 laborers also came from the Chicago area, where a strike had kept them from employment. They used dynamite to excavate boulders, with blasts heard 16 miles away in Mansfield.[19] Building materials included woodwork from native timber, limestone from

Bedford, Indiana,[20] and individually wrapped bricks imported from Holland, which had served as ballast on the ship. Custom-tinted mortar gave a more uniform appearance to the façade.[21]

Periodic problems ensued. In October the men lit dynamite fuses to remove tree stumps. Dry grasses caught fire, spreading quickly to a shed where they stored 2,000 pounds of additional dynamite. Several brave men extinguished the fire in the shed. The fire had come close enough to singe the dynamite boxes.[22] Later, a scarcity of building stone delayed the work schedule.[23] And one Sunday evening at the Allerton boardinghouse an intoxicated Chicago carpenter chased others around with an axe.[24]

The cornerstone of the house was put into place in September 1899 with "appropriate ceremonies"[25] attended by Sam, Agnes, and friends. During construction Robert kept his little cottage, but frequently visited his parents in Chicago before embarking on his winter trip overseas.

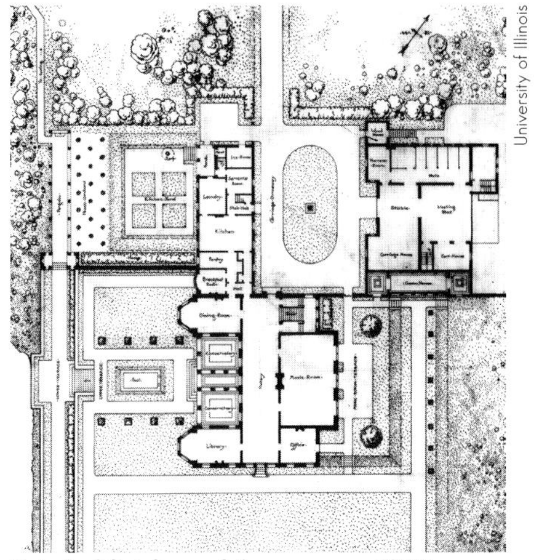

University of Illinois

Detail of first floor of the mansion, 1899 rendering by John J. Borie, III.

During his absence, in March 1900 the boardinghouse built for the laborers burned down, but work continued.[26] By April the mansion had been enclosed and the plasterers were hard at work,[27] as Robert journeyed homeward from Europe. In May the carpenters began constructing a barn.[28]

With the exterior of the home completed, Robert ordered that the lintel above the back terrace doors be carved with the year 1900, rather than 1899, finding the double zeros more appealing to his sense of symmetry.[29] Another lintel topped the Conservatory entrance, with the year 1900 engraved in Roman numerals. Another three years would pass before work on the interior itself would conclude.

In 1902 Borie opened an office in the St. James Building at 1133 Broadway, New York City.[30] He sent plans to Illinois when Robert required revisions and additions. Within a few years he redesigned the mansion's roofline, removing a parapet that allowed water to drip down the interior walls. Despite other architectural corrections to come, Borie's general layout of the mansion and grounds provided a solid foundation for decades of refinement and embellishment, allowing Robert's creativity to thrive.

Guests would approach from the Allerton private road (today's Old Timber Road). At the turn to the mansion sits the two-story, red brick Gate House designed by John Borie in 1903 for the head gardener. Despite its modest function, its style and detail seamlessly introduce the Georgian Revival mansion. Two columns topped by ornamental pineapples, a traditional symbol of welcome, mark the entrance to the grounds. Following the lane from the Gate House for a few hundred yards, guests would arrive

Courtesy of Bonnet House Museum & Gardens

The Allerton mansion before the parapets were removed and the roofline was redesigned in 1908.

Michael Holtz

The home of Allerton's head gardener, designed by John J. Borie, III in 1903. The building, facing the entrance lane to the mansion, is now called the Gate House.

at the mansion's small, sparsely adorned courtyard, enclosed on three sides by the entry door to the main house, a servants' wing on the right, and a detached stable on the left.

Construction of the magnificent stable began in 1901—a year after Robert had moved in. It had taken nearly all winter to haul the required 400,000 bricks six miles west from the Monticello depot.[31] Located immediately adjacent to a glass-roofed conservatory, the stable would hold six horse stalls, a wood house, harness room, washing shed, carriage house, cart house, hayloft, two additional conservatories, and three second-floor bedrooms for staff.

The crowning cupola, a feature usually reserved for public buildings, may have been Robert's homage to his father's immense Prairie Avenue stable—but Sam hated Borie's design. Sam reinforced his opinion by mispronouncing Borie's name as "Vories."[32] Perhaps he was taunting Robert by comparing his mansion to "Voorhies Castle," another elaborate farmhouse being built that same year in Piatt County. [33]

Robert was unhappy with Borie's many starts and stops on the stable construction during the summer of 1901. In several letters to a friend, he complained that Borie failed to reveal his whereabouts. He wrote: "In the meantime, all work has been stopped here owing to his sending us new plans. Really, he is too much. I am furious with him."[34]

Courtesy of Bonnet House Museum & Gardens

The courtyard entrance to the mansion, showing the stable to the left.

That fall Robert stayed in what he simply called his "farmhouse" just long enough to get the feel of it. The large rooms were never adequately heated by the two coal furnaces located at opposite ends of the house. Land owner or not, with the crops in, he wanted to escape the harsh Illinois winter.

Early on, his trips focused particularly on England and France, but soon branched out to Asia. On his earlier European trip with Borie, Robert had purchased some items for the interior of his planned mansion. Now, with the mansion built, he was ready to scout seriously for artwork and the rest of his furnishings.

Stopping in New York before sailing in 1900, Robert may have visited his sister Kate. On Christmas Day she and Hugo became the parents of a nephew for Robert, named Allerton Johnstone.*

Robert traveled with a friend, C. Russell Hewlett,[35]* a New Yorker who had studied in Paris while Robert and Frederic were there. Their trip lasted several months, with Robert sending back Baroque and Rococo furniture from Italy. In China he purchased ornate furniture and scroll paintings to fill his many empty walls.

That trip set the pattern for his lifelong winter travels, searching for art and enjoying warmer climates.

CHAPTER FIVE
Interlude: A Visit to "The Farms"

...remarkable among American successful houses.

House Beautiful, on Robert Allerton's Home, 1904[1]

A TOUR OF THE MANSION

Wealthy citizens in Monticello now had a new standard to meet. From the mid-1800s through the 1930s, wealthy bankers, farmers, and businessmen built gracious homes along the town's main thoroughfares—particularly on Charter Street, and North State Street, called "Millionaires' Row" by the locals. Many of the owners had Thompson-Allerton ties. A brick Gothic Revival home with slit windows at 915 North State Street was constructed for Preston C. Huston in 1873, the year Robert was born. The first Monticello house with electricity, running water, and central heating, by 1909 it was home to his maternal uncle, Charles Nelson Thompson and family.[2] In 1898 Charles' daughter (and Robert's cousin), Jessie Thompson Dighton, and her husband, William Dighton, built a Queen Anne house at number 707 for William's widowed mother, Sarah. The back door at number 707 connected via a sidewalk to 719 North State, built in 1906 by William Dighton's sister, Mary Dighton Burgess, and her husband, Louis Burgess. Their home included a ballroom in the basement and a central vacuum system.[3]

But no home in Monticello could match Robert's. In 1904 *House Beautiful* magazine featured his mansion, commenting on its "consistent good taste and beauty" and calling it "remarkable among American successful houses."[4]

The mansion's first floor plan follows a basic "H" design. The grand Gallery, approximately 20 feet wide and over 90 feet long, forms the main axis. Robert occasionally used this dramatic entry as a dining room for very large gatherings. A stairway, massive Music Room, and an office sit to the left; to the right, the Conservatory balances the size of the Music Room, flanked by two rooms in oriel bays.

The courtyard door to the main house originally opened directly into the Gallery.

University of Illinois

Allerton mansion Gallery, circa 1935.

Unfortunately, when the front door opened, gusts of wind would blow straight down its length.[5] John Borie, who had moved to England in 1907, corrected the problem in 1916 by adding an entry corridor that also connected the stable to the house. Tiled in a diamond pattern of black and white marble, the new space was furnished with bookcases and cabinetry.

The gracious stairway divides into two at the landing. Mahogany banisters and double-scroll trim typify its American Colonial style. Located near the Gallery's main entrance, it allowed Robert and his guests to come and go from the carriage court to the five main upstairs bedrooms without disturbing those in the downstairs rooms.

University of Illinois

Gallery stairway, undated photograph.

The Music Room, next to the base of the staircase on the first floor, is approximately 50 feet long and 30 feet wide, with an impressive 23-foot ceiling height. Within the first decade, Robert furnished it with a Steinway grand piano,[6] luxurious tapestries hung high above the paneled lower walls, and French and Italian furniture. He covered the floors with Persian and Turkish rugs, and used crimson brocade for the draperies.[7]

University of Illinois

Music Room, photographed before 1920.

Tall French doors open onto the Music Room terrace. Outside, two *Caryatid* statues guard the entrance. More accurately called "terminal busts," the term "caryatid" generally refers to a complete male or female figure designed as a structural support in lieu of a column. Robert purchased the sculptures from an antique shop in Rome shortly after he completed the mansion. They either came from the Pope's Villa or they are copies of ones that were there.[8]

Michael Holtz

One of two *Caryatid* sculptures on the Music Room terrace.

University of Illinois

Music Room terrace, circa 1915. Borie's gargoyles decorate the stable façade, and two *Caryatids* flank the Music Room doors.

One wall of the stable, adorned with two whimsical gargoyle-like faces, encloses an adjoining side of the Library Terrace. Such decorations are not typical of the Georgian style, but they were Borie's specialty; he later designed gargoyles for the University of Pennsylvania men's dormitories.

The Oak Room, as it is now called, functioned as Robert's office. Located beyond the Music Room, French doors to the Music Room terrace have since been replaced with windows. A portrait of Sam by

Michael Holtz

Gargoyle on stable greenhouse façade.

University of Illinois

John Borie's rendering of a gargoyle for the exterior of the stable greenhouse. The drawing was incorrectly dated May 1st 1891, rather than 1901.

University of Illinois

The Oak Room, photographed before 1920.

Ellen Emmet Rand, now in the mansion's Gallery, once hung over the Oak Room fireplace.

The Pine Room, across the Gallery from the Oak Room, is paneled in native wood and outfitted with rows of shelves from floor to ceiling. Robert referred to it as his "Front Library," but his collection of books became so extensive that he soon outgrew the space. He eventually lined the Gallery and several other rooms with bookcases to hold them all, and in later years, converted the Music Room to that purpose. In the 1940s, the Pine Room became John Gregg's office.

University of Illinois

The Pine Room, or Robert's "Front Library." Undated photograph.

The Conservatory, set back between the oriel bays, balances the size of the Music Room on the opposite side of the gallery. Its floor-to-ceiling windows allow both ventilation and a vista of the pond and meadow to the southwest. A reciprocal view of the mansion from the grounds defines the formal façade of the house. Shortly after moving in, Robert realized the full impact of the sun beating down through the glass ceiling onto the brick floor. In 1919 he employed Robert Work,[9] an associate of noted Chicago architect David Adler,* to design a proper roof and a paneled interior ceiling.[10]

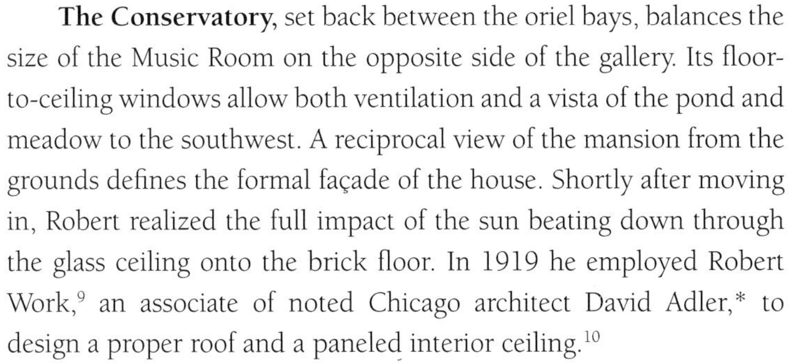

University of Illinois

This 1938 photo of the Conservatory shows large columns that were later removed.

Robert frequently used the Conservatory, a room that could set fifty, for casual entertaining. He dedicated one end to open air dining and furnished the other end with a casual arrangement of wicker chairs.[11]

The Butternut Room, named for its paneling of native white walnut, occupies the oriel bay across from the staircase. Above the fireplace, a carved pineapple symbolizes hospitality. Designed as a formal dining room, it could seat twenty. Instead, Robert used it as his "Back Library."

University of Illinois

A painting of the Three Graces hung over the Butternut Room fireplace, circa 1946.

The Breakfast Room, between the Butternut Room and the servants' wing, served as an intimate winter dining room because it could be warmed with a small electric heater.[12] The term "breakfast room" was a misnomer. Robert always took his breakfast (of orange juice, tea, and two graham crackers) in bed.

The servant's wing, to the right of the front door, housed a pantry, kitchen, laundry, ice house, meat and dairy rooms, staff dining room, and a porch facing the kitchen yard. The second floor of the staff's wing held four bedrooms, two bathrooms, and a morning room. The 1900 census listed only one employee for Robert, a Chinese cook by the name of James Linglong. Ten years later eight employees worked there.

An electric plant and artesian wells rounded out the self-sustaining property. Innovation and attention to detail extended to the greenhouses and conservatories. Depressions in the floor held heated water to increase humidity, a feature flower-lover Agnes must have endorsed.

A 32,000-square-foot mansion with a servant's wing, two conservatories, a long gallery, and a multitude of rooms—one could wonder whether this was the kind of "getting in touch with a farm somewhere" that Sam had in mind. Completion of the mansion marked Robert's first major achievement, but it was only the beginning; he had just begun his lifelong and worldwide quest for art and beauty.

HOW THE GARDENS GREW

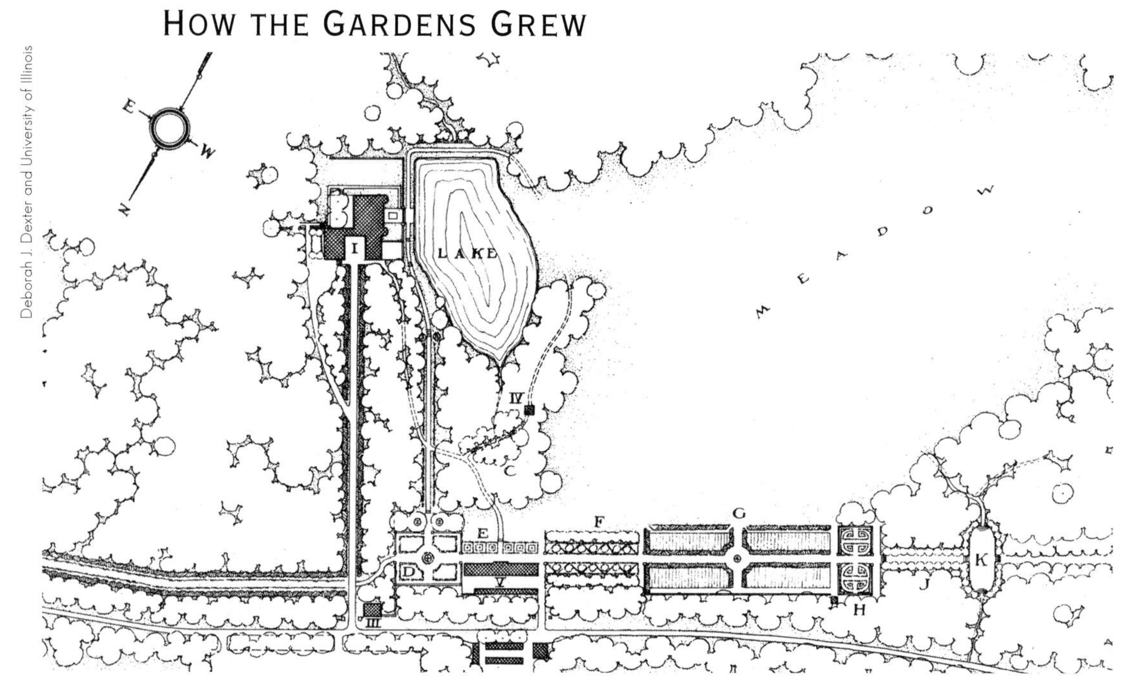

Deborah J. Dexter and University of Illinois

Detail of a 1947 drawing by Robert La Follette Zander (1913-2003). I, Mansion; III, Gate House; IV, Gazebo; V, Greenhouse (current Visitor Center); C, Spring Garden; D, Brick Wall Garden; E, Square Parterre Garden; F, Triangle Parterre Garden; G, Seasonal Gardens (Annual Garden, Bulb Garden, and Peony Garden); H, Chinese Maze Garden; J, Avenue of the *Chinese Musicians;* K, Sunken Garden.

John Gregg Allerton said of Robert, "He created a picture in the garden. Yes, he painted with vegetation instead of oil and canvas."[13] The gardens reflect Sam's devotion to agriculture and Agnes' interest in horticulture, but the final expression is Robert's alone. At first glance, the geometric framework defined by John Borie in 1900 sets the tone for a formal garden, a reminder of Robert's stay in Munich and his travels throughout Europe. Closer observation reveals his Midwestern practicality, blended with influences of twentieth-century style, and his own eclectic taste.

Robert was as restless as Nature herself, changing the gardens through the seasons and years. Only the most massive of the sculptures have enjoyed permanent homes; he repeatedly shuffled the smaller pieces from site to site. His theory about installing artwork in the home extended to the outdoors. "If you leave the same picture on the wall all the time, you never see it anymore."[14] Without thorough documentation, it is difficult to envision how a particular garden appeared at any given time, but the most dramatic difference from 1900 to the present is the overall backdrop. Today we walk trails cloistered in timber, much of which had been clear-cut for farmland when the mansion was built.

The Conservatory Terrace marks the origin of most strolls through the gardens. Robert was ahead of his time, incorporating a pool into the design. A decade after it was built, many members of Chicago society were just discovering the joy of having their own swimming pools. While Robert's pool is small by today's standards, its striking view of the pond and meadow and its decoration with sculpture provided guests with an elegant and novel experience.

University of Illinois

Pool on the Conservatory Terrace in the 1920s.

Two limestone *Sphinxes* designed by John Borie top the steps from the Conservatory Terrace to the pond. The image of the sphinx, in both Greek and Egyptian form, appears in revivals of various architectural styles as guardians to the entrances of temples, palaces, or tombs. Normally, they would face approaching visitors, but Robert reversed the direction, preferring a view of women's faces rather than lioness haunches from the Conservatory windows.

Michael Holtz

Two *Sphinxes*, designed by John J. Borie III around 1900, face the pool and the Conservatory.

In Greek tradition, the Sphinx possessed sacred knowledge and posed riddles to those wishing to enter the gates of Thebes. With a correct answer, the visitor could enter; for an incorrect one, the Sphinx would strangle and then devour the traveler. Fortunately, John Borie's *Sphinxes* have a less intimidating demeanor. Borie's design coincided with (and could have been inspired by) the much-publicized death of Oscar Wilde in November 1900. Wilde had resurrected the theme of the Sphinx in poetry and story in the 1890s.[15]

The Avenue of the Formal Gardens, designed by John Borie, leads from the base of the steps at the pond to the first of the gardens. At the turn of the twentieth century, a single

University of Illinois

The Avenue of the Formal Gardens, looking toward the mansion, photographed between 1915 and 1922.

Photo courtesy of Bonnet House Museum & Gardens

Robert standing at lattice benches (removed in 1910) on the Avenue of the Formal Gardens, midway between the mansion and the Brick Wall Garden.

row of Irish junipers lined the sunny, open path. The walkway has since been widened and has become quite shaded. It gracefully meanders in the direction of the Gate House and the road, coming to a resting point midway to its destination. There, until 1910, a pair of lattice arbors housed long benches. Four steps lead upward to a straighter continuation of the path, providing a formal approach to the Rose Terrace and the Brick Wall Garden, west of the Gate House. In 1915 two stone benches replaced the lattice arbors, with a Korean *Fu Dog* sculpture behind each. In 1922 the *Fu Dogs* made way for enlarged versions of Glyn Philpot's *Primitive Man* sculptures.

University of Illinois

The Rose Terrace as it appeared in 1908. Once a home for the *Chinese Musician* sculptures, the Rose terrace area has displayed the *Sea Maiden* sculptures by Richard Kuöhl since 1936.

The Rose Terrace, 24 feet wide and 232 feet long, stretched along the sunny southeast side of the Brick Wall Garden. Its rear wall, added soon after 1905, doubled as the entrance to the Brick Wall Garden and provided an espalier backdrop for the roses. Two pea gravel paths with brick edging, borders of low hedges, and classical urns showcased the rose beds.

The Brick Wall Garden began as a vegetable garden in 1900, but its humble purpose did not exempt it from ornamentation. Borie's iron gates adorned two of the original three walls (the south wall was added in 1905, where the *Sea Maiden* sculptures stand today). The Allerton initial "A" in his design echoes the motif used in the mansion's balconies. In 1908 Borie redesigned the east entrance as a niche topped with two stone fruit baskets.

Accents such as junipers and perimeter plantings of flowers and vines became more important features over the early years. Privet hedge replaced a border of carrots in the 1920s. Twenty years later, Robert converted the vegetable beds to turf, creating a more dramatic design. In 1933 he removed the original centerpiece of the garden, a dipping pool,[16] replacing it in 1942 with Lili Auer's sculpture, *Girl with a Scarf.*

University of Illinois

The Brick Wall Garden originally featured a dipping pool, shown in this photo, circa 1915.

From the center of the Brick Wall Garden, Formal Gardens extend almost a quarter-mile to the southwest. Built sequentially, six more gardens follow in a straight line, parallel to Old Timber

Road. Robert would create a total of fourteen gardens on the premises.

The Square Parterre Garden began in 1902 as a narrow path parallel to the greenhouse (now Allerton Park and Retreat Center's Visitor Center and Gift Shop) and slowly transformed into a garden with the addition of topiaries and potted plants. In 1918 it became a parterre, literally meaning "along the ground." Parterres rely on strong geometric or maze patterns for visual interest and frequently feature no flowers at all. Robert used 2,251 privet plants to create the square design.[17] The first sculptures placed in the garden were two rustic, early nineteenth-century lead figures, the *Shepherd* and *Shepherdess*,[18] adapted from the typical style of John Cheere.[19]

University of Illinois

The Brick Wall Garden in 1915, with iron gates and fruit baskets designed by John Borie.

University of Illinois

John Borie's 1905 drawing for the iron gates, specified "Everything to be wrought. Nothing to be rivetted. No foliage work."

University of Illinois

The Square Parterre Garden in 1918, featuring *Diana* and the *Ephebe*.

During the 1920s Robert replaced the *Shepherd* and *Shepherdess* with *Diana* (the goddess of the hunt) and an *Ephebe* (her young, male companion), each with a hound. The concrete figures, approximately five feet tall, were a gift to Robert from his friends, Charles and Frances Pike* of Lake Forest, Illinois. In their honor, Robert nicknamed the sculptures "Charlie and Frances."[20] In 1925 he installed them atop columns at the entrance from Monticello Road, filling their previous positions in the Square Parterre Garden with urns on pedestals.

Michael Holtz

Diana and the *Ephebe*, the sculptures Robert called "Charlie and Frances," now top the Allerton Park entrance gates.

The Triangle Parterre Garden began in 1908 as a gravel pathway between the Square Parterre Garden and the Seasonal Gardens, lined with evenly spaced Irish junipers, later replaced with arborvitae. In the mid-1920s triangular plantings of Amur privet and gravel in a formal pattern replaced low mounds of hedge. He later replaced the sweet corn border—an unconventional choice for a formal garden—with yucca and lilies.

In 1918 Robert added pairs of columns to the east and west entries of the Triangle Parterre Garden, each topped by lead urns. In 1922 he replaced

University of Illinois

East entry of the Triangle Parterre Garden as it appeared in 1930, with garlanded lead urns atop the columns.

Michael Holtz

Limestone *Assyrian Lions* now top pairs of columns at the east and west ends of the Triangle Parterre Garden. The two currently on the west are replacements, carved in Indiana in 1976.

the two urns on the west with limestone *Assyrian Lion* sculptures, carved in Chicago from prototypes in his collection.[21] He added the identical second set on the east by 1935.[22] The sculptures are only carved on the front side, indicating that the originals were designed as ornamentation for a wall or doorway.[23]

Robert had the north, south, and east sides enclosed with lattice walls in 1920, then added a stair tower into the northwest corner, leading to a walkway atop the northern wall of the neighboring Annual Garden. The stair tower has been closed for many years, and the lattice tower is a replica, smaller than the original, and arched with an ogee rather than a half-circle.[24]

University of Illinois

The northern wall of the Seasonal Garden, displaying iris in bloom, photographed in 1918.

The Seasonal Gardens originated in 1908 and assumed their current layout in 1922. Four rectangular quadrants comprise the 560 foot-long garden, each section named for a season: Spring for Robert's favorite peonies, Fall for chrysanthemums, Winter for fir trees, and Summer for perennial bulbs. A replica of Auguste Rodin's *Adam,* acquired after 1924, marks the intersection of paths between the four gardens. Almost hidden in the rear of the Peony Garden now stands a limestone copy of Germain Pilon's *The Three Graces,* commissioned in 1916 and moved from a previous location on the grounds.

The Chinese Parterre, also called the Chinese Maze Garden, is enclosed on all sides by a high concrete wall, originally espaliered with apples and pears and punctuated with urns at the top. In 1930 Robert relocated the two sets of Borie's iron gates from the Brick Wall Garden to the east and west openings of the Chinese Parterre. In a narrow chamber formed between the east concrete wall and the wooden wall of the next garden, two stair towers once provided a stunning view of the hedge layout below. The pattern of Robert's favorite silk pajamas supposedly inspired the design.[25] Over a half-mile of plants replicate twin sections of a variation of the ancient Chinese symbol "Shou," an ideogram that represents longevity. If symbols have power, this one proved effective—Robert lived to be an old man.

Chinese porcelain *Fu Dogs* originally guarded the center of each circular hedge motif. In 1925 Robert replaced them with a pair of marble goldfish fountains,[26] purchased from a Peking dealer with the provenance that they once decorated the garden of a prince. The goldfish remain in position today, but they have never functioned as fountains.[27]

University of Illinois

The Chinese Parterre in 1915. *Fu Dog* sculptures anchored the center of each motif.

The Avenue of the *Chinese Musicians,* at first a simple gravel path curbed with concrete, had previously ended the formal gardens. Six pairs of orb-topped pillars, removed in 1925, marked intervals of its length, backed by a wall of sheared evergreens.[28]

Michael Holtz

Michael Holtz

The limestone *Chinese Musicians* comprise a nomadic tribe of sculptures. Now in their third location (and some in their third incarnation), they were moved to the current garden in 1977.

Robert purchased ten of the original *Chinese Musician* sculptures in England, sometime before 1923. Shortly thereafter he commissioned two additional ones from tombstone carver, Lew Wagy,[29] who worked from a shop on West Washington Street in Monticello. Those twelve statues stood in a row on the Rose Terrace from 1925 until 1932 when he placed them along the path to his new Lost Garden.[30] In that woodland environment, squirrels, vandals, and the weather soon damaged the statues beyond repair. The *Chinese Musicians* now line a path to the Sunken Garden (constructed in 1915). The current statues are all copies, made and installed in 1977.[31] Six additional statues now stand in niches inside the mansion Library.

As Robert acquired sculpture over the years, new gardens arose in more remote locations on the estate: the *Fu Dog* Garden, the Lost Garden, and magnificent settings for *The Death of the Last Centaur* and *The Sun Singer*. Each site provides the guest a sense of discovery.

Michael Holtz

In 1925 Robert replaced the *Fu Dogs* in the Chinese Parterre with two marble *Goldfish* purchased in Peking. He moved John Borie's iron gates from the Brick Wall Garden to the Chinese Parterre in 1930.

CHAPTER SIX
A Time for Romance

Passion is universal humanity.
Without it, religion, history, romance and art would be useless.

Honoré de Balzac (1799-1850)

MAKING THE ROUNDS

Upon Robert's return from Europe and China with Russell Hewlett in early 1901, Robert was spotted three times in March with Miss Hazel Martyn.* They first appeared together on Tuesday evening, March 12 when Robert hosted a dinner party at high society's popular watering-hole, The Annex, followed by *The Gay Lord Quex—A Comedy in Four Acts* at the Powers' Theater.[1] Other guests of his included two Chicago matrons, one of whom was the renowned society leader, Delia Caton, wife of Arthur Caton.

Hazel Martyn, a striking redhead, ranked as one of the great beauties of her day—but forty-eight-year-old Delia Caton had long been the talk of the town. The Caton home faced Lake Michigan, with the backyard bordering Marshall Field's home. Rumors claimed that an underground tunnel ran between the two houses, facilitating a lengthy affair between Delia and Marshall Field, right under the eyes of Delia's husband, Arthur. After both their spouses died, Delia and Marshall Field married, but Field died only months later, still grieving his son's sudden death.[2] (Another resident of the street, Arthur Meeker,* fictionalized the Caton-Field affair in his 1949 novel, *Prairie Avenue*.)

The following week on Tuesday evening, March 19, Delia and her sister, Abby Eddy, hosted a costume party for Abby's son, Spencer,* at the Eddy's 1601 Michigan Avenue residence.[3] Spencer had grown up with Robert and Frederic Bartlett, attended the same schools, and had also recently returned home from Paris. Spencer's grandfather and Frederic's father were partners in the hardware business of Hibbard, Spencer, Bartlett & Co.

The costume party was nowhere near as spectacular as the Mikado Ball of 1886, but thirty young adults attired themselves in Austrian peasant garb. Spencer's Aunt Delia and his mother transformed the dining room into a Tyrolese inn, spreading the supper on long tables with benches.[4] The guest list included Helen Birch* (an Eddy relative and later second wife to Frederic Bartlett), Potter Palmer, Jr., Robert Allerton, and again, Hazel Martyn.

While we have no record of Robert's costume, a hint appeared years later in a letter from Spencer's sister Catherine about a different costume ball. Then Robert wore a pale-blue Bavarian officer's uniform, and she, a beautiful Lancret dress.[5] Madame X speculated on the appeal of costume parties in a 1914 column:

> *The fancy dress seems to unlock the prison doors and let out that other subconscious self which enjoys an outing in the social world. Especially does the masquerader doff his stiff Puritan ancestors and if there be any Latin or Celtic strain in his blood it is sure to show itself.*[6]

On March 20, the afternoon following Spencer's costume party, Robert made a third appearance, this time at a matinee of *A Pair of Spectacles*. The group accompanying a "Mrs. Birch"[7] included eight married women, two couples, a Miss Hooper, Robert Allerton, and Hazel Martyn.[8] If matchmaking was the goal, perhaps Miss Hooper filled in as a backup to Hazel.

These three social events offered opportunities for Hazel and Robert to spend time together, etiquette codes restricting unmarried women from dating. They could attend events where unmarried men might be, but never without a chaperone.

With the right pedigree and a mutual interest in art, Hazel may have been a perfect match for Robert. Her father served as Vice President of the Union Stock Yards and was a confidential associate to Philip Armour until Martyn's death in April 1897. Nevertheless, she seemed to quickly drop out of the picture.

Robert's friends circled from Chicago to New York to Europe in various combinations of the same old families. This made it even more curious that he chose Monticello, 150 miles downstate, for his home. But his friends didn't seem to mind his location. By 1901 he had begun entertaining guests at The Farms, luring them from their weary travels to the fresh, country air.

ELLEN GERTRUDE EMMET

One of Robert's earliest guests was an intriguing young woman—like Hazel Martyn, a redhead—named Ellen Gertrude "Bay" Emmet.[9]* With a determination and sense of purpose inherited from her father's great-uncle, Irish nationalist Robert Emmet, she was about to throw Robert's life off course.

Ellen was among the first generation of women to be accepted as professional artists in the late nineteenth century. Her work met with impressive critiques early on, and by age eighteen she was earning a respectable living as an illustrator for *Vogue* magazine, *Harper's Weekly*, and *Harper's Bazar.*[10]

Courtesy of Ellen E. Rand

Ellen Gertrude Emmet

Hood Museum of Art, Dartmouth College, Hanover, NH; gift of Abby Aldrich Rockefeller.

The Architect, a portrait of John J. Borie III by Thomas Eakins (1844-1916) painted between 1896 and 1898. Oil on canvas.

Like Robert's, Ellen's childhood was marked by tragedy—her father died in an accident when she was nine years old. Her mother remarried, and her new stepfather moved the family to England. Over the late 1890s her mother's marriage faltered and her stepfather stopped supporting the family.[11] Ellen became the breadwinner, earning enough from portrait commissions to refuse offers of financial assistance from a cousin.[12] Struggling on with her studies, she lived with her sisters in Paris through the autumn of 1900.[13]

Word of Ellen's talent spread quickly, and to all the right people—among them, architect and family friend Charles Follen McKim and American expatriate John Singer Sargent. Sargent relayed his favorable opinion of her work to his friend, author Henry James, a cousin of Ellen's mother. Ellen first met Henry James on a summer visit to England in 1897. He promptly wrote to his brother, psychologist and philosopher William James, about Ellen's impressive talent.[14] Henry took a deep interest in the lives of the Emmets and tried to help Ellen obtain portrait opportunities, including commissioning her to paint one of him.

Ellen's mentor in Europe, Frederick MacMonnies, held classes in a converted barn. Ellen, his only female student at the time, "found nude male models standing ever ready, saw tame rats roaming freely about, and discovered a fierce young leopard was kept in a cage as a pet."[15] In 1898 she studied in Paris with Raphael Collin. There her work caught the attention of James McNeill Whistler and Augustus Saint-Gaudens. In 1900 she won a bronze medal at the Exposition Universelle in Paris, with many more awards and honors to follow.

Frederic Bartlett could easily have met Ellen Emmet any time between 1898 and 1900 while they were both in Paris. John Borie may also have met her during his studies. In the autumn of 1900 Ellen returned to New York City and rented an apartment/studio in the Ireland House in the Washington Square neighborhood[16] where Robert had earlier taken an apartment for a season. Apparently the two met through mutual acquaintances.[17] In the fall of 1900 she wrote to her sister (Edith) Leslie, mentioning having attended an opera with an endearing, hearing-impaired young man who was the son of a Chicago pork-packer. His collection of horses and fourteen dogs appealed to her love of animals. She planned to paint his portrait shortly after Christmas for a fee of $500.[18]

University of Illinois

Robert at his writing desk in 1904. Above the desk hangs a framed portrait of his mother, Pamilla Thompson Allerton.

By May 1901 Robert began writing to Ellen, continuing with increasing frequency throughout the following months. He addressed his first letter, "Dear Miss Emmet," arranging to meet her in Lake Geneva, where she would paint a portrait of Sam that Robert would hang over his fireplace.

I am delighted you are coming a little later as I will now miss none of your visit.... You have got to stay a week at least here. Don't think you can get out of it!... The time is getting short before you will be out here.[19]

Formality dropped away in the next letter in late June, addressed, "Dear Ellen," in which he wrote about a thunderstorm that she would have enjoyed, appealing to her love of danger and excitement. He described the storm:

> *That the farms is standing to day [sic] is a miracle. In the first place the kitchen wing was struck by lightning, tearing the roof all to pieces. Such a crash and then such a shaking with great balls of fire rolling across in front of the house. The library and my bedroom came next. The windows [were all] blown out... they were ankle deep in water. Then the new awnings broke and then the pergola which was just about finished fell with the most splendid crash. Everything looks this morning as if there had been a great battle. Trees, branches, etc. in ruins.... I wish you were here and could have seen the storm approach. The sky was blood red and such a blowing of wind and then a solid wall of water and hail. Really a magnificent sight.* [20]

In the storm's aftermath, he agonized over preparation for a party for 250 of Monticello's leading citizens and wished she were there with him. In mid-July, after visiting her in New York, he wished, "you were here or I where you are." He ended with, "I miss you so dreadfully," sending his love to her and her family.[21]

Robert's letters to Ellen from May 1901 through September 1901 show a man who felt he had found his soul mate. She spent most of that time period at an Otsego, New York country house called "The Wigwam," located near the home of Emily Borie Ryerson, John Borie's sister. Borie made appearances at his sister's house while Ellen was painting Emily's portrait, and Robert's letters make little attempt to conceal his jealousy. "I am sure Borie must be at Otsego as you never write when he is there."[22]

Returning from visiting Ellen at the end of July, his agony was even more evident. "You never write where you are or what are you doing. I hate New York. You simply forget all about me now you are there."[23] He responded with joy and delight when he did finally receive a letter from her, putting aside his frustration with New York City when she told him she had taken an apartment there. He anticipated visiting her in the fall, but worried that he might not be able to afford a winter trip abroad. A drought had taken its effect on his crops, and thus his funds, and he seemed almost desperate to see her.

His vulnerability unmasked, he thanked her for how much she helped him to come out of his shell.

> *Do you know since I have known you[,] life has become so much easier... clarity... was always an inward struggle[.] Now knowing you and seeing you has made it all seem so simple and natural. To know and be intimate with two people like you and my mother, well it's the greatest of joys outside of everything else. You know perfectly well I am dying to visit you in September and will if I can.*[24]

University of Illinois

Mrs. Anna Rathbone on the Conservatory Terrace of the mansion, circa 1910.

He tried to encourage her to come by telling her about his horse, Prince, who was "dying to carry you once more." He promised "a new dog for you to meet and your devoted R.A. to do all in his power for your pleasure."[25] After his godmother, Anna Rathbone, left from her visit to Monticello, he wrote to Ellen, "I hate to have any woman here after you. You make them all seem such small potatoes."[26]

Ellen once told Robert that she liked to eat leftovers from the icebox late at night. Maybe she really enjoyed cold food. Or perhaps it was her way of telling him that she prided herself on being a Bohemian who was content to scrounge, and that she was a bit uncomfortable with servants bringing gourmet meals to a formal table on a daily basis. In Robert's desire to cater to her every wish, he missed the point entirely. He ordered that on her visits, full meals be prepared for her and left in the icebox.[27]

During that time, Borie's delays with changes in the stable's design caused no end of grief for Robert. He told Ellen how glad he would be to see the last of Borie. Meanwhile, he contented himself tending a newly-christened Ellen Garden where he planted poppy seeds she had sent him, probably hoping more than flowers would blossom.

Early that summer Ellen had visited him. A snapshot of Ellen on horseback at The Farms shows her in her true element. Like Agnes, Ellen was a country girl at heart. Since her days in Paris, she had nurtured a dream of owning a small farm as a rural retreat for her extended family. If nothing more, Robert certainly had an enticing farm to offer.

University of Illinois

Ellen Emmet on horseback at The Farms during one of her early visits.

As Robert's letters to Ellen in the summer of 1901 show, he seems to be chasing her more than she was pursuing him. Possibly his urgency to have her near had proved a stumbling block. He clearly expressed his frustration at Ellen's living so far away, but her career depended on being in New York. It was the center of America's art world, and her social connections there enhanced her career. That year she would forge a lifelong friendship with the young debutante, Eleanor Roosevelt.* Years later, she would paint President Franklin Roosevelt's official portrait.

Robert's friendship with Ellen demonstrated no small degree of reconciliation with his own artistic limitations. Her talent, like Frederic's, left him far behind—although she appreciated his knowledge and taste in selecting fine art.[28] In his first act as a patron, his commissioning of two portraits from Ellen—that of Sam and of himself[29]—may have been simply a ploy to lure her to Illinois. With or without his help, Ellen was hardly at a loss for clients.

Being the breadwinner had become central to Ellen's character. Nonetheless, wealth was on her list of criteria for a husband.[30] So what else did Ellen see in Robert? We have her portrait of him, hanging in his Butternut Room, as evidence. His presence as master of the domain is inescapable. He gazes down from above the fireplace, his unblinking eyes following the visitor's every move. Impeccably groomed in his brown suit, at first he seems unusually stern and solemn for a man in his late twenties—but the corners of his mouth, almost hidden by a moustache, reveal a slight, enigmatic upturn.

Visiting Robert's farm was a good trial run, but true to her independent nature, Ellen did not wait for Robert to make her dream of a country home come true. In 1903 she bought her own piece of land near Salisbury, Connecticut, naming it "Barack Matif Farm." She stayed there intermittently with her family, and Henry James visited in 1904.

University of Illinois and Ellen E. Rand

Portrait of Robert Allerton by Ellen Gertrude Emmet, 1901.

For Better or For Worse

In the spring of 1903 Robert was preparing the mansion for special summer guests. In a spectacular wedding on June 10 at St. Paul's Episcopal Church in Cleveland, Ruth Hanna, daughter of Senator Marcus Alonzo Hanna of Ohio, married Joseph Medill McCormick* of the *Chicago Tribune* newspaper family. President Theodore Roosevelt led the mother of the bride down the aisle, followed by his daughter, Alice. As a close friend of the groom's for several years, Robert served as an usher. After a wedding breakfast for 150 guests, the young couple journeyed by train to Robert's Monticello estate where they planned to honeymoon for two or three weeks.[31]

Courtesy of Sean Johnstone

Robert's sister, Kate Allerton Johnstone, with her son, Vanderburgh.

A few months later, marital bliss for Robert's sister took an unfortunate turn. Only seven months after her second son, Vanderburgh,* was born, Kate and Hugo's marriage floundered. In August 1903 the *Washington Post* reported that she filed a divorce suit against Hugo. Kate discovered that he had maintained a burlesque actress, Nina Farrington, in a New York house, supplying her with carriages, automobiles, jewelry, and a monthly stipend of one thousand dollars[32] ($24,000 in 2007 purchasing power).Apparently neither family duty nor Kate's buying him a seat on the New York Stock Exchange had won his loyalty. Two weeks later, Ms. Farrington's husband, Sidney Love (Hugo's cousin and best friend), found a package of letters between Nina and Hugo. He, too, filed for divorce.

Courtesy of Sean Johnstone

Kate's husband, Hugo Johnstone.

Authors' collection

Picture postcard (Schloss, New York, circa 1903-06) featuring burlesque actress Nina Farrington.

East and west-coast newspapers reminded readers throughout 1903 and 1904 that Kate was the daughter of the millionaire, S. W. Allerton, but Robert's name remained untainted. Chicago readers continued to learn of every social event that he attended.

His friendship with Ellen continued. He attended an opera with her and other friends in 1905.[33] Ellen and her family swam in Robert's sea of friends. Letters sent between the artistic Emmet family members discussed Dickey Borie, Roger Quilter, Russell Hewlett, and Henry James (always by his full name). During 1905 Ellen's cousins and their mother mentioned Robert's plans for Thanksgiving and also that he was sailing on the same steamer[34] as one of their friends.[35]

One letter from Russell Hewlett in December 1905 informed Ellen's London-based cousin, Jane Emmet von Glehn[36] that he would be sailing around the world with Robert, returning by the end of May. Hewlett wrote that he "felt quite homesick at going away again so soon, but I decided that it would be too stupid to miss such an opportunity to see all the wonderful and beautiful things of the East."[37] And an exotic trip it was. The two went to a "thieves market" in Peking. By torchlight, they sorted through stacks of stolen scrolls, giving either thumbs up or down to each piece.[38]

Russell Hewlett must have scribbled something about Ellen (using her nickname of "Bay") in a 1905 letter to Jane's mother, because she reported to another daughter: "It is plain from Russell's letter that Robert Allerton is not to marry Bay this time."[39]

Appearance of the 1906 "Richest Bachelor" article confirmed that Robert's friendship with Ellen hadn't made much headway. Sam must have despaired of Robert ever settling down and producing more Allerton grandchildren. Considering Sam's friendship with the McCormicks, owners of the *Chicago Tribune,* he may have initiated the article. However, perhaps it backfired. Some of the sentences may have kept women away. One such negative example: "Samuel Allerton did not look upon the 'business' of painting pictures with much favor."[40] Another description might have raised more questions than it answered: Robert was "well liked as a man likes another man."[41]

Today's celebrity magazines cannot compare to a 1907 *Chicago Tribune* article that appeared the year after Robert's "Richest Bachelor" section, giving him another chance with women. The full-page spread featured Gibson girls hovering with fishing poles, some of them reeling in men from an immense birdbath. The article, titled "Matrimonial Chances for Chicago Girls," named Chicago bachelors with incomes from $1,500 to over $100,000 per year.

Robert's was the highest, at $150,000. At thirty years of age, he was a stock-broker and "the son of the millionaire and one of the finest fellows in town, as well as probably the wealthiest." Excerpts mentioned the variety of bachelors:

> *... aldermen, brokers, lawyers, merchants, athletes, one or two who think they are invalids, politicians, millionaires, salaried men, bon vivants, golfers, automobilists, skat players, firemen, and detectives... There are no objectionable characters among them. There are some who drink, but none of them so far as*

their friends know ever get drunk and smash up the furniture. Some of them are large packages. One weighing over 250 is said to be worth his weight in gold... They are broken in. They know that women like to be petted.[42]

Photo courtesy of Elisabeth Bartlett Sturges

Robert with his godson, Clay Bartlett (son of Frederic and Dora), circa 1910. (Shoulder length hair was popular for boys during the Lord Fauntleroy craze.)

One bachelor was "an excellent catch; has more money than he knows what to do with, so has his portrait painted occasionally." A twenty-seven-year-old man was "undersized, but has an extremely pleasant manner." Another was "not much used to the company of girls," and yet another had a "tendency toward corpulency." One fellow didn't "care much for girls, but probably could be coaxed." Yet another "works in his father's bank, but not too hard." Robert clearly appeared to be the best bet.

Robert may have had slim prospects for a family of his own, but he was about to become a godfather. In 1907 he returned to New York for Christmas, attending the christening of one-month-old baby "Clay" Bartlett at Frederic Bartlett's home.[43] Childhood friends Will Hibbard and Catherine Eddy also became Clay's godparents.

Soon after the christening Robert sailed for Europe again, spending time with Ellen's family in London. Shortly after New Year's, Ellen's aunt remarked to her daughter, Jane, that Robert Allerton was visiting and Ellen seemed very happy.[44] During his time there, he commissioned Wilfred von Glehn to "do a decorative panel for over the mantel in a paneled room in his house."[45] No such panel is found today in the house. Perhaps it was a trumped-up reason to keep company with the Emmets. Robert achieved one of his heart's desires that month—while visiting with the von Glehns, he met the celebrated artist, John Singer Sargent.

Most Emmet relatives and friends enjoyed Robert, surmising that he and Bay had a future together. According to one letter from Jane Emmet to her mother: "Henry James... likes Robert Allerton very much and thinks Bay is going to marry him someday."[46] However, one person wasn't impressed. The following week Jane received a letter from her own mother, stating, "I am glad you like Robert Allerton. It is a shame in [sic] Aunt Elly [Ellen's mother] to hold on to Bay and prevent her from marrying Robert."[47]

Perhaps Ellen was not ready to consider marriage. Maybe Robert was not the right man for her, or as an artist she had misgivings about living so far from New York City. Ellen was not easily steamrolled, but one of her grandchildren noted that had Ellen wanted to marry Robert, her mother—like Hazel Martyn's—would have wielded a power difficult to ignore.

CHAPTER SEVEN

Love and Loss

There is no remedy for love but to love more.

Henry David Thoreau (1817-1862)[1]

ENTERTAINING AT THE FARMS

Throughout 1910 Madame X continued to keep readers apprised of Robert's whereabouts. Robert could now entertain on his own terms, ignoring society conventions. His visitors usually arrived from Chicago or New York. He rarely included his Monticello friends and relatives (the Lodge, Dighton, Evans, Kirby, and Kratz families) at weekend parties, preferring not to mix them together at the "castle" (as it was sometimes referred to by the townspeople).[2]

Periodically he invited Monticello schoolteachers to afternoon teas at the mansion, escorting them around the grounds. The teachers later regaled their friends and families with stories about Robert's amiability and the English maids dressed in black dresses with white aprons and caps. Otherwise, he literally distanced himself from Monticello townsfolk, traveling twenty-five miles to Champaign just for a haircut. Perhaps Champaign had a better barber. Or maybe it was because the Monticello barber's wife was a reporter for the local newspaper.

Robert's gatherings usually afforded out-of-town guests the opportunity to dress in costumes, still all the rage in the cities. In 1908 Ellen hosted a costume carnival for 150 people in her New York studio,[3] but Robert's masquerades were much more casual and impromptu. Often the guests arrived on a summer weekend, hot and tired. To refresh them, Robert would suggest that each guest pick out an appealing costume from the many he had collected during his journeys.[4]

Robert originally stored the costumes in his library. Later he moved the cupboard, a wooden closet with locker-like separations, into the conservatory attached to the stables (later accessible via the new hallway). Guests could choose to become a mandarin, matador, German officer (probably the suit he wore to Delia Caton's party), Japanese bride, or harem girl. Kingfish feathers decorated a Chinese bridal outfit.[5] Both men and women enjoyed the togas and kimonos, feeling freer from their starched shirts, stiff collars, and corsets. As John Gregg Allerton remembered it, "the women... put on more clothes and men put on less."[6] Visitors had favorite costumes. Mrs. John T. McCutcheon* preferred a kimono that flowed easily on her tall frame.[7]

University of Illinois

Guests enjoying Robert's costumes at The Farms.

Robert also kept a supply of low-heeled walking shoes available, along with umbrellas and capes hidden away in shelters around the property.[8] He insisted that his servants be as invisible as possible, but the upstairs maid would respond to a guest's ringing for help. Staff stayed out of the way unless otherwise requested; the upstairs maid served the guests breakfast in bed and the butler served the other meals.

Robert kept guest books from the beginning, inviting his visitors to scrawl a poem, dash off a sketch, or write a nice note. He also pasted in postcards and pictures from his travels, including photos taken at The Farms. "It was a record of his life," John Gregg Allerton said. "He always told his staff that if the house caught on fire, the first thing to save was the guest books."[9]

His sister Kate rarely visited, but Robert sometimes entertained Sam or Agnes or both. He set aside the front bedroom, at the head of the stairs, for them. Occasionally Sam would annoy Robert by arranging his toupee on top of a bust of Caesar stationed at the bottom of the stairs.[10]

A Dark Day

With Madame X's columns constantly reminding the reader that Robert commanded land and money, she should have added "matchmaker" to her resume. She listed him first in an article about gentleman farmers who were making lots of money. But this time, instead of elaborating, she contented herself with reiterating that his farm was one of the country's largest and "brings him an income sufficient to gratify his artistic and expensive tastes."[11]

If Madame X still thought of Ellen Emmet as a match for Robert, she had to turn her efforts elsewhere after January 15, 1911. On that day *The New York Times* scooped *The Chicago Tribune*:

> *Announcement has been made of the engagement of Miss Ellen Emmet, daughter of the late Christopher Temple Emmet, to William Blanchard Rand, son of the late George C. Rand of this city. Mr. Rand is a member of the Rockaway Hunt Club. No date has been set for the wedding.*[12]

Five days earlier Robert and another relative had attended his cousin Henrietta's small wedding in New York City.[13] He may or may not have read the notice before he sailed for Europe on his annual excursion. He returned from his trip in April on the *Lusitania*, arriving on the 14th.[14] Two weeks later, on April 29, *The New York Times* published a notice of Ellen's upcoming wedding to Rand, set for the following week in Connecticut. On May 6 it described the Episcopal wedding as a small affair for family members, with no attendants. The article also noted that, "Mr. Rand has purchased Butterly Farm, and will there establish a training stable, keeping a string of 100 horses. Mrs. Rand has painted portraits for many noted families, including the Roosevelts."[15]

Madame X barely concealed her opinion of Ellen's marriage:

> *Besides being a genius of no uncertain quality, the bride in question has a personality of unusual charm and magnetism, which has rather crowded her life with enthusiastic and devoted friends. Those are full of speculation as to the ultimate outcome of this marriage, because of the difference in the ages of the couple, the groom being twelve years the younger of the two. In ordinary cases this would probably result in eventual unhappiness, but the unusually vivid personality of Bay Emmett [sic] sets her apart from others of her sex. Just as in her youth she was mature, so in her maturity she will preserve her youth.*[16]

Years later, John Gregg Allerton mentioned that Robert had not been warned of Ellen's marriage. If he was already in Europe, he would not have read the January announcement—but it seems unlikely that mutual acquaintances would have failed to tell him. Nonetheless, Robert's chauffeur, Elmer Priebe, called it a "dark day"[17] when Robert learned of it.

Over the years rumors have floated that he and Ellen had been unofficially engaged, but in reality, he never pursued marriage with her. No matter how strong his earlier feelings were towards Ellen, Robert had said that he was reluctant to burden any woman with a near-deaf husband.[18] Although he treasured Ellen's friendship, he realized she might not visit The Farms again after she married. In any case, he had already found other relationships to fill the void.

ROGER QUILTER

Previously, while socializing in London with Jane Emmet von Glehn (Ellen's cousin) and a singing teacher named Victor Beigel, Robert met a young English composer named Roger Quilter.* A man of delicate constitution, Quilter was four years younger than Robert. Robert quickly felt drawn to him, and he nurtured the younger man's musical ambitions.

Roger Quilter, copy of 1923 bromide print by Herbert Lambert.

While traveling in Europe immediately after the announcement of Ellen's engagement, Robert suggested that Quilter come to America and use the quiet majesty of The Farms to help him compose music. At first the idea appealed to Quilter. He wrote to a friend, "I want to go very much & yet I hate the idea of the journey—& I don't want to be away from you for very long but also, I fear, I do want to be away from family etc (nice as they are)."[19]

Quilter offered several excuses why he couldn't come: orchestra rehearsals, his father was not well, and he was feeling ill himself. The truth was that he cowered at the thought of crossing the ocean and being away from the comfort of his immediate circle. No matter how much he tried to rationalize it and how close their relationship, he couldn't convince himself to visit America.

In February 1911, while visiting Munich alone, Robert still thought Quilter's visit was possible. He sent this very revealing letter:

> *23 Feb 1911 Robert Allerton, Hotel Vier Jahreszeiten, München*
> *to RQ c/o Thomas Cook & Son, Cairo, fwd Savoy, Luxor*
>
> *Dearest Roger when I came in … last night and found your first letter… life has been different since. I never dreamt I could so madly long to hear from any one before. How I wish you were here to hear all the good music and go to the funny balls. We went to a long one last night and feel quite jaded this morning from so much dancing - Susan Metcalf has a concert here tomorrow night we are going of course - It is the most beautiful weather warm and sunny like spring. Do write me what your one act opera is going to be about. I love your music dear Roger all I have heard. It's too heavenly.*
>
> *To think of all the nice things you are going to compose next summer at the Farms what a divine time we will have together there by ourselves riding over the farm and taking long walks with the dogs. You will like it I haven't a doubt. There won't be any of these beastly seperations [sic] what hell they are. Think what a beautiful time we might be having together now but I must not complain. It's so wonderful to have found you and we have a long life ahead. Life is so much nicer now we are friends and so much more besides even though we are apart you blessed old darling. I do so love you Roger every body that knows you must but no one can as much as I.*
>
> *Your devoted Robert*[20]

Quilter's biographer, Valerie Langfield, learned what little more we know about the relationship through a discussion with the son of one of Quilter's acquaintances. According to that man's father, Quilter's relationship with Robert "was very important and the only homosexual one that Quilter admitted."[21]

TITANIC

The following year, on January 24, 1912, Robert sailed from New York to Southampton onboard the *Olympic.*[22] The passenger list included Mr. and Mrs. John Jacob Astor IV. Robert planned to spend the winter in London, then visit Berlin before returning.[23] No records can be found for the actual date and ship on which he returned, but one anecdote recounts that Robert missed catching the *Titanic* by an hour. The *Titanic* sailed from Southampton on April 10, 1912, the usual time for Robert's return journeys. Unfortunately the Astors did sail then. Both Mr. Astor and John Borie's brother-in-law, Arthur Ryerson, died as the famous ship sank. It would have surely been a topic of conversation at The Farms when Borie visited Robert that summer.[24]

GLYN PHILPOT

Just before Robert left for his winter trip, the Art Institute of Chicago hosted a "Loan Exhibition of Portraits for the Benefit of the Passavant Memorial Hospital." Ellen Emmet Rand showed three portraits at the exhibition, including one of Alexander James, the son of William James. Frederic Bartlett loaned a portrait of his son Clay by Von Zumbach.[25] Rue* (Mrs. John Alden*) Carpenter had secured several portraits from England, including Glyn Philpot's *The Tragedienne*. Philpot would soon figure prominently in Robert's life.

Glyn Warren Philpot's self-portrait, painted in 1908.

Glyn Philpot* did not attend the 1912 exhibition in Chicago. However, Robert would have known his name and work when they became acquainted in London in 1913.[26] The two men shared a love of music. Philpot had a rich baritone voice and once considered a career as a singer.[27] He played and composed for the piano without having had formal instruction.[28] The allegorical, religious, and mythological themes of opera echo through the Symbolist style of his work, especially in his later years.

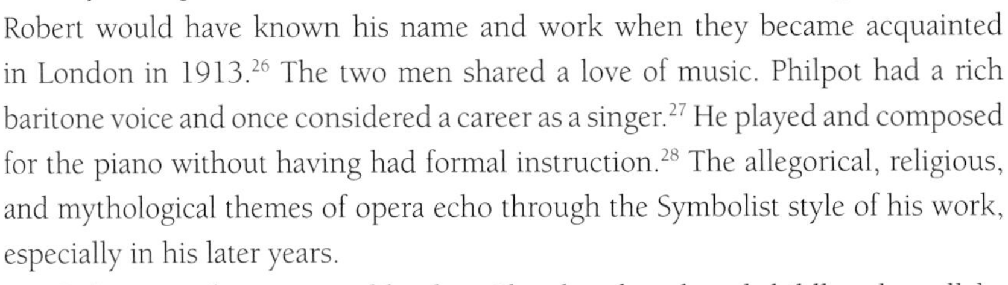

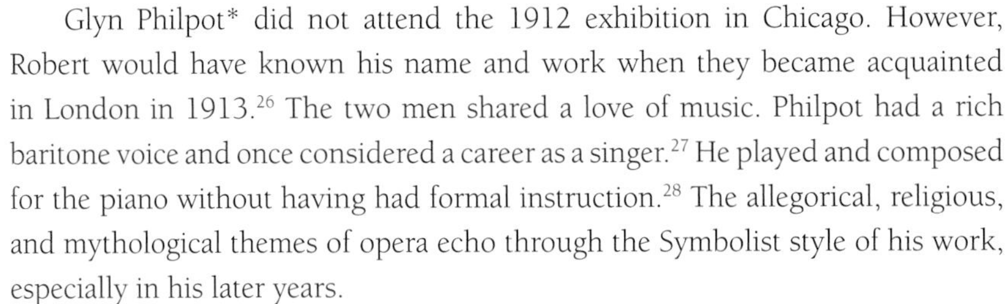

Robert was eleven years older than Glyn, but they shared childhood parallels. At age seven, Robert and Glyn each had suffered the death of their mothers. Both their fathers had then married a sister-in-law, each of whom had helped manage the respective households.[29] Robert's stepmother, Agnes, fueled his interest in art; in Glyn's case, it was his sister Daisy who nurtured his talent and career. In contrast to almost all of Robert's other friends, Glyn was born to a middle-class family. His precocious talent was recognized early, but he had enjoyed none of Robert's advantages.

As their friendship progressed, Robert invited Glyn to visit him in Illinois. Unlike Roger Quilter, Glyn eagerly accepted Robert's invitation. He sailed on August 26, 1913, traveling with another friend, Walter Creighton. Glyn wrote to Daisy that he was avoiding the "really silly steamship amusements," but that he was "awfully excited at the prospect of seeing Robert."[30]

Much to his surprise, when he arrived in New York, Robert was nowhere to be found. Instead he was greeted by Rue and John Carpenter, who informed Glyn that Robert was busy hosting John Borie at The Farms, as he had the previous summer. Whether Glyn was acquainted with Robert's guest or only knew him by name, he described the architect to Daisy as "Borie—that beast."[31] Instead of going directly to Illinois, Glyn detoured to Vermont at the invitation of the Carpenters. He wrote again to Daisy of his disappointment, saying the Carpenters had reassured him that Robert was "simply longing" to have him there.[32]

Glyn arrived at The Farms in September and began working in the studio that Robert had prepared above his stable. But after only a few days in the Monticello countryside, Glyn wrote that he felt "terribly depressed, home-sick and so dull." He added that Robert was "disappointed with me and [me] simply worshiping him all the time."[33]

He was amused by a Madame X article that compared his sensitive and exotic features (Glyn was of mixed English and Spanish heritage) to early portraits of Shelly or Byron.

> *He is not afraid to look the artist when in the country, and wears a most becoming and effective sublimation of the skirt [shirt] worn by Venetian gondoliers, open throated, with soft, flaring collar turned back over the coat. In evening dress, however, he is entirely the conventional young Briton. His manner is quiet, with a tranquil poise about it that is very refreshing in this country of energetic social intercourse.*[34]

His mood further improved by his birthday party on October 5 in Chicago. Robert treated him to a baseball game, dinner with a birthday cake, and an assortment of gag gifts.[35] The following weekend, Robert and Glyn toured the Bartlett farm and detached studio (all owned by Frederic's father) in Lake Geneva.

After spending nearly three months with Robert, Glyn feared overstaying his welcome. Robert convinced him to stay, but the situation became so stressful for Glyn that he experienced an attack of eczema requiring medical attention. He decided not to leave until he felt he absolutely had to, and then expected to regret his departure. In a letter to Daisy in late October, we obtain a rare glimpse of the Robert Allerton that he knew:

> *Robert had a long talk with me last night & he gave me such wonderful advice.... He says things so simply & yet you know he has been thinking quite a lot before he says anything.*
>
> *I've certainly never had a friend who was so interested in my welfare. He has no opinion whatever of his own importance & says the most childlike things about himself—and yet through it all there comes out the most beautiful wise mature character. I wanted to tell you all this... to show you that it is not just a silly infatuation I have for him. Another thing is—he never flatters me at all.*[36]

In his biography of Glyn Philpot, J. G. P. Delaney considers this letter to be Glyn's first acknowledgement to Daisy of his homosexuality, which he made little attempt to conceal publicly in later years. Delaney felt that Glyn was deeply attracted to Robert's almost paternal care and guidance. Robert counseled Glyn to not repeat his achievements simply to attain

© Tate, London 2009

Painting (oil on canvas, 1913) of Robert Allerton entitled *The Man in Black* by Glyn Warren Philpot (1884-1937).

material success, but to stay focused on his true direction as an artist. Delaney stopped short of speculating whether Robert reciprocated Glyn's feelings, saying that the extent to which the relationship progressed remains an "unanswerable question."[37]

Glyn had intended to redecorate Robert's music room, but never accomplished it. He chose instead to paint an oil portrait of Robert, which he titled *The Man in Black.* Robert is dramatically costumed in a black fur cap and cloak. Strongly lit against a stark background, he gazes off to his right, his slightly raised eyebrows revealing his interest in something or someone we cannot see. The red of his lips and blush on his high cheekbones give him an appearance of youth belying his forty years. In 1916 the National Gallery in London chose to hang it, a great honor for Philpot. A *Chicago Tribune* correspondent using the pseudonym "Cinderella" declared it:

> *a portrait which the sitter did not like well enough to buy.... But the National Gallery did, so therefore debonair and much traveled Bobby Allerton hangs high with those gorgeous high living Rembrandts and high tempered Goyas and high bred Van Dycks.*[38]

Robert secured a portrait commission for Glyn in the Chicago suburb of Lake Forest to paint Miss Isabelle McBirney,[39] daughter of Hugh McBirney. The McBirneys had lived on Prairie Avenue and were part of the Allerton social circle. Glyn couldn't seem to escape the relatives of "Borie—that beast." (John Borie and Isabelle McBirney were related through their sisters' marriages to Ryerson brothers.[40])

The McBirney portrait neared completion in November, and Glyn finally decided the time had come to leave Illinois. He took the train to visit his brother in Santa Barbara, California—a three-day ride that he had dreaded. He planned to stop in Pittsburgh and New York before returning to England, but he abruptly left California and canceled his side trip to Pittsburgh's Carnegie Institute. He claimed to have received news by cable that required his immediate return home, but no record or further mention of a cable has ever surfaced.

His two-year involvement with the Carnegie Institute was professionally important. He had exhibited one painting there in 1912 and another in 1913 (*The Marble Worker,* which won first prize in the prestigious International Competition). The Institute had invited him to serve on the Selection Committee for a future International Exhibition, but in his letter canceling his visit, he also declined that honor.

Coincidentally, Robert received news on November 11 that his friend Russell Hewlett had died in Pittsburgh. Since their travels together more than a decade earlier, Hewlett had become Dean of the School of Applied Design of the Carnegie Institute of Technology and was President of the Pittsburgh Art Society. According to his obituary, he had won recognition for his versatility in both art and music. He was described as "a bachelor member of the old Hewlett family... after which the town of Hewlett on Long Island was named."[41] After contacting Frederic Bartlett with the sad news, Robert rushed to New York, arriving in time to attend the funeral in Brooklyn on November 14.[42]

Whether Russell Hewlett and Glyn Philpot were acquainted, Glyn would have known about him through the International Competition and through Hewlett's friendship with Robert. But Glyn's letters home to Daisy offered no clue whether Hewlett's death in any way affected his plans. Perhaps he thought he might coordinate another quick visit with Robert in New York, or maybe he was simply anxious to return home. In any case, his hasty change of plans leaves an air of mystery.

Robert returned to Illinois immediately after the funeral. Frederic Bartlett's wife, Dora, met with Agnes Allerton and Robert on November 29, when he bid them good-bye before leaving the next morning for another trip around the world.[43] Glyn departed from New York for England on December 3, sailing on the *Lusitania*. Thus, both Glyn and Robert left the country the same week, if not the same day, but Glyn made no mention to Daisy about having traveled with Robert.[44]

Glyn did not return to the United States for another ten years, but when he did, he again visited Robert and produced several works of art.

Robert's trip that winter of 1913-1914 may have started off well, but it was a journey that would end sooner than he expected. His relationship with Roger Quilter helped him cope with what was to come.

THE DEATH OF SAMUEL ALLERTON

Robert was traveling on February 22, 1914 when his father died in his sleep. Although Madame X reported that Robert was in Moscow at the time, Agnes and Kate finally contacted him in Tahiti,[45] postponing Sam's burial until Robert could arrive. Hurrying home via Peking (today Beijing), through Bremen, Germany, and lastly Paris, he wrote to Quilter from his ship. He was unsure at that point whether his final destination would be Chicago or California. He scoffed that the ship's passengers consisted primarily of "dressmakers, etc." The vibrations of the old ship and the choppiness of the Atlantic combined to prevent him even escaping to the comfort of a book.

Feb 1914 Robert Allerton, Norddeutscher Lloyd, Bremen
RQ 7 Montagu St

Dearest Rog I feel so depressed and sad I had no business to write but your lovely letters - I simply must tell you what a comfort and help they have been. No one could be more lucky than I am to have such a good true dear friend as you are dearest Rog and how I do appreciate it. Words could never explain how much it means to me. I gess [sic] you know don't you dearest Rog. It's the most terrible dissapointment [sic] not to see you. I have been all [?] so looking forward to it. If you could only manage to come over to the Farms this summer - I can't yet believe I will never see my dear Father again he must have been ill only a very short time as all along have been most cheerful happy.... I feel I shall have a violent reaction when I reach my destination.... Thomas could not have been nicer and was the greatest comfort. Eddy was so lovely and I think it was so wonderful of Billy to come over to Paris although I really much preferred not to see anyone but of course he could not have known that. This is a beastly ship. Years ago I crossed on her and swore I never would again - and here I am so grateful to have caught her!... All the love in the world darling Rog I do love you so

Your ever devoted Robert[46]

One can only imagine Robert's sadness as he cruised into Hoboken, New Jersey early in the morning of March 4 onboard the *Kaiser Wilhelm II.* There his friends, George Porter, and Frederic and Dora Bartlett met up with him, the Bartletts having postponed their trip to Phoenix for a week.[47] After lunching at the Ritz, Frederic and Dora joined Robert traveling via the *20th Century Limited* to Chicago, where he would visit with friends until Agnes and Kate arrived on March 13. Dora and Frederic took special care of him, inviting him to join them for dinner or drives "in the motor."[48] Shortly before Robert's mother and sister arrived from Pasadena, the Bartletts departed for Phoenix, leaving Robert forlorn in their absence.[49]

Michael Holtz

The Allerton family tombstone in Graceland Cemetery, Chicago.

In California, Universalist Church pastor Reverend A. R. Tillinghast had conducted a simple funeral service for Sam. On March 14, the day after Agnes and Kate arrived, Sam was buried with great ceremony at Graceland Cemetery. Reverend Rufus A. White presided over the 11:00 interment, attended by more than 150 of Allerton friends and business acquaintances. The Imperial Quartet provided music.[50]

With the loss of his ambitious, rough-speaking father, the cultured-yet-shy Robert would inherit more land, money, and property. He was already an expert at spending money. But what to do with it all... and himself?

CHAPTER EIGHT
Wealth and Responsibility

For unto whomsoever much is given,
of him shall be much required

Luke 12:48

SAMUEL ALLERTON'S ESTATE

The Chicago Tribune estimated Sam's estate at $4 million (2007 purchasing power of over $85 million).[1] Robert and his stepmother Agnes served as executors; his sister Kate waived her right, being out of the country during that time. Both Agnes and Robert received shares in the First National Bank of Chicago and Pittsburgh Union Stock Yards. Agnes inherited the Lake Geneva property, and Robert inherited the Prairie Avenue home and the remainder of the Piatt County farmland not already in his name.

Contrary to the facts, John Gregg Allerton said: "Kate might have gotten a little more because she was the favorite and the oldest. First born and all that, at least Robert always felt she got the first choice."[2]

Sam left shares in the Omaha Union Stockyards to Kate's husband, Hugo Johnstone, despite the notoriety he had brought to the family. He also left modest bequests to his loyal servant, Julia Moynihan, and his attorney and friend, William P. Williams.[3]

In 1914 the Prairie Avenue neighborhood showed signs of decline. Many homeowners were selling and moving elsewhere, and Robert did the same. In September 1915 he sold the prime northwest corner lot to the Hump Hairpin Company for a factory.[4] To keep a Chicago base, he and Agnes chose an apartment at 1315 Astor Street on the fashionable North side where many of their friends had relocated.

Besides money and property, Robert also inherited positions of power and responsibility in various institutions. He held his father's spot on the Board of Directors for the First National Bank of Chicago, and served as President at various times for the First National Bank of Allerton, Illinois, and the First National Bank of Spaulding, Nebraska. Other presidencies included the Pittsburgh Union Stock Yards, the Pittsburgh Provision Company, the Art Marble Company, and the A. T. Land Company.[5] In addition, he held a position with the First National Bank of Monticello.

GIVING TO PIATT COUNTY

Robert's philanthropies commenced as soon as he moved to The Farms, ramped up throughout the war years, and continued for the rest of his life. He preferred his contributions to be his own idea, turning away many people with a standard donation of five dollars, but he gave quite generously to provide a better quality of life for citizens of Piatt County.

In 1903 he and other citizens pledged funds toward a new Piatt County Courthouse. While most of the leading citizens offered $200, Robert subscribed $500 toward its construction.[6] Three years later, he contributed funds for the decoration of a new building for Monticello's St. Philomena Catholic Church.

In 1921 he purchased a brick house on Monticello's South Charter Street for use as a Community House. The building, rent-free for three years, served groups such as the Community Club, Woman's Club, Camp Fire Girls, and Boy Scouts.[7] In 1952 Monticello citizens voted to renovate Township Hall, the North State Street building that housed Allerton Public Library (established by Agnes and Sam in 1897). The library moved into a larger room, and other spaces were converted to serve organizations previously using the Community House. Robert sold his Charter Street building and used the proceeds to help refurnish Township Hall.[8]

Ralph Edward Marquiss

Monticello Community House on south Charter Street, as published in the *Marquiss Community Handbook of Monticello* of 1921 and 1922, page 49

Robert helped fund the first farm-to-market road in Illinois. Frustrated with the circuitous route into town (north, then east, then south), in December 1915 he donated $500 to Piatt County toward building a road from the southeast gates of The Farms into town, known today as Allerton Road. The right lane leading to Monticello was paved with brick for wagons filled with grain; empty wagons would return on the unpaved side.[9] It took 100 men and 50 horses to complete the job.[10] The county finally blacktopped the brick lane in 1981—a tribute to the quality of the original workmanship.[11]

To further improve the approach to The Farms (both for the townspeople and for his guests coming from the Monticello depot), Robert added new trees to those previously planted by his father. Evenly-spaced, towering Norway spruce trees still line the final half-mile stretch of public road to his gates and nearly a half-mile after the turn (his private road to the Sangamon).

When Robert moved to The Farms, only a simple ford provided crossing at the Sangamon. Robert hired Joseph Corson Llewellyn's* architecture firm to design and build a one-lane, arched concrete bridge. Arthur T. Porterfield, one of Llewellyn's engineers, produced the design, and the bridge was constructed in the summer of 1915.[12] In all, Robert paid $80,000 for the brick road and concrete bridge.[13] By 2001 severe deterioration and concerns for safety necessitated closing the Allerton Road entrance and Llewellyn's bridge. Visitors to Allerton Park must again follow the same roundabout route from Monticello that Robert spent so much money and effort to rectify.

University of Illinois

Bridge over the Sangamon River on Robert Allerton's estate, constructed in 1915. The bridge is currently closed to traffic.

In May 1919 Robert joined with several local citizens—Allen F. Moore, William Dighton, John N. Dighton, and C. A. Tatman—to establish the Piatt County Fairgrounds. Each donated $2,000 to defray the $20,000 cost for the land, known today as Forest Preserve Park.[14]

In November 1915, using funds from selling the Prairie Avenue property that he inherited, Robert established the Dr. Howard R. Chislett Trust Fund benefiting Passavant Hospital. Dr. Chislett, a leading surgeon and faculty member at the hospital, had cared for Sam during one of his last illnesses.[15] As the Trust document stated, income from the trust was strictly for Dr. Chislett's use "for the benefit of such cases as in his judgment may seem worthy and deserving of philanthropic assistance in the way of services and attention."[16] Robert also donated $200,000 for the hospital's building fund. Later, after Passavant changed names to Hahnemann Hospital, he served on the Board of Trustees, eventually being named an honorary trustee for his long association with the hospital.[17]

Knowing that Piatt County citizens had been considering the need for a home for tuberculosis sufferers and "tired mothers and crippled children,"[18] in July 1919 he made an offer to the county supervisors. He proposed selling almost ten percent of his Piatt County land (1,200 acres, worth approximately $400,000[19]) and contributing the proceeds to the county for construction of the needed building. Several days later newspapers noted that two and one-half fertile acres of Robert's land, located northeast of town, would be an outright gift to Piatt County. The property had been the long-time residence of Sam's farm manager and friend, John Phalen, who had died on July 25, 1919. Profits from farming the land would sustain the sanitarium, and residents of the Old Peoples' Home would pay no more than $500 for life care. Construction was expected to begin in the spring of 1920.[20]

A trust agreement was drawn up on November 21, 1919 to create The Samuel W. Allerton Farm Memorial, The John Phalen Old Peoples' Home Memorial, and provide for a County Tuberculosis Sanitarium location. The agreement did not mention including a home for tired mothers and crippled children.[21] In 1945, after decades of trying to unsuccessfully implement the plan, the land was sold. Until 2007 the trust managed the monies, earmarking them to help Monticello's Kirby Hospital's charity cases. The trust was liquidated in 2007 and the fund is now managed by Kirby Hospital. Robert's ninety-year-old gift to the county, modified from its original form, still benefits its citizens today.

Michael Holtz

In 1650 the sundial now in the Deland, Illinois Cemetery was an ornament on a bridge in Monmouthshire, England. Later it was placed in a sanctuary. The John Wanamaker Stores of New York purchased it in 1890. Robert used it in his garden before donating it to Deland's cemetery.

Following in the footsteps of Sam's and Agnes' philanthropy to Monticello's library, in 1918 Robert donated funds to Cisco's Women's Club to establish the Willow Branch Township Library. A section of the Cisco drugstore initially housed the books. Tax-supported since 1920, the library changed location several times over the years.

In 1912 nearby Deland, Illinois already had the Goose Creek Township Library, and was the smallest town in Illinois to earn a library grant from Andrew Carnegie.[22] Robert donated an English sundial for the town's cemetery in 1927.[23]

When Robert learned of a young woman who was a top student from a large family without the funds for her advanced education, he paid for her studies at Illinois State University in Normal, Illinois.[24] Such local gestures reflect Robert's caring and love of learning. However, they pale in comparison to his later gifts of scholarships and bequests to cultural institutions and universities.

THE GREAT WAR

By April 6, 1917 the United States was just entering the war. At forty-four years old, Robert might have been eligible for the draft, but his hearing loss and his management of a vital agricultural enterprise eliminated him from consideration. But he still wanted to do his part. He and Agnes each began by donating $1,000 to the Red Cross.[25] The following month he wrote this letter to President Wilson:[26]

Monticello, Ill. May 3rd, 1917
Woodrow Wilson, President of the United States
Washington, D.C.

Dear Sir:

This is the time for every good citizen to do his duty.

This is the time for practical manifestation of Loyalty and Patriotism.

I am a farmer and own, approximately, thirteen thousand acres of land in this State. About ten thousand acres are under cultivation.

I hereby tender to the Government, for its use and benefit, and without cost to it, the net profits of all crops that may be raised on this land, this year.

Hoping you can and will accept this offering, I am, with personal regards and best wishes,

Robert Allerton

Robert contributed another $200 to Monticello Township's Red Cross drive. Dighton and Kratz family members topped him with donations of $250 each,[27] but Robert also donated a knitting machine to the Piatt County Red Cross to help speed production of scarves, mittens, hats, and sweaters for American soldiers.[28] To a charity bazaar in Chicago collecting funds for "Our Boys in France Tobacco Fund," Robert gave $100.[29]

While in New York early in 1918, he donated a Red Cross ambulance to the Army, christening it the "Piatt County Ambulance."[30] He gave another $100 toward purchasing an ambulance in Italy. (In those days an ambulance cost less than $250.[31])

The first Piatt County Liberty Loan Drive set its goal at $350,000. Robert surprised everyone with his subscription of more than half—$200,000 worth of bonds.

One of Robert's Chicago friends, Andrew Courtney Campbell, served in the French Lafayette Escadrille. When he died in an air battle, Robert, Agnes, and the young man's cousin (Mrs. McBirney) established a fund to build a French hospital bearing his name. Each contributed $500,[32] equal in 2007 purchasing power to almost $69,000.

In 1918 Robert fell seriously ill in Chicago.[33] After a two-month stay at Hahnemann Hospital for a painful ear infection, he returned home. Although rumors surfaced about a mysterious poisoning, the hospital cleared up the confusion.[34] The ear infection had evolved into a case of blood poisoning.[35]

There was room for such worry. As the war was winding down, the Influenza Pandemic of 1918-1919 was spreading across the globe. Ultimately the disease killed 675,000 Americans, ten times more than died during the war itself. The threat prompted Monticello's Allerton Public Library to close its doors on October 25, 1918 until the danger diminished.

WORKING FOR ROBERT

Robert hired several employees who stayed with him for decades. In spite of his reputed fair treatment, not all stayed as long. His first employee, a cook, came on board in 1900. By 1910 another employee, James Shield, managed four groundskeepers: Roy Milligan, A. McNaughton, James Louis, and John Aldt. The inside staff included Catherine Murray as the cook, a German butler named Ranholt[36] Richards, and the butler's Canadian wife, Sachi, as the housekeeper. With the war overseas, anti-German Monticello townspeople pressured Robert around 1915 to let Ranholt go.

After that, Robert began to hire staff from England. Stanley Gollop, one of the first, became Robert's butler. He and Robert met at a New York hotel where Gollop worked as a bellhop. Gollop recruited other family members to work at The Farms, including his sister, Edie Cackett, and her family, until Robert fired Stanley in 1921 for "misbehaving."[37]

Edie Cackett filled the housekeeper position. Her husband, Arthur Cackett, worked for a time as the chauffeur and later as assistant butler. Their six-year-old son, Cyril, recalled that whenever Robert was in residence, he always tried to devote the hour between six and seven o'clock to him. During "Cyril's Hour," they played baseball or games Robert had brought from his trips. Knowing that the child needed transportation to Shady Nook School over two miles away, Robert gave Cyril a bicycle.[38] But, as one employee's daughter recounted, Robert typically showed no interest in befriending young children, especially little girls.[39]

Another Gollop sister, Emily, worked for years as Robert's laundress.[40] With only copper boilers to heat the water, Emily's days ran long, especially with guests in the house.

Edward (Ted) Page, another Gollop relative,[41] first arrived as a guest. As a teenager living in England, he suffered from tuberculosis. He met Robert when his Uncle Ted (Stanley Gollop's brother) accompanied Robert on a trip to England. Realizing that young Ted needed a better environment in which to recuperate, Robert invited him to Monticello, and Ted gratefully accepted. During his recovery, he stayed on the estate premises in a room with a screened-in porch. After regaining his health, he joined the staff as a houseboy and later worked as gardener, chauffeur, and butler.

Ted enjoyed fishing, as well as hunting for frogs by dangling a red string and hook from a pole in likely hiding spots. One day, Robert caught him in the act and asked what he had been doing. "Hunting for frogs, for frog legs, for dinner," he replied.

"Hunting with what?" Robert asked, staring at the pole.

Ted answered with some hesitation, thinking he might be in trouble, "The red string. It attracts them."

Robert said nothing more about it, but several nights later, Ted caught a glimpse of him walking along the edge of the pond with a fishing pole—and a red string hanging from the end.[42]

Robert wandered the estate early every morning with his dogs, while his guests usually slept in. Sometimes almost until noon. It always annoyed him that his guests wasted so much of the day in bed. Eventually the guests would ring the upstairs maid for breakfast. The houseman, in addition to keeping the coal furnaces going, would clean and shine their shoes, placed outside their bedroom doors.

University of Illinois

Robert with one of his dogs at The Farms, in 1915.

The houseman also transported garbage on a trolley from the house to the garage. In the early years, the horses then hauled the garbage to the estate's dump, at the far end of the formal gardens. During the winter, estate laborers cut ice from the Sangamon River to store in the ice house.[43] Well-packed in layers of sawdust or straw, it would last for several months.

Besides the Cacketts and the Gollops, other workers shared family ties. At one point four Priebe siblings held jobs on the premises: Willie as chauffeur, Albert as gardener, Emma, and finally Elmer.

Emma Priebe married John Ashby, who operated the dairy barn at The Farms. The couple first lived in a little frame farmhouse on the site where Robert later constructed the House in the Woods. Raising chickens and selling eggs to The Farms to supplement her salary, she cooked for nine workers, in addition to Robert and his guests, three times a day.[44]

When Elmer Priebe arrived, working as a laborer, he lived briefly with the Ashbys. Later he became the chauffeur when his brother, Willie, returned to Indiana. In addition to driving, the chauffeur was expected to fix the car. For three months during the winter of 1904, Elmer lived at the Prairie Avenue house while Sam and Agnes stayed in Pasadena, learning to maintain Sam's castoff crank-start Stevens-Duryea automobile. Three years later Robert gave it to a Monticello contractor and purchased a Packard. The new car came complete with a modern starter instead of the crank, but required another round of maintenance training for Elmer.

University of Illinois

Employees at The Farms in 1916: John Ashby, Della Hillert, Juanita Ashby (age eight), Elizabeth Shaw, Emma Priebe Ashby, Pauline Ashby Shonkwiler (age two), Minnie Camereth, and Albert Priebe.

Unfortunately, the Packard did not have a gas gauge, making it unreliable on long trips. But with a vehicle instead of a buggy, Elmer could drive Robert into Champaign or Decatur in about an hour. Once a week he also drove the employees there to shop and run errands. Each October he would jack up the car and cover it, using the horse and buggy until spring arrived.[45]

Emma Priebe Ashby's daughter, Pauline Shonkwiler, recalled hazy childhood memories of Robert as the lord of the manor. He would stroll into the farm house that they rented from him, without knocking, to converse with her mother. She also remembered her Uncle Elmer driving Robert and his guests to the Monticello Depot. Robert did not allow Elmer to acknowledge friends or family as he drove guests, but he managed to wink at Pauline when she waved at him.

When Robert and Elmer traveled alone, Elmer was as much a traveling companion as a chauffeur. Elmer drove him to Detroit, Montreal, New York, Boston, and Atlantic City, where they swam in the ocean. The two would stay in equally fine hotel rooms, share meals, and attend shows together. On one trip, Robert also brought his female bookkeeper and the butler.[46]

University of Illinois

Elmer Priebe in Robert's 1907 seven-passenger Stevens-Duryea Big Six Touring automobile. Photographed in front of the stable in 1914.

Because Robert was a bachelor, some thought he must have hated women—a notion roundly denounced by Elmer's wife, Irene.[47] When Elmer announced his plans to marry her, Robert congratulated them and told Elmer that he greatly approved of marriage. He inspired only positive comments from "Mrs. Elmer," as he called her. Her notes about Robert substantiated his generous nature, and that he was philanthropic for the sheer joy of being kind to others, not for self-aggrandizement. Irene presented Robert as a sincere man, but one not afraid to laugh at himself. Once he imitated how a model from a Paris fashion show teetered across the stage in her heels and tight clothing.[48]

Life on The Farms included hours of walking. In the afternoons, Robert and his guests explored the estate, usually from two until five. They meandered through the gardens and the seven miles of woodland paths in the south part of the estate that Elmer and Robert had cleared with hatchets. He wanted his guests to have fun, discovering sights and sounds while walking.[49] If it was too hot, his guests could stay close and canoe in the pond. For staff relaxation, the farm hands would saunter down to a nearby swimming hole.

As the years passed, Robert became more liberated in his manner of dress, sometimes walking barefoot, sometimes bare-chested, in the woods. At other times he could be seen on the grounds or in the woods, his shirtless torso gleaming bronze, but wearing spanking-white slacks and white shoes. On one occasion, little neighbor girls encountered him walking—completely nude—in the woods. One of the girls recalled his anger that the children had trespassed in his woods; only his guests were allowed freedom to wander.[50]

Later, as he grew older, other neighbors found him pleasant and chatty. He liked sunbathing in the nude around the pool and would casually retreat into the house au naturel, but only when no guests were visiting.[51] Apparently that habit led to rumors that visitors could be found lying nude around the house in the mornings after parties the nights before. Robert deplored heavy drinking, in particular inebriated women, so it is highly unlikely that their parties were so unrestrained.

Each morning, the housekeeper would leave the menu for the day on the back porch for Robert to approve before he left with the dogs for his morning walk. Robert preferred some manner of eggs for lunch every day. Although not much of a cook himself, he did invent a few simple recipes—for instance, peeled eggplant, thinly sliced and dipped into a mixture of cracker crumbs and beaten eggs. The coated slices were fried, stacked like pancakes, topped with a poached egg, and covered with a spicy sauce of tomatoes and wine.[52] Another favorite was eggs poached in red wine and meat stock, served in a small bowl.[53] He enjoyed American, French, German, Italian, Amish and other cuisine—anything but Mexican. A guest, a distant relative, was less than thrilled with one of Robert's favorite dinners of liver and onions and discreetly fed his portion to a dog passing by the table.[54]

University of Illinois

Costumes in one of the special closets Robert constructed for that purpose, photographed in the 1920s.

One day a stray dog wandered onto the estate and a temporary gardener kicked at it. Robert supposedly fired the man immediately. But dogs weren't always Robert's best friends. He once sought medical assistance after trying to break up a fight between two of his animals. He had been severely bitten by both and the local doctor was rushed to the estate to care for his wounds.[55]

Robert's staff commented that he was fair but strict, and didn't tolerate cruelty or sloppiness. He welcomed employees' relatives who asked to visit. He extended half-salary when he closed the house for the winter. The staff would clean the mansion from top to bottom before heading out on their own vacations, one or two at a time, many to Florida. When only a handful of staff remained, neighborhood children would sometimes venture close and peer into windows. One remembered being thrilled at seeing the exotic costumes through the panes. Another was occasionally allowed even greater liberties by the staff, carefully playing dress-up in the costumes.[56]

CHAPTER NINE
Myths and Misperceptions

It isn't what we don't know that gives us trouble,
it's what we know that ain't so.

Will Rogers (1879-1935)

"SOME LION'... OR SOME LYING"

Although the newspapers teemed with articles about the European war and relief efforts, not all news in July 1917 dealt with the bloody conflict. Monticello citizens had a more immediate worry. In June a Champaign County farmer had reported seeing a large animal prowling his grounds, scaring his dogs. He was convinced it was a lion and that it must have escaped from a recent carnival performance.

Five weeks later, the butler, Stanley Gollop, was picking flowers on The Farms. He suddenly yelled for help, claiming he had been attacked by a lioness. Although *The Chicago Tribune* reported that Gollop was "all but devoured,"[1] Allerton's staff delivered him to a doctor with only minor slashes and cuts. With many sightings already reported, more than 1,000 men volunteered to hunt for the beast. Three hundred marksmen were chosen from Decatur, Lincoln, Mount Pulaski, and Piatt County. The hunters, carrying .20 caliber pistols, old squirrel guns, and rifles used by veterans during the Civil War, were commanded by two veterans of the Spanish-American war.[2]

In addition to a $500 reward offered by a carnival company, Robert—feeling forced to open his estate to the hunters—offered his own $250 reward. The search continued over several days, with the beast supposedly appearing as far north as Ravinia, near Chicago. Newspapers reported that everyone in the state was living in terror. One frightened Central Illinois man caught a glimpse of the lion's eyes in the dark and shot his rifle in its direction. Unfortunately, the eyes were really a car's headlights, and the bullets hit the car hood instead of an animal.[3] Frustration turned to elation when hunters found what they thought was the lion's lair. But traps baited with poisoned meat lay untouched the following day.[4]

Spurred onward, one of the searchers sent a telegram to big-game hunter and ex-president Teddy Roosevelt at his home in Oyster Bay, Long Island.

> *You are invited to come to Decatur immediately and hunt the big lioness which is roaming through the 300 acre timber tract on the Robert Allerton estate, near Monticello. If you come, a big hunting party will be organized under your direction.*[5]

Teddy never answered the call to arms.

One columnist quipped: " 'SOME lion' on the Allerton estate. Or some lying'."[6] More stories proliferated. Two boys rowing on the Sangamon River spotted an animal that matched the description. Even *The Los Angeles Times* weighed in, stating that Robert would try to lure the lioness with a mate, provided by the Chicago Lincoln Park Zoo.[7] *The Washington Post* quoted a zoo spokesperson as offering several opinions:

> *What if it ain't a lion, but a goat that's gone wild...? The beast... may have been a large yellow dog or anything else... I think a better idea... would be to tunnel carefully under the woods, drive the lioness into the tunnel and starve her into submission.*[8]

The scare ended three days later. One of Robert's tenant farmers claimed that his collie attacked the passing lion on the banks of the Sangamon. Both animals "engaged in a fierce struggle"[9] and the lion's body dropped in the water and drifted downstream. The farmer said he had dragged the lion's body out of the water and planned to claim all rewards—but he never produced the carcass.

Whether a lion had been loose or a wildcat had wandered into the area, one will never truly know. The butler's injuries were sparsely documented, but one story revealed that an Allerton maid caught Gollop peeking into a window as women were changing their clothes. She chased him away with a rake, scratching him in the process.[10] Another rumor suggested that a runaway dog, not a lion, knocked him over.[11] And yet another claim surfaced that the "lion" had been a collie with a coat trimmed to resemble that royal animal. A "lion on the loose" proved a better story than the truth.[12] However, wildcats were sighted in the area after 1950, with one such animal surprising a man near The Farms in the 1960s.

An employee's wife later recounted that when Robert realized that the search had turned into an opportunity for outsiders to trespass, he put an end to the hunt. A Chicago reporter expressed skepticism about a lion in the countryside, but was more astonished to find a butler![13] The Monticello newspaper staunchly defended the townspeople's actions:

> *... there are two things that neither he nor any other reporter can get around. We have the footprint of the beast, for we dug it up in the oiled road. We*

are going to have a plaster cast made of it, and send it over to the lionologist of the University, for his diagnosis. Besides that haven't we a clawed butler?[14]

Although the "lion's" fate was never satisfactorily resolved, the newspapers declared both the animal and the story dead. More sobering news fill the front pages—the names of men being drafted into the war in Europe. Robert may have fumed over the invasion of people onto his property, but perhaps the hunters, in the back of their minds, were practicing for the serious carnage to come.

A Load of Rattlesnakes

Many local citizens still believe that Robert Allerton imported rattlesnakes to deter trespassers. One man claimed that, as a boy, he had witnessed crates of the creatures being unloaded from a boxcar at the depot, bound for delivery at The Farms. Such a scheme would have made no sense. Robert would not have needlessly risked his own safety on his twice-daily walks in the gardens and woods, nor that of his guests.

Rattlesnakes did naturally inhabit the property. One gardener claimed he had killed seven of them on the premises.[15] A farmer's wife, while hanging wash on the line, thought she had dropped a stocking and picked it up. According to the story, the "stocking" bit her and she died.[16]

An employee's daughter said that rattlesnakes proliferated at the river, sunned themselves on the road, and curled up inside potato bins or across the back of the outhouse seats. Black snakes hung from tree limbs. One morning Elmer Priebe found a snake tucked into bed with him, warming itself against him. Ted Page's daughters sometimes walked on stilts to avoid them. Typically they armed themselves with a hoe wherever they went, but Robert wanted the snakes left alone.

The eastern massasauga rattlesnakes (also known as the "great river mouth") prefer river bottom forests and continue to make The Farms their habitat, albeit in small numbers. By 1994 they were an endangered species in Illinois, with The Farms considered one of the last places in the state where they, and the Kirtland snake, can be found. In 2002 researchers captured an adult male massasauga and implanted it with a radio transmitter to monitor its movements. Within several years, two female snakes bore over twenty offspring.[17] By August 2008 none were found, but researchers continue to survey the property.

The shy massasaugas, members of the pit viper family, are more venomous than the timber rattler, but with their small amount of venom, their bites rarely cause extreme harm to human adults. Nearby neighbors claimed that Robert's hogs, allowed to run wild, kept the rattlers in control. That isn't as far-fetched as one might think. Hogs are effective snake predators. Their thick layers of fat protect them from the snakes' fangs.

Visitors slipping past hidden snakes may want to look closer at the ground. On a weekend visit many decades ago, a female guest went horseback riding across the meadow and through the wooded trails. When she left Robert's mansion, she was wearing a diamond brooch, but when she returned, she noticed that it had slipped off her clothing. Never recovered, the valuable jewelry may still be lying under layers of leaves and branches somewhere on the estate, waiting to be claimed.[18]

GUESTS AT THE FARMS

The Chicago Tribune

Flamenco dancer "La Estrellita" rehearsing with Chicago Junior League members for the "Fete Espagnol." The *Chicago Tribune* headline proclaimed, "Fox Trot Toes to Twinkle in Fandango: La Estrellita Improvises Costumes for Fete Espagnol Dancers." (April 5, 1918, page 3)

With visitors coming and going, rumors circulated that Robert brought trainloads of performers to The Farms to amuse the guests. Some of his guests were performers themselves. One in particular, a flamenco dancer named "La Estrellita,"[19]* offered a diversion for the staff. Elmer Priebe recalled the dancer arriving from Chicago one weekend with a group of Robert's friends. After dinner Robert invited everyone, including the servants, to gather in a circle on rugs and sofas in the stable studio.[20] For half an hour they watched the tall and lithe beauty dance around the room, clicking her castanets.

Robert and La Estrellita (born Stella Davenport in Cincinnati) may have become acquainted through their mutual interest in collecting art.[21] She was enough of a star at the time that Jack London compared one of his characters to her in his 1917 story, "The Kanaka Surf."

"She carries her body like a Spanish dancer," Mrs. Patterson said to her husband...

"By George, she does," Stanley Patterson concurred. "Reminds me of Estrellita. Torso just well enough forward, slender waist, not too lean in the stomach, and with muscles like some lad boxer's armouring that stomach to fearlessness. She has to have them to carry herself that way and to balance the back muscles. See that muscled curve of the back! It's Estrellita's."[22]

Another guest, Carleton Smith,* founded the National Arts Foundation of New York. Having grown up in Bement, seven miles south of Monticello, Carleton knew Robert. Once he brought opera star Lily Pons (wife of composer Andre Kostelanetz) with him to visit The Farms.[23] (Smith is most famous in Piatt County for bringing Marilyn Monroe and Carl Sandburg to the Bement Centennial in the summer of 1955.)

Robert's circle included one very famous architect's wife. Bessie Springs Smith White, Stanford White's wife, was a distant relative by marriage to Ellen Emmet. Although a 1906 newspaper claimed that Bessie White had been visiting Robert on June 25—the same night her husband was murdered in Madison Square Garden—they were wrong. Stanford White's son recalled that it took him until 3:30 in the morning to reach their Long Island house where Bessie lay asleep. He waited outside her bedroom until daylight before informing her of his father's death.[24]

Most of Robert's weekend guests might have been unknown outside Chicago, but other names may still be familiar today, especially the Potter Palmers (Jr.), ballerina and choreographer Ruth Page,* Colonel George Langhorne,* and assorted members of the McCormick family. Caroline Kirkland (Madame X) visited as well. Illinois governor and presidential candidate Adlai Stevenson[25]* and Secretary of State William Jennings Bryan also came to The Farms. Elmer Priebe drove Mr. Bryan to a Chautauqua at the county fairgrounds.[26]

A great many of Robert's visitors were Chicago members of the Arts Club of Chicago. This group of associates, both friends and colleagues, engaged Robert in the challenge of introducing Modernism to the Midwest and defining Chicago as its capital.

University of Illinois

Colonel and Mrs. George Langhorne on the Conservatory Terrace of the Allerton mansion in the 1940s.

CHAPTER TEN
The Arts Go Hog Wild

We have made our money in pigs...
is that any reason why we should not spend it on paintings?

Charles Hutchinson[1]

THE ARTS COME OF AGE IN CHICAGO

In the rubble of the 1893 World's Columbian Exposition, the Columbian Museum of Chicago (now home to the Museum of Science and Industry)[2] and the Art Institute of Chicago remained standing—an acknowledgement by the city fathers that culture is essential to growth. Chicago had the rails, the resources, and the strategic location. Soon it would build new cultural and educational bases: the John Crerar Library,[3] a new home for the Newberry Library,[4] the Chicago Orchestra,[5] and the University of Chicago.[6] But among these grand endeavors, the Art Institute of Chicago would anchor the Midwest as a cultural capital, second in the nation only to New York City. Frederic Bartlett and Robert were poised to become major players in the effort to build the museum's collection, and the competition was keen.

A New York reporter threw a jab at the Art Institute's first president, Charles L. Hutchinson,* who along with trustee Martin Ryerson* had made a bulk acquisition of Old Masters paintings:

> *[Hutchinson] probably paid $1,000 a foot for his Rubenses, Rembrandts and Van Dykes, and we presume the citizens of Chicago will give him a triumphal procession along the lakefront when they arrive, carrying them and him in huge floats, drawn by a team of milk-white Berkshire hogs.*[7]

Clearly Chicago had a public relations problem. Patrons like Marshall Field and Berthe Palmer rose to the challenge, donating major art collections. Imparting their expertise, they dictated regional taste and determined Chicago's standards for artistic propriety (or at least, its public display of it). In the process, they could enjoy the thrill of the hunt and then shelter their personal acquisitions from theft and personal property taxes in the museum.[8] Most gave equally to hospitals, orphanages, and educational institutions, greatly benefiting the general public.

The next generation continued philanthropies of all types, but a few of them took a radical turn. Looking at all those paintings led to the inevitable consequence—they began to take art seriously. To complicate matters, their cultural awakening heightened during a revolutionary period in the history of art.

Early twentieth-century postcard showing the entrance to the Art Institute of Chicago.

Art historian Sue Ann Prince said of the new generation of Chicago collectors, many of whom would soon open their eyes to Modernist trends, "assembling works of art was more than just a fashionable pastime: it was a conviction, an end in itself."[9] Frederic Bartlett had called his love of collecting "a habit—a disease."[10] In 1902 he and Dora built a new home on Prairie Avenue to hold it all.[11] *The Chicago Tribune* quickly made "Dorfred House" the talk of the town,[12] and Sam could surely see that Robert was headed in the same direction.

Frederic's father, Adolphus Bartlett, had assisted in the development of the Art Institute,[13] but only reluctantly allowed Frederic to study painting in Munich. Perhaps he hoped it would be a passing fancy. Imagine Adolphus and Sam several years later, finishing a lunch at the Chicago Club. They fold their napkins in resignation, and Sam tells Adolphus about a ride through The Farms with Robert.

Robert had wistfully commented on a beautiful sunset.

Sam had told him, "Look at the corn and wheat. That's where the money is."[14]

Benjamin "Old Hutch" Hutchinson had cornered the wheat market and become Sam's associate in the First National Bank of Chicago.[15] It was his son, Charles Hutchinson, who presided at the Art Institute—the butt of the New York reporter's Berkshire hog joke. Old Hutch was no less able to resist the livestock theme, reminding all within earshot of who had earned the fortune in the first place.

"Think about him!" Old Hutch said, "A son of mine! He paid $500 apiece for five painted sheep and he could get the real article for $2 a head!"[16]

Twenty years Robert's senior, Charles L. Hutchinson straddled the generations of Sam and Robert. Hutchinson was a family friend, philanthropist, art collector, authority on architecture, and lover of nature. He had boldly guided Chicago into a new era, and must have served as a role model to Robert.

In 1881 Charles Hutchinson and his new bride, Frances Kinsley, settled down the street from the Allertons at 2709 Prairie Avenue.[17] The families shared ties to the Universalist Church in Chicago, Hutchinson being an active leader. The church building of the new St.

The Chicago Tribune

Illustration from a March 11, 1906 *Chicago Tribune* article featuring Dorfred House, Frederic Clay Bartlett's Chicago home.

Paul's on the Midway Universalist complex was dedicated to the memory of his mother, Sarah Ingalls Hutchinson, and Robert's mother, Pamilla Thompson Allerton.[18]

In 1900, just as Robert completed his mansion at The Farms, the Hutchinsons built their summer home, "Wychwood," at Lake Geneva. Next door, Frederic Bartlett had participated in the design of his father's summer home.[19] Millionaires around the country had settled in various vacation colonies—in the mountains, on lakes, on the coasts, and even in the desert. Rugged individualists such as John Muir and Teddy Roosevelt[20] ushered in the new century with attention to the glory of nature and the need for conservancy. Those at Lake Geneva paid homage, but they were hardly "roughing it." For Chicagoans, the natural setting of Lake Geneva provided enough fresh air to revive the spirit and enough fashion to satisfy expectations. It was Prairie Avenue, recreated and plunked down in a more appealing spot.

Frances Kinsley Hutchinson's books describe the couple's devotion to gardening and nature and her husband's preoccupation with architectural improvements. Hutchinson led others on the lakefront to a higher aesthetic ideal.

Robert's mansion followed the convention of his day, but his home was not one in a string of mansions, competing for honors along a shoreline. His location on the downstate prairie set him apart, literally and figuratively.

As Robert continued the philanthropies of his parents, Charles Hutchinson set an even higher standard. His donations frequently equaled half his annual income.[21] Over time he was involved at some level with at least seventy different Chicago organizations, serving as president of six, treasurer of twenty, and director or trustee of over forty.[22] Robert's legacy eventually covered all the same bases, albeit on a slightly smaller scale.

During Hutchinson's tenure as president of the Art Institute, Chicago gained stature as an arts center, just as Modernism exploded onto the scene. The 1913 International Exhibition of Modern Art, better known as the Armory Show, is now recognized as one of the most (if not *the* most) important American exhibitions in the history of modern art. First held at New York's 69th Regiment Armory, the show introduced avant-garde works of the Impressionists, Cubists, and Fauvists to record crowds. A slightly smaller version of the exhibition arrived at the Art Institute of Chicago in March (just before Glyn Philpot's August visit to Illinois), and then traveled to Boston.

In all three cities the show sparked public and professional debate: what qualified as art and what did not? Art Institute students held a mock trial of Henri Matisse and then stabbed and dragged an effigy of "Henri Hair Mattress" through the museum terrace.[23] It is to Chicago's credit that the show came to the Midwest at all, and that the Art Institute would gain a strong reputation for its collection of twentieth-century art.

Robert's role in the Chicago scene grew steadily after his studies in Europe. He joined the Art Institute in 1894 as an annual member, and in 1902 he became a governing life member.

In 1918, five years after the Armory Show, he was elected trustee. Frederic Bartlett became a trustee in 1923.

Frederic intended his early acquisitions for his homes, but as time went on he selected art with the museum in mind, determined to introduce modern French art to the public.[24] In the annals of art history, Frederic Bartlett is named among Chicago's "Modernist Five," along with Martin Ryerson, Arthur Jerome Eddy, Annie Swan Coburn, and Joseph Winterbotham.

Robert's acquisitions were not as adventurously Modernist as Frederic's, but his cumulative gifts would be equally striking in quantity and scope. His early collecting consisted of sculptures for The Farms—nothing of major note, but simply what appealed to him at a particular time. Many of his garden pieces are copies by regional artisans or works by lesser-known artists. In 1911 he donated to the Art Institute of Chicago a sculpture by John Donoghue (American, 1853-1903) entitled *Young Sophocles Leading the Chorus of Victory after the Battle of Salamis.* His most notable gifts to the Art Institute began in earnest in the 1920s and continued steadily throughout his life.

THE CLIFF DWELLERS

In November 1907 Robert became a charter member of the Cliff Dwellers Club, founded by Chicagoans to emulate New York's Players Club.[25] The brainchild of writer Hamlin Garland, the group has been described as offering, "the solid comfort and good food of a men's club as a base for conversations and as a snare for visiting artists."[26] Frederic Bartlett was appointed to the first Executive Committee. The charter members (all of them men) first met at the Fine Arts building on Michigan Avenue, kicking off with a lighthearted program of spoofs and skits. Later they created a permanent home, a "bungalow" and roof garden on top of the new skyscraper being built for International Harvester at Michigan Avenue and Harrison Street.

The early membership mixed businessmen, artists, and those who bridged the two worlds through their institutional positions or patronage. Most early Cliff Dwellers were only known regionally, but today many of the names are legendary: Daniel H. Burnham, Frank Lloyd Wright, Louis Sullivan, Carl Sandburg, James Whitcomb Riley, Daniel Chester French, Lorado Taft, Booth Tarkington, and Otis Skinner.[27]

ON THE HEIGHTS

Hail! Ye men of lofty station
Looking down upon the nation,
From your eyre of elation
And relief;
Hail! Ye dwellers in a far land,
On a peak and up near starland,
With you Hamlin-culture's garland
For a chief!

From a 1910 handbook published by The Cliff Dwellers. Poem contributed by Brander Matthews of Columbia University.

THE ARTS CLUB OF CHICAGO

The Arts Club of Chicago was founded in 1916 to raise standards among professional artists, provide exhibition space, and link artists with patrons and art lovers.[28] Founding members Charles Hutchinson and Martin Ryerson forged a strong and mutually beneficial alliance with the Art Institute.

Robert and Frederic served on several committees of the Arts Club of Chicago and socialized with friends such as John Alden Carpenter, Hugh McBirney, and Edgar Lee Masters.[29] Eventually Robert became a director, along with Katherine Dudley, Mrs. C. Morse Ely, Mrs. Pauline Palmer,* Mrs. Arthur Ryerson (John Borie's sister, Emily), and Caroline Kirkland (Madame X).[30] Other members of the Club included such high-rollers as the Wrigley and Swift matriarchs.

Under the leadership of Rue Winterbotham* and Alice Roullier,* the Arts Club promoted a sustained interest in the avant-garde movement, sponsoring the first showing of Picasso in Chicago and his most significant in the United States. (Years later, in 1939 they exhibited Picasso's masterpiece *Guernica* for one week). In 1923, in addition to Picasso's exhibition, they featured a showing of Rodin. And the following year they showcased the work of Georges Braque and Henri de Toulouse-Lautrec, the first exhibition in the United States of Lautrec's art.[31] Over the years the members together pooled personal and club funds to purchase over fifty works of art to be placed in the Art Institute.

The Arts Club charged two different types of dues from members. Those who could afford it paid a significant fee to belong; struggling artists paid only a token amount. This appealed to Carl Sandburg and other writers, artists, and musicians.[32]

In January of 1918 Robert and architect David Adler assembled a show at the Arts Club of Chicago featuring antique tapestries and furnishings owned by Chicago families: Mrs. R. T. (Florence Higinbotham) Crane, Jr.,[33]* Mrs. C. Morse Ely, Emily Borie Ryerson, Mrs. Ogden Armour, and others.[34] The following year, Robert and Adler redecorated the Art Institute's Gallery 47 with a stain of "deep misty blue" against white woodwork. The color showcased the work of decorative designer John Flaxman (1760-1800), who began his career as a designer for Josiah Wedgewood.[35]

The Performing Arts

Robert began serving on the Chicago Opera Company's board of directors at the end of the war.[36] In 1919 committee leader Mrs. John Borden needed to rent two hundred boxes for a successful ten-week season. For the previous three years, Robert had never followed through on his promise to rent a box. Because of his hearing impairment, he preferred a first row seat. On other occasions, he would share a friend's box. However, for the spring 1919 season, he rented a box for those who could not afford that luxury, the recipients of his generosity to be chosen by the Friends of the Opera. Perhaps this encouraged others to fall under the spell of Robert's friend, Mary Garden, the attractive, Scottish-American soprano who performed at the Chicago Opera from 1910 through 1931.[37]

In 1923 Robert joined Mrs. John Borden, Mrs. Rockefeller McCormick, and Mrs. Emily Borie Ryerson in their promotion for a Chicago "civic theater."[38] In 1926 he and many Chicago friends, including Frederic Bartlett and several of the McCormicks, sponsored the Chicago Play Producing Company, a "Little Theater" under the leadership of Marion Gering. Familiar names from the Arts Club of Chicago also joined the board of directors.[39] During that interim he joined many of the same people in backing the production of a Russian ballet,[40] with music written by John Alden Carpenter (Rue Winterbotham's husband).

Robert also belonged to the Chicago Club, Union League Club, Casino Club, The University Club, Saddle and Cycle Club.[41] Comparing the membership lists of these elite societies and executive boards, one finds more or less, the same names in differing combinations. Untangling the networks of marriages, business relationships, and addresses would be daunting; suffice it to say that the rosters corresponded time after time to Robert's lists of associates and guests at The Farms.

Private Collection

Charcoal portrait of Robert Allerton, dated 1921, by Leopold Gould Seyffert (1887-1956). Seyffert studied at the Pennsylvania Academy of the Fine Arts under Cecilia Beaux and William Merritt Chase. He was an instructor at the Art Institute of Chicago from 1917-1927, during which time he received numerous awards for his artwork. Among subjects of his other portraits were Andrew Mellon, Charles Lindbergh, Samuel Gompers, Leopold Stokowski, and Chicagoans Julius Rosenwald, Marshall Field, Jr., Potter Palmer, Jr., John McCutcheon, Charles L. Hutchinson, and John A. Carpenter.

CHAPTER ELEVEN
One for Me, One for You

But I grow old among dreams,
A weather-worn, marble triton
Among the streams.

From "Men improve with the Years"
by William Butler Yeats (1865-1939)[1]

In the Spirit of Art

Throughout his decades of collecting and experimenting with the gardens, but particularly as a middle-aged man, Robert never seemed to be satisfied with just one of anything. His sense of balance in design—and even in his life—required pairs. Much of the collection that filled his estate consisted of replicas of major works that he had donated. Others were multiples of lower-valued sculptures. In the rare instance that a single piece sufficed, the artwork frequently fulfilled a purpose beyond his personal delight in the object: caring for the emotional well-being of a friend or family member, or patronage to a particular artist. His innovative techniques in landscape and residential architecture satisfied his own curiosity, but his ideas also served as proving grounds for those who accepted his challenge. For Robert, the art of collecting and gardening had matured into a means of expression—a way of filling an emptiness in his own life and in the lives of those he loved.

One example of this can be found both in Wisconsin and at The Farms. In 1916 Reinette Thompson McCrea,[2] his maternal aunt, passed away. In her honor, Robert commissioned Chicago stone mason Charles Laing[3] to copy a sixteenth-century sculpture by Germain Pilon, *The Three Graces,* for her grave in Oak Hill Cemetery in Lake Geneva, Wisconsin. He was so fond of the piece that he commissioned Laing to make a second copy for The Farms. It has been moved several times over the years, arriving in 1970 at its current location in the Peony Garden.

THE SUNKEN GARDEN

Before 1915 the chain of Robert's formal gardens ended without punctuation. An unadorned allée of trees led to a ravine, used as the estate's landfill and composting field. It was an eyesore, to say nothing of the odor in the muggy Illinois summer. Robert recruited his friend, architect David Adler, to transform the site into an exclamation point—a new garden at perpendicular orientation to the others.

University of Illinois

Construction of the Sunken Garden in 1915.

The drama of the new garden derives not from sculpture or plantings, but from the very restrained use of those features. More an amphitheater than a typical garden, it is almost entirely devoid of plants except for evergreens on the upper level. In fact, the centerpiece of the garden is the visitor who happens to stand in the center of it. Art historian Dr. Muriel Scheinman has compared the Sunken Garden to a swimming pool.[4] If one can imagine the flat, green lawn as water, fish sculptures appropriately support the theme (however, the fish were a later addition). In its earliest stages, stairs led down from the east side to the floor of green turf, surrounded by concrete walls.

Michael Holtz

In Greek mythology, these three daughters of Zeus personified joy, charm, and beauty. This version of *The Three Graces* is a limestone copy of a sculpture by Germain Pilon (1530-1590) that was commissioned by Catherine de Medici. The original supported a gilt funerary urn that held the heart of her deceased husband, French Henry II.

Robert had no shortage of available laborers—1915 was a year of heavy flooding, and local fields were too waterlogged to work. He hired a crew to clear the ravine, lay drainage tile, and level the site with hand shovels.[5] William F. Lodge,* Robert's Monticello friend[6] who led many of the other garden construction projects,[7] had little experience at the time with using poured concrete—it was a relatively new technique in the area. Marks from the board forms showed, requiring a resurfacing of the walls.[8]

University of Illinois

The Sunken Garden in 1917, shortly after completion. Only the lower walls are in place. Stairs led to rustic, wooden gazebos at each end.

Lattice gazebos topped stairways on the north and south, and pairs of ceramic *Fu Dogs* guarded the perimeter of the lower level. In 1925 and again in 1932 the garden underwent extensive redesign and more impressive features were added.

University of Illinois

By 1925 lattice gazebos appear atop larger concrete houses, and upper walls have been constructed around the garden.

Robert had visited Beijing

when he began the garden, and he may have been influenced by a particular feature of the Temple of Heaven. Its House of the Heavenly Lord is surrounded by a wall that produces amazing acoustic effects—a person at one end can clearly hear a person at the other, approximately 65 meters away. In Robert's Sunken Garden, a normal speaking voice is perfectly audible across the garden's length. With his hearing disability, perhaps he found the concept intriguing.

THE HOUSE IN THE WOODS

Michael Holtz

Joseph Corson Llewellyn designed the House in the Woods for the Allerton Estate. Built in 1917, the stucco home quartered the head gardener and his family.

The year 1917 was an industrious one at The Farms. Robert also built a new home down the road from the Gate House for the head gardener and his family, calling it the House in the Woods. The project, designed by Joseph Corson Llewellyn, provided him an opportunity to experiment with construction of hollow tile covered with stucco, rather than wood. Despite the building's modest function as staff housing, Robert made sure it reflected his aesthetic standards. He incorporated the mansion's original front door, recycled from the 1916 remodeling, and around 1925 he moved the *Shepherd* and *Shepherdess* sculptures from the Square Parterre Garden to decorate the exterior.[9] Coincidentally, the Lake Geneva summer home that Frederic Bartlett designed for his father in 1906 was also known as The House in the Woods.[10]

THE BARTLETT FAMILY

Given the parallels in Robert's and Frederic's lives, competition could have strained their relationship. Robert had followed his friend to study painting, bowing to his superior talent. In the early 1900s he stood in Frederic's shadow as a voice for the arts in Chicago. Both then owned rural estates and fashionable homes and were beginning to collect art with a grander goal in mind. But in one very important respect, the two were diametrically opposite: Frederic had a family, and Robert remained a bachelor. Even in that regard, the two nurtured each other's growth and their friendship prevailed.

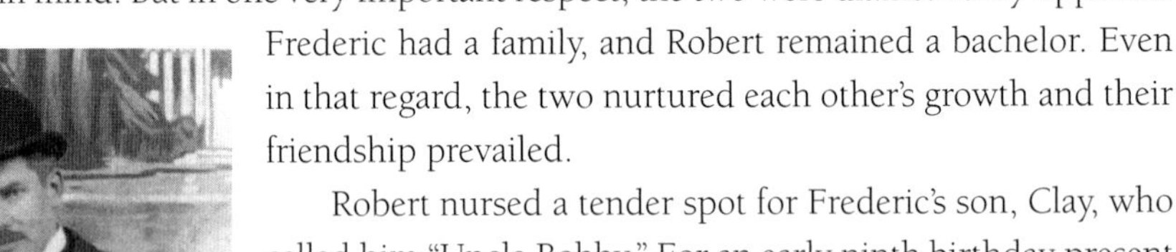

Courtesy of Elisabeth Bartlett Sturges

Dora and Frederic Clay Bartlett in San Francisco, 1915.

Robert nursed a tender spot for Frederic's son, Clay, who called him "Uncle Bobby." For an early ninth birthday present in 1916, Uncle Bobby told the child of a special gift, still in Monticello… a pony which they later named "Merry Legs." Reading behind the comment in Dora's diary ("It took us a long time"), the Bartletts may not have been thrilled with the drive down to Monticello on June 3 with a cart to transport the pony.[11]

The Bartletts and Robert found time to see each other practically every month, especially when he spent part of January 1917 in New York. The Bartletts had moved there two years earlier after selling their Prairie Avenue home.[12] After dining and seeing an opera with Robert on January 12, 1917, the Bartletts said their goodbyes.[13]

A month later Madame X reported that Robert was "disporting himself in Honolulu... where, garlanded with... flowery trimmings... he has been enjoying all the delights of that land of lotus eaters."[14] Two weeks after that article appeared, he received shocking news. Dora died at home on March 3, 1917, falling ill after helping Clay recover from a bout of pneumonia.[15]

The passing of Dora in 1917 added to the deaths of loved ones that Frederic already experienced. After losing his mother in 1890, he had mourned his brother's demise in 1900. Twenty-year-old Frank Bartlett had been visiting the recently-married Frederic and Dora in Munich that summer when he fell ill with appendicitis. He died on July 15, 1900, immediately after an operation.[16] Six years later in 1906, Frederic and Dora grieved the deaths of their baby twins. Now his beloved Dora was gone.

Frederic took a new bride on January 22, 1919. His marriage to Dora's friend, Helen Birch, came as no surprise to Chicago society. Thirty-seven-year old Helen had socialized with many of Frederic's friends and acquaintances for decades. Catherine Eddy Beveridge,* Frederic's good friend and Helen's cousin, held the ceremony at her Boston home.[17] Among the few guests were Robert and Delia Caton Field, widow of Marshall Field.[18]

Courtesy of Bonnet House Museum & Gardens

Clay Bartlett (Robert's godson), Hugh Taylor Birch, Helen Birch Bartlett, and Frederic Clay Bartlett.

In 1922 Frederic suffered the loss of his father, Adolphus. In spite of Adolphus Bartlett's dismay at Frederic's decision to become an artist, he served a trustee of the Art Institute of Chicago from the 1880s until 1917[19] and bequeathed it the sum of $10,000.[20]

Like Robert, Frederic's father-in-law, Chicago attorney Hugh Taylor Birch, loved nature and had donated over 1,760 acres to wilderness preservation organizations. As a wedding gift, he gave Helen and Frederic a thirty-five acre stretch of undeveloped land in Fort Lauderdale, Florida. Frederic designed a restful winter home on the property, innovatively tuned to his artistic style and the wild setting. Helen's father suggested that they name their winter retreat Bonnet House after the bonnet lilies that grow on property.[21]

Frederic and Helen began collecting art with a new passion. Robert did the same, selecting some pieces strictly for his own pleasure and others for the public to experience.

THE RETURN OF GLYN PHILPOT

In 1921 Glyn Philpot returned to America, his fourth trip abroad since the end of the war. He would visit The Farms again, accompanied by Vivian Forbes, his companion since

Courtesy of Juanita Gale

Robert's butler, Edward "Ted" Page, who posed for the *Primitive Man* sculptures in 1921.

Michael Holtz

Glyn Warren Philpot sculpted a small version of the *Primitive Man* as a study during his stay at The Farms in 1922. The two life-sized versions at Allerton Park are the work of Chicago sculptor Charles Laing.

1915. Vivian, a man younger than Glyn by eight years, was by all accounts unstable and emotionally manipulative, and their lifelong relationship eventually took its toll on Glyn. More mature and sobered by the war, Glyn visited Robert with much less giddiness, but with no less warm friendship.

Vivian sketched a charcoal portrait of Robert, and Glyn painted an over-mantel canvas, a picture of a faun and satyr. Robert posed for an oil sketch, most likely a study for that piece. Robert asked Glyn to paint to a frieze on that theme for the mansion. Glyn agreed to the subject, but chose to sculpt instead of paint.

Using Robert's butler, Ted Page, as a model, Glyn produced a small plaster study of man in his most primitive state, pushing himself up and out of the earth. To simulate the action, Ted posed nude for several hours each day, balancing a pile of heavy books on his shoulders. For all his hard work in the cold studio, Ted (whom Robert nicknamed "King Edward") received the not-so-kingly sum of five dollars.[22] In 1922 Robert commissioned Chicago stone mason Charles Laing[23] to translate Glyn's study into the pair of full-size limestone *Primitive Man* statues that we see today near the mansion and pond, facing one another on opposite sides of the Avenue of the Formal Gardens. Although Ted Page wished he had been able to wear clothes during the pose, he felt proud for being the model. But later, as he pondered how little he received for the work, he wondered, "What in the world did I do that for?"[24]

In a 1923 exhibition at London's Grosvenor Galleries, Glyn Philpot exhibited as a matched pair the small studies of the *Primitive Man* that he produced at The Farms.[25] With a penchant for symmetry, Robert frequently placed sculptures in pairs—but it is not clear whether the idea of duplicate statues was Robert's or Glyn's.

The Distinguished Benefactor

Robert was elected the first Distinguished Benefactor of the Art Institute of Chicago in 1923. A bronze tablet installed near the museum's entrance at that time acknowledged Robert Allerton, Florence H. Crane, Cyrus Hall McCormick, Annie S. Coburn, and George W. Sheldon as donors of more than $25,000 each.[26] His election coincided with remarkable gifts in 1923 and 1924 of works by the artist Auguste Rodin (1840-1917), including small bronze castings of his 1891 *Fallen Carytide* and his 1882 *Sorrow,* and drawings from the artist's later period. But the most impressive donation was a bronze casting of the 1881 *Adam,* slightly larger than life-size, that Robert purchased from the artist's studio after Rodin's death.

With permission from the Art Institute of Chicago, Robert commissioned Charles Laing of Chicago[27] in 1924 to create a copy of the *Adam* for his own Garden of Eden. It was damaged in transport to The Farms, but installed successfully in the Seasonal Garden where a large elm tree once stood. In 1975 a visitor to the Park toppled the sculpture in an attempt to climb it, damaging it beyond repair. The current replica was created by an Indiana stonemason who, in an effort to increase the strength of the piece, left the stone uncut between the legs and between the right hand and body. Understandably, the artistic finesse of the reproduction is no match to the original.[28]

Michael Holtz

Robert donated an original bronze casting of Rodin's *Adam* to the Art Institute of Chicago in 1924. This 1977 limestone copy is the second to be installed at Allerton Park.

THE DEATH OF AGNES

Robert's stepmother Agnes was involved in an automobile accident in Pasadena in May 1910. The chauffeur had lost control of the vehicle and crashed into a trolley. She was not badly hurt, but the *Chicago Tribune* reported it as third-page news.[29] Unlike the rest of her family, her name had rarely appeared in the papers.

Her health began to decline around 1922, supposedly from liver disease. On December 19, 1924, Agnes passed away at her Astor Street residence.[30] At that time, Robert's sister Kate was staying at The Drake Hotel, conceivably in town with family for the upcoming Christmas holidays.

Robert and Kate held a private funeral service at Agnes' apartment on December 22 and interred her ashes next to Sam's grave at Graceland Cemetery. The bulk of her $2-million estate[31] fell to Robert. Income from a $400,000 trust fund was distributed to her sister (Phoebe Wysong of Canton, Illinois) and her four nieces: Kate Johnstone, Jessie T. Dighton of Monticello, Berintha Greene of Winnetka, Illinois, and Pamilla Clark of Pasadena. At their deaths, the women's surviving children, if any, would receive their mother's principal. Agnes also left trust funds for Chicago, Pasadena, and Lake Geneva employees, other relatives, friends (such as Mrs. Anna Rathbone), and several churches and hospitals.[32]

Her sister, nieces, and Mrs. Rathbone were additionally bequeathed jewelry. Robert received the contents of her Lake Geneva and Pasadena homes and donated some of it to the "Holiday Home," a local Lake Geneva charity. He distributed the rest to relatives and employees.

One whole section of his stepmother's will is devoted to Robert, mentioning their mutual affection and the kindness he had shown her over the years. She considered him her son, and she his mother. Everything else belonging to her now fell to him, as did the residuary estate of the trust funds after death of the individual beneficiaries.

Robert brought Mrs. Rathbone and his Chicago secretary, Mrs. Helen Murphy, to both Pasadena and Lake Geneva to help him choose what to save and what to toss. Many items at The Folly didn't appeal to him, so he gave them to friends, family, or staff. Statues made of him as a little boy, he destroyed with a hammer. Other items—including a silver tea set—he placed in a "big basket and walked out at the end of the pier and dumped"[33] into the lake.

University of Illinois

Agnes Thompson Allerton's bookplate, pasted in a scientific book on soil fertility, expresses her love of horticulture and reading. A verse above the engraving of roses reads:

A Blessing on the Printers Art
Books are the Mentor of the Heart,
The Burning Soul, the Burdened Mind,
Alone in Books Companions find.

Robert brought the remaining contents to The Farms, filling the stable room with trunks of linens, silver, and clothing.[34]

When The Folly stood empty, Robert had it razed. He didn't need the house to keep his childhood memories alive, but neither did he want anyone else to live in it. The Pasadena house held no strong memories for him, so he left it standing.[35]

By this time, Robert had established a pattern of destroying or abandoning physical representations of his life and memories: his paintings in Europe, his Prairie Avenue home, The Folly, statuettes of himself, even silver tea sets. Many among some older generations were known to chop up furniture for kindling or burn family possessions rather than let them fall into the hands of others. Robert simply did it on a more massive scale.

On many levels, Robert used objects of art to fill voids in his life. But the largest void of all—the one Agnes had helped fill—resulted when Pamilla, his birth mother, died when he was seven. His unceremonious destruction of the family heirlooms may have been his way of demonstrating, if only to himself, that no object in the world could replace the loss of either Pamilla or Agnes.

CHAPTER TWELVE
Father and Son

Fate or a wise man knew that we needed each other.

John Wyatt Gregg Allerton[1]

From 1919-1923 Robert participated on the University of Illinois Campus Plan Commission, a group assembled by the Trustees. This early service to the University would mark two significant beginnings: a life-changing personal relationship and an enduring connection to the public of Central Illinois.

As part of the University's continued expansion, the Commission recommended a new football stadium, scheduled for completion in November 1923. The new Memorial Stadium, honoring World War I veterans, would replace the 4,000-seat Illinois Field.[2] To mark the upcoming closing of Illinois Field late in 1922, the Trustees invited the Commission participants to attend the November Dad's Day celebration. Pre-game luncheons sponsored by fraternities were a normal part of Dad's Day events.

Robert's good friend from Monticello, William F. Lodge, served as President of the Dad's Day Association. Lodge's son (William T.), Asler C. Dighton* (Robert's second cousin) and Asler's roommate, John Wyatt Gregg,* were Zeta Psi Fraternity brothers.[3] Together, the three young men often visited Monticello, twenty-five miles away, occasionally popping in on Asler's Cousin Robert at The Farms. Being supportive, Will asked his father to invite Robert to Zeta Psi's luncheon as a stand-in father for John.

John's family consisted only of his brother, Scranton, and his sister, Katherine. His mother, Katherine Scranton Gregg,[4] died from breast cancer around 1916.[5] His father, James Richmond Gregg, died during John's junior year (1921) at the University of Wisconsin. John had enrolled there as a student of chemical engineering after completing his military service in World War I. Upon the death of his father, he quit school to earn his living. He had chosen chemical engineering on the guidance of his brother. With a preferred interest in architecture, he took a job with a Milwaukee architect, Alexander Eschweiler.[6] Before long, he realized he

University of Illinois

University of Illinois Zeta Psi brothers, photographed for the 1926 *Illio* yearbook: John Gregg (bottom row, far left), Asler Dighton (second row, far right), and Will Lodge (top row, far left). That year, football star "Red" Grange was also a Zeta Psi member.

would need to return to school to pursue his new career in earnest.

In 1922 John transferred to the School of Architecture at the University of Illinois. Because he had belonged to the Zeta Psi Fraternity in Wisconsin, he continued with the Illinois chapter. At age twenty-two, his maturity earned him dual positions as the fraternity's bookkeeper and commissary steward. Compensation in the form of room and board[7] augmented his occasional income as a part-time librarian at the University's Ricker Library.[8] In his junior and senior years, he also worked as a teaching assistant.

When John arrived at the University of Illinois, Robert's stepmother, Agnes, was ill.[9] Sam had been dead for eight years. Robert was lonely for family... as was John. The two established an immediate kinship. John always felt that their lifelong relationship started with that luncheon. As he said years later, "Fate or a wise man knew that we needed each other."[10]

John Gregg was elected vice president of the Architectural Society[11] in 1924 and president by 1926.[12] During that time, he studied for the State Board Exam. Most students would not have been eligible to take the test before graduating, but working in Alexander Eschweiler's architectural office had given him a leg up on other students. John took the test in November 1926 and passed immediately, thanking his fortunate timing. He claimed the exam became more difficult in later years.[13] He obtained his license on January 3, 1927.[14]

Immediately after graduation, funded by a gift from Robert, John sailed to Europe on a freighter with a friend.[15] Overseas, he lived as frugally as possible, then returned to Illinois and contemplated his future. One of his professors[16] had relocated and offered him a job teaching architecture at the University of Cincinnati. Robert advised John to the contrary, counseling him to expand his practical experience.[17] Like a good "son," John followed Robert's advice, probably knowing full well that Robert wished him to stay nearby.

University of Illinois

John Wyatt Gregg in World War I uniform, 1918.

In 1926 John joined the office of Robert's good friend from the Arts Club and Art Institute, David Adler. A well-known and popular architect to high society, Adler occupied offices in Orchestra Hall. John first held a position as a draftsman. He rented an apartment on Hermitage Avenue,[18] eventually moving into Robert's Astor Street apartment to save money—at Robert's suggestion. During the summers, John lived there alone while Robert stayed mostly in Monticello. However, during the winters, Robert joined John at Astor Street, using it as his base between travels.[19]

Remembering how much John benefited from his European travels before starting his job, Robert convinced David Adler that John would become a better architect by seeing more of the world.[20] Adler agreed and allowed John time off to join Robert on a trip to Hawaii.[21]

John continued working for Adler until 1932, spending weekends and vacations at The Farms. Adler, disheartened by the death of his wife and the worsening economy, closed his firm that year. Robert rescued John with an offer to help the farm manager, by then Elmer Priebe, to run The Farms.[22]

John never worked a paying job again, exacerbating an increasingly uncomfortable relationship with his brother, Scranton. Scranton worked hard as an engineer to support his family, and he felt that John no longer contributed to society. It surely hurt that John had lucked into a relationship with a very wealthy man who seemed to supplant their own biological father.

Robert, and the newspapers as well, frequently referred to John as Robert's foster or adopted son, but the difference in last names caused confusion. Robert wanted to legally adopt John, but Illinois law did not yet allow adults to adopt other adults.

John felt close to his siblings, but his claim that he was essentially an orphan did not sit well with his brother. Scranton rarely visited The Farms, but John would bring Robert along on visits to Scranton and his family in Milwaukee. Katherine Courtenay, John's sister, visited Monticello on a number of occasions, enjoying her time there.

Realizing that other students would benefit from travel as John did, Robert established a scholarship for architectural students. Commencing in 1929, the Allerton Traveling Scholarship awarded $400 each to two high-ranking junior-year architectural history students. They would travel during their summer vacation and study architectural form, typically in New England and the East Coast areas. At the end of the summer, the students were to submit reports—now stored in Ricker Library at the University of Illinois.

Robert always held a spring open house for Landscape Architecture and Architecture junior-year students and staff—typically more than forty people—at The Farms. There they could wander the grounds and examine his art collection.

University of Illinois

The dashing Robert Allerton, circa 1920.

CHAPTER THIRTEEN
Through Art, Life Endures

I Arise from Dreams of Thee

Roger Quilter[1]

FREDERIC, ALONE AGAIN

While Pauline Palmer and other guests visited Robert at The Farms in October 1925, Robert received a letter from Frederic Bartlett, who was falling into despair over the illness throughout the summer of his second wife, Helen.[2] On October 24, after only six years of marriage to Frederic, forty-three-year-old Helen died in New York of cancer.[3] Their circle of friends grieved the loss of Helen, and they worried about Frederic's emotional wellbeing.

In a touching preface to Helen Birch Bartlett's only volume of poetry, *Capricious Winds,* poet and editor Harriet Monroe acknowledged not only Helen's profound talent, but the depth of her love for Frederic. "Undoubtedly life meant more than art to Helen Birch Bartlett. Her last seven years especially were too rich in happiness to permit the full indulgence of her creative impulse toward either music or poetry."[4]

It was Helen who first turned Frederic's attention to the Post-Impressionist artists. Following Robert's notable gifts, in 1926 Frederic donated a stunning collection of twenty-four Post-Impressionist paintings to the Art Institute of Chicago, naming it the Helen Birch Bartlett Memorial Collection. The collection included George Seurat's *A Sunday on La Grande Jatte,* Vincent van Gogh's *The Bedroom,* Henri de Toulouse-Lautrec's *At the Moulin Rouge,* and Paul Cezanne's *Basket of Apples.* True to Frederic's meticulous attention to detail and his sensitivity to interior design, he insisted that the frames of the paintings in the collection all be painted white, unifying the works visually.[5] To complete the modernist environment, decorative moldings were removed from the room. With the Bartlett collection, the Art Institute led the way for modern art in the United States—New York City would not open the Museum of Modern Art for another three years.

Starting in the early 1920s, before Frederic's tremendous gift, Robert began donating to the Art Institute. In 1922 he offered a nativity painting by Paul Gauguin. In 1923 he gave Auguste Rodin's bronze *Head of Pierre de Wissant,* following it in 1924 with Rodin's bronzes of *Sorrow* and *Fallen Carytide.* That same year he donated seven other pieces: four paintings by André Derain, and one each by Pablo Picasso, Amedeo Modigliani, and Constantin Brancusi. By the end of 1927 he had donated at least twenty-four significant works to the Art Institute, including pieces by Georges Braque, Raoul Dufy, Eugène Delacroix, and Suzanne Valadon.

Beginning in 1925, Robert served as Vice President of the Art Institute of Chicago.[6] That year, he and David Adler organized an exhibit of Chinese pottery at the Art Institute, showing the progress of eastern art.[7]

Courtesy of Bonnet House Museum & Gardens

Helen Birch Bartlett died in 1925, after only six years of marriage to Frederic Clay Bartlett.

THE AGNES ALLERTON GALLERY OF TEXTILES

In January 1928 the Art Institute's Decorative Arts Department, of which Robert was chairman, opened a new wing dedicated in memory of Agnes. Robert funded the five galleries as well as the continued upkeep of the Agnes Allerton Gallery of Textiles, designed by architects Coolidge and Hodgdon. At the time the Needlework and Textile Guild considered the gallery one of Robert's most important gifts. His insistence on bronze for all the cases, fixtures, and even the doorknobs, delayed the gallery's completion.[8] The Guild joined with the Antiquarian Society on January 28, 1928 to preview the exhibit. He donated many rare pieces to enhance the collection, including an 18th Bérain tapestry.[9] They are only part of the more than 13,000 textiles owned today by the Department of Textiles: needlework, velvets, laces, and clothing dating from hundreds of years B.C. to the present time.

He also joined with Chicago friends, such as Mrs. Tiffany (Margaret) Blake,* Pauline Palmer and Carter H. Harrison (son of his father's mayoral opponent) to acquire, among other pieces, Paul Gauguin's *Tahitian Woman* and Giovanni Antonio Guardi's *The Masked Ball.*

THE JUNGLE ROOM

Any competition between Robert and Frederic was congenial; they remained close throughout the years. After a winter trip with Frederic, Robert suggested that his friend help redecorate the Music Room at The Farms, with a jungle mural. John Gregg recalled Robert saying, "Why don't you paint a fresco all around up above where the tapestries were, in the Rousseau style, and then we'll paint all the woodwork banana color to match it and we'll get new furniture."[10]

Courtesy of Bonnet House Museum & Gardens

In 1927 Frederic Clay Bartlett painted a jungle-themed mural on the upper level of Robert's Music Room. Robert later replaced the murals with bookcases.

It took Frederic months to complete, but Madame X enthused over the murals in 1927:

> *Mr. Bartlett has created a thoroughly sophisticated, somewhat formal, but very brilliant jungle. It is… the sort of decoration that does not permit of much other furnishing, so Mr. Allerton has banished most of the art treasures that*

> *formerly adorned the room and left it with some luxurious couches and chairs covered with velvet of a vivid mandarin hue, a tint that appears in the frescoes above in a few giant blossoms....*
>
> *Analyzed, the frescoes reveal the glossy, rich foliage of the tropics.... Chanel blue lotus or salmon pink amaryllis gives touches of color to the otherwise dusky, though vivid, equatorial foliage behind and through which a sky of sunset saffron glows softly...*
>
> *To find such a house, with its frescoes and art treasures.... It is like meeting a beautiful woman of the world... sitting by the wayside in the desert of Sahara.*[11]

Years later, after Robert discovered that many of his guests avoided the room because of the heaviness of the colors, he redecorated it a third time. This time the room turned into a library with an upper gallery. The murals were covered in 1940 by a thin coat of white wash, but eventually the gallery bookcases hid many of them, where they stay today. Others were rolled up and stored in one of the barns.[12]

Shortly after Frederic completed the jungle murals, he and Robert traveled together to Sweden, Germany, France, and other countries, probably collecting more art. Whenever possible, they preferred to fly. Lindbergh had not yet completed his solo flight across the Atlantic, but since 1914 commercial passengers were trying the new mode of travel.

Old Relationships and New

While Robert was busy consoling Frederic, other deaths hit close to home. In November 1925, a month after Helen's death, John Borie died. Even after his frustration with the architect's delays in finishing the stables, Robert had kept up his friendship. Six months after Borie died, Robert's beloved Aunt Lois passed away at the age of 100.[13] As these lives were flickering away, another name from the past popped up.

During the fourteen years since he had urged the composer, Roger Quilter, to visit The Farms, Robert must have remained especially dear in his thoughts. In 1928 Quilter completed a new piece, dedicated to Robert. The title: "I Arise from Dreams of Thee." He orchestrated the passionate Shelley poem, ripe with love, kisses, and a heart beating "loud and fast." Perhaps he wanted to rekindle their relationship, or maybe he was just indulging in sweet nostalgia.

Whatever Quilter's reason, he was too late. By then Robert and John were already linked in the newspapers, but as father and foster son.

Years later, Frederic Bartlett's third wife, Evelyn Fortune Lilly Bartlett,* mentioned that everyone suspected John and Robert's relationship was other than father-and-son, but it didn't matter to her or their friends. That public facade defined their relationship both to society, and in some respects, even to themselves. They did indeed function as father and son, with Robert pointing the way and John, for the most part, following.

CHAPTER FOURTEEN
Feathering His Nests

The ideal of happiness has always taken material form in the house, whether cottage or castle. It stands for permanence and separation from the world.

Simone de Beauvoir (1908-1986)

THE VINE WALK AND GAZEBO

Robert gave bursts of attention to The Farms throughout his life. Even when he may have thought his gardens were complete, a new idea would occur to him and he would reorganize the location of statues, or change an entire area. The Vine Walk was one of those opportunities for change.

In 1915 he focused on grassland located northwest of his mansion. The Vine Walk consisted of an allée of eight-foot wire trellises, planted with vines to create a shaded walkway through the sunny open prairie. Nowadays rows of cedars tower along each side and the trellis vines curl thickly through the wires. The path originally extended from the Gate House area and followed alongside Old Timber Road. The western half was removed decades later to accommodate a parking lot entrance. Two Korean *Fu Dogs,* relocated from the benches on the Avenue of the Formal Gardens in 1922, sit atop columns at the end of the walkway, guarding a one-story, concrete gazebo that was built in 1915.

During his stepmother's last months in 1924, Robert had attended a funeral at Graceland Cemetery in Chicago. On the way home, he passed a large house where sections of cast iron fencing had been discarded in the front yard. He learned it was originally from New Orleans and purchased it immediately.[1] The cast iron would create a perfect second story for the Gazebo, the center of which consists of a stair that spirals up to a lookout, which he completed by 1925.

The first guardians of the Gazebo were twin sculptures of Greek origin, flanking the southwest door at the end of the Vine Walk.[2] These *Charioteers of Delphi* are second-generation limestone copies. The original bronze, excavated at Delphi in 1896, resides at the

Michael Holtz

One of the two Korean *Fu Dogs* atop the posts at the end of the Vine Walk.

University of Illinois

In this 1925 photo, the *Charioteers of Delphi* occupied the west steps of the Gazebo at the end of the Vine Walk (now called the House of the *Golden Buddhas*). Robert later moved them to the top of pillars at the northwest entrance of the estate.

Michael Holtz

Robert's two *Charioteers of Delphi* were carved of Bedford limestone around 1924.

Delphi Museum and has one arm, holding a rein. Robert's sculptures each had one arm, faithfully replicating the ancient original. But he thought they looked odd (especially with no reins to hold and no chariots to drive), so he had the two single arms "amputated." The Art Institute of Chicago owns a terra cotta copy[3] from which Robert's two limestone statues were modeled. In the 1930s Robert and John expanded the gardens at a perpendicular turn to the southeast and added new Asian sculptures to the Gazebo, renaming it the House of the *Golden Buddhas*.

Redesign of the Sunken Garden (1925)

After a trip to Bali, Robert and John were inspired to redesign the Sunken Garden. According to John, "it was a combination of not being satisfied with the way it was and wanting to give me a job so that I wouldn't feel that I was wasting all the talent I'd been trained for."[4] Prior to 1925 Robert and John added a ramp to the surrounding upper terrace. By 1932 John designed new stairways in the clean, modern Art Deco style with pylons soaring twenty-four feet from the upper terrace. Robert and John first saw prototypes of *Guardian Fish* atop the roof of Nagoya Castle in Japan and commissioned Yamanaka and Company to produce sixteen to top the pylons.[5]

Michael Holtz

The original Japanese *Guardian Fish* are bronze, originally covered with three layers of gold leaf, each approximately 40 inches high. Japanese palace roof ornaments of tiger-headed fish, or "kinshachi," symbolized protection from fire. Several *Guardian Fish* in the Sunken Garden are replacements for the 1931 originals.

University of Illinois

Robert added upper walls and circular stairs to the Sunken Garden in 1925. This photo, circa 1933, shows the Japanese *Guardian Fish* atop pylons and eight copies of the Chinese Parterre *Goldfish*.

Eight new copies of the *Goldfish* in the Chinese Parterre replaced the *Fu Dogs* on the lower level of the Sunken Garden, one at each end of four concrete benches that John added to the lower level. The copies, made from the same Indiana stone that was used for the Field Museum, were the work of Charles Laing of Chicago.[6] By 1938 lattice panels were added to the upper walls of the garden.[7]

A Change of Apartments

Toward the end of 1928, Robert invested in a new kind of building just down the street from his 1315 N. Astor Street apartment. The proposed fifteen-story structure—a co-op—at 1301 North Astor would soon be his new Chicago home.[8] Designed by Philip B. Maher, the building is a wonderful example of the Art Deco style. The exterior alternated black marble pilasters with a gray limestone façade. Joseph Llewellyn, one of Robert's architects at The Farms, designed public areas inside the building.

The Winterbothams occupied the penthouse and terraces with the Potter Palmers (Jr.) three floors below them. Continuing downward, the occupants, in order, were the Frank Hibbards, the Tiffany Blakes, Mrs. C. Morse Ely, the James M. Hopkinses, the Howard Gillettes on the fourth floor, Robert on the third floor,[9] and Frederic Bartlett and his son Clay on the second.[10] (Frederic would only live there a few more years until his marriage in 1931 to his third wife, Evelyn Fortune Lilly.) David Adler designed several of the apartment interiors, including those of Mrs. Ely and the Palmers.

Courtesy of Bonnet House Museum & Gardens

Frederic Clay Bartlett and his new wife, Evelyn Fortune Lilly, on their honeymoon in 1931.

MAKING THE BEST OF THE DEPRESSION

Robert was more occupied with business affairs and stock investments than the daily running of his Piatt County property. Content to stay involved only with major decisions, he turned over the running of his seventeen local farmsteads to an on-site manager.[11]

His fortune allowed him to be cavalier about insurance. He refused to purchase coverage for his farms and out-buildings, feeling it would be more cost-effective to self-insure. A bookkeeper in Chicago assisted him with his financial paperwork, reminding him of coupons to clip and making suggestions about possible stock purchases. He may not have spent every waking hour focused on finances as his father did, but he did not neglect monetary responsibilities.

Robert's involvement with the banks and knowledge of the stock market prompted him in 1929 to warn his employee, Elmer Priebe, of potential bank closures. Elmer and his brother heeded Robert's guidance and safeguarded their money, but Robert was not so lucky. Elmer later claimed that Robert's large stock holding in Monticello's First National Bank might have provided the means for it to re-open earlier than others.[12] Unlike many businesses during the Depression, however, the First National Bank of Chicago never closed. Having been burned by his losses in the Monticello bank, Robert wrote all future checks from the Chicago bank that his father helped create[13] and where he and Kate held 3.5% of the stock.[14]

Robert and John enjoyed trips to New England, the East, and Michigan (many Illinoisans summered at Charlevoix—including Adlai Stevenson's family) between their major journeys. Typically they spent November 7, John's birthday, at The Farms, sometimes staying through Thanksgiving. By then, because of the cold, they used the back part of the house for their living quarters.[15] Two bathrooms had also been installed for them. John affirmed that by Christmas, they usually traveled to the other side of the world.

As with Robert's travels, the onset of the Great Depression had little effect on his development of the gardens. In fact, he was beginning to collect and install his most notable pieces.

CHAPTER FIFTEEN
Masterpieces for the Gardens

The glade was geometric, circular, gold,
No brush or weed breaking that bright gold of leaf-fall.
In the center it stood, absolute and bold
Beyond any heart-hurt, or eye's grief-fall.
Gold-massy in air, it stood in gold light-fall

From "Gold Glade" by Robert Penn Warren (1905-1989)[1]

THE DEATH OF THE LAST CENTAUR

By 1929 the chain of gardens reached from the mansion to the Sunken Garden in one direction, and to the House of the *Golden Buddhas* in the other. But one of Robert's most impressive acquisitions was yet to come. He went searching this time for sculpture to mark the intersection of two paths, one climbing up from the river bank, the other extending from the Sunken Garden.[2] In Paris, Robert and John had visited the studio of Émile-Antoine Bourdelle, a friend and former student of Rodin. There Robert commissioned a bronze casting of Bourdelle's 1914 sculpture, *The Death of the Last Centaur,* shortly before the artist died in 1929.[3]

Robert asked John, who was working for David Adler at the time, to design the setting at the top of the dramatic ascent from the river. From the riverbank, the beginning of the formal walk is a rectangular "room" of trellised vines, the rear wall marked by four soaring, concrete pillars, each originally topped with a cast iron torch urn. Sixty steps lead up from the pillars. Each fifth step forms a landing, adding pauses in the climb. At the top of the steps, the statue stands on a two-tiered octagonal base, surrounded by benches that repeat the shape. A smaller set of matching pillars marks the opposite end of the walk, approximately one hundred yards away, near the road.

At first the white pillars appeared too stark, distracting from the sculpture. John piled small amounts of copper sulfate on top, allowing it to drip down and stain the concrete. The

Michael Holtz

The Death of the Last Centaur by Bourdelle represents Chiron, a Centaur born of the gods. Chiron was more refined than his cohorts—a mentor to Hercules, musician, skilled archer, and physician (represented by the herb under the hoof). Hercules mistakenly shot the immortal creature with a poisoned arrow, leaving him doomed to an eternity of pain. Chiron offered to sacrifice himself in exchange for the release of Prometheus. Zeus accepted the bargain and lifted Chiron to the heavens to become the constellation Sagittarius.

urns that topped the pillars were copies of ones from Sweden that Robert had donated to the Art Institute of Chicago, reproduced by David Adler for plumbing manufacturer William E. Clow of Lake Forest.[4]

The Death of the Last Centaur has aged gracefully, its patina rubbed away by visitors who feel compelled to touch the hooves or fingers, as if to ease his pain. Those spots glisten, revealing tiny flecks of gold imbedded in the bronze—a technique outlawed in France shortly thereafter due to the toxic fumes it created in the foundries.

Michael Holtz

The bronze *Sea Maidens*, created by Richard Kuöhl in 1930, are each approximately six feet high. John Gregg designed their towering, fluted pedestals at the entrance to the Brick Wall Garden in 1932.

The Sea Maidens

In 1930 Robert and John traveled to Hamburg, Germany where they happened to spot a statue by Richard Kuöhl in a kiosk. The bronze female figure, delicately draped in a gossamer gown, held a miniature Viking longboat in her outstretched hands—an advertisement for Hamburg American Line passenger ships. Robert, as usual, asked the artist to create a pair for The Farms. Kuöhl proposed a male and female, but Robert thought the male lacked the grace of the female figure. Kuöhl agreed to mirror images of two maidens, and at Robert's suggestion, designed each to hold a bowl and a garland of seaweed instead of a ship.[5]

Richard Kuöhl is best known today for his controversial (and repeatedly defaced) Hamburg World War I memorial. Commissioned in 1936 by the Nazis, its inscription, a verse by Heinrich Lersch, translates as, "Germany must live, even if we have to die."[6] In spite of the notoriety it received, Robert and John purchased several other pieces of Kuöhl's work—so many, in fact that John said, "No wonder Kuöhl never became famous because we have so many of his creations hidden away."[7]

The Sun Singer

On the recommendation of Chicago architect John Holabird,[8] Robert and John visited the studio of sculptor Carl Milles[9] on their 1929 visit to Stockholm. Impressed by the artist's work, Robert promoted the *Triton Fountain* to a group of prominent Chicagoans of Swedish heritage, who donated the work to the Art Institute of Chicago the following year.[10] He became interested in a different sculpture by Milles for his estate.

Their stay in Stockholm's Grand Hotel placed Robert and John very near the site of Milles' *The Sun Singer* statue. It was mounted on a pedestal overlooking the bay on the Stromparterre, in front of the Royal Palace. Robert thought a smaller version—the same size as one in Milles' own garden—would be perfect on the library terrace in Monticello. The model in Milles' garden had no arms or head. Using a translator, Robert asked if Milles could make a version exactly that size, but with arms and a head, like the one in the harbor. Milles agreed.[11]

University of Illinois

Snapshot from Robert's photo album of *The Sun Singer*'s arrival in 1932.

The Sun Singer arrived at The Farms in 1931 in an enormous crate. To everyone's astonishment, the statue inside was the same size as the figure in the harbor—over fifteen feet high! Either the translator erred, or Milles misunderstood. Installed on the terrace, *The Sun Singer* would have peered into the second-story windows.

Michael Holtz

Apollo (*The Sun Singer*) and Chiron (*The Death of the Last Centaur*) each represented fine arts as well as the art of medicine in Greek mythology. Chiron raised Apollo's son, the doctor Aesulapius.

Instead, Robert chose a plot of prairie for the colossus, well beyond *The Death of the Last Centaur,* with an open view except for a few neighboring homes. He purchased one house from Mr. Lee Hill and "slid" it down the hill. John then remodeled it for the Hills and added gingerbread ornamentation.[12] Robert also bought the Swartz and Stine houses and tore them down. Mrs. Dodd, an elderly widow, did not want to leave, so he promised her a pension and a house if she would move to Cerro Gordo, a few miles away. She accepted, taking full advantage of his generosity by living quite a long life.[13] In place of the houses, he planted trees.

Robert first planned an axis of four entries to the sculpture site. After building a road up from the river, he closed it off, deciding that *The Sun Singer* should only be approached from the front (east) or from the rear, with a circular path around it. John designed a three-tiered concrete base, inspired by the Temple of Heaven in Beijing. *The Sun Singer* stands atop only two tiers; he intended a border of clipped hedge to form the third.[14]

At the installation, some workers played a practical joke. Robert

Song to the Sun

By Esaias Tegnér
(First stanza of an 1817 translation by George Borrow)

A song I'll indite
To the bright beaming one:
Round thy King-stool, O sun!
Thou hast deep in night's blue
Set the worlds, like a crew
Of mute vassals; thine eye
Looks upon them from high—
But thy course is in light.

arrived to see his statue wearing a giant condom. He was not amused at the time, but neither did he lack an eventual sense of humor about the incident. His home movies include title frames, and the footage of raising *The Sun Singer* to its pedestal is called "The Big Erection."

Much of the work of Carl Milles reveals a lighthearted exuberance. *The Sun Singer* is more restrained than most of his art, but its nudity prompted the disapproval in Sweden by both his sponsor and the family of the man it honored.[15] He created the original on assignment for the Swedish Academy in honor of Sweden's poet, Esaias Tegnér. Instead of sculpting a statute of the poet himself, he chose to illustrate the poem entitled "Sång till Solen" ("Song to the Sun"), in which the singer coaxes the sun to rise each day. The young man, nude except for a Greek helmet topped with an ornament of the winged Pegasus, is Apollo. The god Apollo ruled the arts, represented by the nine Muses that embellish the drum-shaped base of the sculpture. A small tortoise hides under Apollo's heel, in reference to the tortoise shell from which he made his first lyre as a youth.

Carl Milles expressed his delight at his statue's Illinois home in a letter to Robert. Calling the setting "magnificent" and asking for photographs, he wanted to use the installation at The Farms as an example of how his work should best be displayed:

> *I wish to show them how you have understood to do that outstanding way of placing a statue in our time. I hope this bronze will stay there in that way till the last man has gone—when the earth is as dead as the moon—and still this is there. Such a dream!*[16]

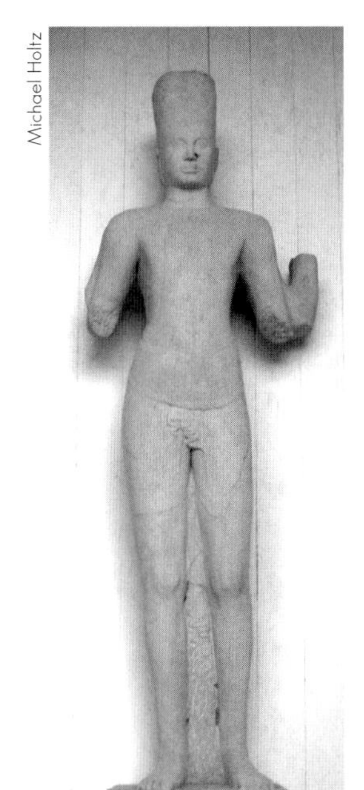

Michael Holtz

Faithful to the Cambodian original, the mutilated arms of the *Hari-Hara* add to its air of antiquity. The craftsman left stone between the legs to add stability.

Robert's Apollo sings to the sun in the far western end of his gardens, while Apollo's twin sister Diana (also known as Artemis) presides over the moon at the eastern gates. Whether by accident or conscious intent, his installation could not be more perfect.

Gardens of the East

The gardens at the eastern end of Robert's property were about to take an even more "Eastern" turn. After Robert moved the *Charioteers of Delphi* to the entrance gates, the Gazebo at the end of the Vine Walk, with its decorative cast iron lookout, assumed a new identity as the House of the *Golden Buddhas.*

On a trip to Siam, inspired by the Buddhas that appeared at every turn, Robert commissioned a pair from the Royal School in Bangkok.[17] He and John toured various temples with the instructor and selected attributes from the many prototypes, including the particular type of head and hand position. For one Buddha, Robert selected the pose of "calming the waters," with palms facing outward. According to art historian Dr. Muriel Scheinman, the meaning of the other's pose, one arm crossing the chest, is not standard to Buddhist imagery.[18] The two resulting *Siamese Buddhas,* now in the Gazebo, were each fashioned from single teakwood logs. After a two-year wait for the wood to cure before carving and gilding, the statues were completed in 1931.[19]

A third sculpture, *Hari-Hara,* arrived in 1934. Robert had it fashioned of stone from a plaster cast he had purchased from the Musée Guimet, a Paris museum of Asian art. He donated the cast itself to the Art Institute of Chicago. The figure is a fusion of two gods, Hara and Hari. Hara is also known as Vishnu, the Creator. Hari, also called Shiva, symbolizes the degenerative process of nature.[20]

The *Fu Dog* Garden began from eleven pairs of cobalt blue-glazed ceramic fu dogs that Robert had collected from various American and European dealers. Fu dogs resemble a breed such as the Chow or Shih Tzu, but they are not really dogs at all. The mythical animals are more akin to snowlions, frequently shown supporting Buddha's throne. Robert's nineteenth- and twentieth-century *Fu Dogs* each weigh approximately 150 pounds and sit atop 64-inch pedestals.

Over the years, Robert had showcased the *Fu Dogs* separately in various gardens, but in 1932 he gathered them into a new garden, a perpendicular extension from the House of the *Golden Buddhas.* John Gregg designed a setting of triangular-shaped privet hedges at the bases of the columns that support each *Fu Dog.* A saw-tooth pattern of concrete curbing replaced the hedges in 1935.[21]

Michael Holtz

Each *Siamese Buddha* wears an unadorned, monastic robe and stands on a richly patterned base. Ornate tiered umbrellas, mounted to the wall behind the figures, protect the heads.

In addition to the twenty-two blue *Fu Dogs,* a granite pair from Korea perch on pedestals at the end of the Vine Walk. A green, porcelain *Fu Dog,* noted for its unusual color, glowers atop a short column in the Cutting Garden behind the mansion.[22]

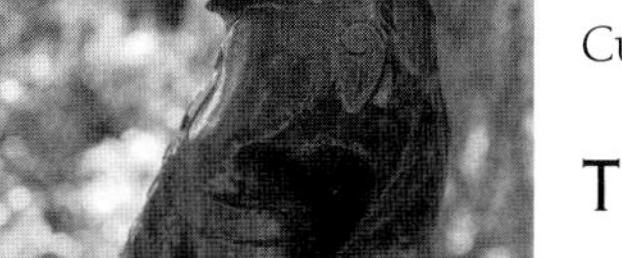

Michael Holtz

The term *fu dog* originated in China, but the mythical animal is common in many Asian countries. The sculptures traditionally appear in pairs, guarding gateways or tombs from evil spirits or standing in front of government buildings as defenders of the law. The male may hold a spear in its paw, and the female usually puts her paw atop a sphere that represents the sun.

THE LOST GARDEN

Robert's final gardens grew along a formal axis, stretching both directions from the mansion to their logical conclusions, at *The Sun Singer* and the *Fu Dogs.* But one garden remained to be built. This one would not be as grand, but would reflect Robert's new comfort and casual joy among friends he held dear.

A simple cable bridge not far from the mansion once connected the formal grounds with the wilderness and prairie south of the river. One spot along the riding path that traversed the area had long been a favorite place to rest or enjoy a picnic. Robert planted one end of the path to the clearing with a double allée of Eastern Red Cedars that joined to a westward continuation, lined with native oaks. In 1932, making way for Richard Kuöhl's *Sea Maidens* on the Rose Terrace, he relocated ten *Chinese Musician* sculptures to this path of cedars in the wilderness.[23] At eastern end of the path, he installed his replica

University of Illinois

The Lost Garden teahouse, as it appeared in 1940.

of *The Three Graces* on a concrete platform. At the western end, a marble statue of *Diana* marked the end of the formal path, later replaced by a marble *Faun*.[24]

Robert and John's journeys in the 1930s included Samoa, the Marquesas Islands, Greece, Jerusalem, Egypt, Africa, South America, Cuba, the West Indies, and Europe.[25] The more exotic journeys probably influenced their plan for a centerpiece for the garden, a tea house (also called the "summer house") that John Gregg designed between 1935 and 1936. Five ogee-shaped openings dominate the facade of the rectangular structure, similar in construction and repeating the lattice theme of the stair towers near the Chinese Maze Garden. Four of the portals framed niches, each painted with a mural and furnished with a bench constructed by Monticello cabinetmaker Francis Brooks.[26] The center niche housed a marble copy of Canova's *Venus Italica*. A spiral stair, hidden in the rear of the structure, led to a sundeck roof that offered a broad view of the meadow.

While John was given free rein to design specific projects, much of their creativity grew from collaboration. In the end, Robert always had the last word, and at least in public he left no doubt about the hierarchy of their relationship. John revealed his feelings in a presentation he made at Allerton Park years later, in which he referred to Robert as "a beloved dictator."[27]

Michael Holtz

Robert's marble *Venus*, purchased from an art dealer in Europe, is a faithful, late nineteenth-century copy of a statue by Venetian sculptor Antonio Canova. Canova based his 1802 *Venus Italica* (at the Pitti Palace in Florence) on a Greek representation of Aphrodite.

CHAPTER SIXTEEN
Death in the Family

The family you come from isn't as important as the family you're going to have.

Ring Lardner (1885-1933)

THE JOHNSTONES

The same year that Robert moved into his Astor Street apartment, a tragedy stunned his sister Kate's family. On June 8, 1929, while attending the Shriners' Convention in Los Angeles, Robert's twenty-eight-year-old nephew, Allerton Johnstone, plunged to his death from a window of his room at Hotel Hayward at Sixth and Spring Streets. The young man, a 316-pound amateur wrestler, crashed to the roof of a one-story section of the hotel. The impact shook the structure, startling the employees. Sustaining internal injuries, broken legs, and a crushed chest, Allerton Johnstone was rushed to a hospital where he died forty-five minutes later. Kate collapsed at his bedside.

Kate's son had brought his chauffeur and a personal trainer to the convention. Since high school, he had been an amateur wrestler at the Pasadena Athletic Club. He had appeared in Elks' Club wrestling matches, toured the country showing off his strength, and appeared in minor film roles, all the while ignoring his family's disapproval.[1, 2]

At the cost of $1,000 (2007 purchasing power of $12,000), he souped-up a Packard roadster, installing a radiator from the car of deceased actor, Rudolph Valentino, and customizing the steering wheel and column to accommodate his girth.[3]

Robert had never been close to his sister. Both Hugo's philandering and his nephew's antics probably fueled the distance between him and his family, but they still continued to communicate and discuss their problems. Although newspapers reported the death as an accident, Kate later told Robert and John that her son had jumped.[4] Robert's great-grand-nephew mentioned that Allerton Johnstone had a history of mental illness and traveled with a nurse. The chauffeur and trainer may have also functioned as caregivers.

Kate held funeral services at her Pasadena home before she and her younger son, Vanderburgh, traveled with the body to Chicago for its interment in Graceland Cemetery.[5]

Courtesy of Sean Johnstone

Kate Allerton Johnstone, Robert's sister and mother of Allerton and Vanderburgh Johnstone.

Vanderburgh rarely spoke of his brother again.

While Robert enjoyed spoiling his "son" John, Kate did the same with her remaining son. During Vanderburgh's years at Phillips Academy Andover and Princeton,[6] Kate would rent a vacation home in Newport, Rhode Island and send a chauffeur-driven limousine to bring him and his friends to visit her. In her enormous dining room, Kate would sit at one end of a very long table (some of that era were up to fifty feet long), and Vanderburgh and his friends would sit at the other. From their faraway seats, they would carry on their own conversations and mock Kate's inability to hear.[7]

Kate finally divorced Hugo on July 10, 1930 after years of separation.[8] Even with all her riches, life with Hugo had offered little satisfaction. Unlike her brother Robert, who humbly listed his occupation on census records as "farmer," Hugo employed the toney title of "capitalist."[9] He may not have appreciated a wife with a serious hearing impairment—almost as pronounced as Robert's. Hugo was tall and handsome, a socialite and a sportsman; Kate was what others may have considered "plain" in appearance. It is possible that she blamed Hugo for the example he set for their sons. Whatever secondary incompatibilities existed between Kate and Hugo, she had endured the primary one—his infidelity—until the crisis of their son's death.

It appears that Robert had little involvement with Kate and her family beyond family and his business dealings with Hugo. Kate, living in California, rarely visited The Farms. The ten-year gap in their ages could explain their detached relationship, but perhaps Robert preferred isolating himself from Kate's problems. Robert's inheriting a larger share of their parent's wealth may have caused friction. Kate and Robert's relationship could have been just like that of many other siblings—distant for many reasons.

A Winter of Sadness

As Robert was traveling the world, collecting art with John, he was hit with news of two deaths during the winter of 1937. His friend, artist Glyn Philpot, suffered a fatal heart attack on December 16. Numerous dignitaries of the art world and famous subjects of his portraits attended his December 22 funeral at Westminster Cathedral. Robert and Glyn's mutual friend, Roger Quilter, provided the music—a special arrangement of Ravel for the organ.[10] A few days later, on Christmas Eve, Glyn's companion, Vivian Forbes, swallowed a lethal dose of sleeping pills. He died in the room where Glyn had passed away.[11]

Then, on December 31, Kate died of complications from brain cancer in Pasadena.[12] The obituary simply mentioned her son, Vanderburgh, and brother, Robert, and that she would be buried on January 3, 1938 in Chicago's Graceland Cemetery.[13]

There is no record of Robert attending either the funeral of his friend or that of his sister. By Thanksgiving of every year, he and John typically were already visiting warmer locales. That winter, their vacation started off in Australia and New Zealand. It would have been impossible to make it back to London or Chicago in time for either funeral even if he had received the news immediately.

Kate left an estate of approximately $320,000 (equivalent today to almost $5 million). Of that, $200,000 was held in trust for Vanderburgh, living at the time in Las Vegas, New Mexico. His twin sons, Crane* and Vanderburgh II,* also received property and cash from Kate, as did several friends.[14] In her will, she asked Vanderburgh to give Robert any of her personal belongings "which he may desire to keep as a remembrance."[15] Other than that, he received nothing. Her will noted that Robert already had received substantial funds. Strangely enough, she also left $600 per month to her ex-husband, Hugo.

Within two months of her passing, an estate auction held over a five-day period gave others the chance to purchase "a breath-taking selection of… Silver, Furniture, Objects d'art, Paintings, and more than 200 ITEMS OF JEWELRY."[16] The jewelry itself would be offered only on the afternoon of the third day. Apparently Kate's family didn't believe in tossing valuables into a lake.

Courtesy of Sean Johnstone

Kate and Hugo's son, Vanderburgh Johnstone.

CHAPTER SEVENTEEN

The Lawai-Kai Years

The peace of great prairies be for you.
Listen among windplayers in cornfields,
The wind learning over its oldest music.

The peace of great seas be for you.
Wait on a hook of land, a rock footing
For you, wait in the salt wash.

From "For You" by Carl Sandburg (1878-1967)

A New Find

In 1937 when Robert and John started on their annual winter trip, they undoubtedly picked their retreats because of brewing conflicts elsewhere. Several years earlier, Italy had invaded Ethiopia, supported only by Germany. Then Germany converted Austria into a satellite state. Europe turned a blind eye when Hitler remilitarized the Rhineland in 1936. And Hitler and Mussolini supported Generalissimo Franco's nationalist forces against the Soviet-supported Republican troops in the Spanish Civil War. Japan and China began fighting each other in 1937. With the cauldrons of fear in both Asia and Europe, safe travel possibilities had narrowed.

Robert and John spent the first six weeks of 1938 exploring Australia and New Zealand. In mid-February their trip home included a ten-day stopover in Honolulu before boarding the SS *Mariposa.* In what would become a life-changing twist of fate for Robert, the manager[1] of The Halekulani Hotel had overbooked—Robert and John could have a room for only the first nine days.[2] They needed lodging for the last night.

Robert's childhood friend who lived in Honolulu, Mrs. Walter (Louise Gaylord) Dillingham, suggested they fly to the garden island of Kauai[3] and stay at Philip Rice's boarding house, the Lihue Inn. At the time, the Inn served as the only hotel on the island.[4]

Michael Holtz

The house that John designed at Lawai-Kai. Queen Emma's cottage is to the right of the main house.

Knowing Robert's penchant for landscapes, Louise arranged for them to visit an intriguing garden property—listed for sale—at the south end of the island. Among its attractions was a crescent-shaped white-sand beach leading to a lush valley. Nearby, the "Spouting Horn" blowhole spewed water through a natural tube in the lava.

The beachfront property's owner, bachelor Alexander McBryde, had died in 1935, but innkeeper Philip Rice, McBryde's executor, showed them around the estate on Lawai Beach. John later said, "The charm and beauty of the place struck us dumb and we hardly spoke to each other although we stayed there almost an hour."[5] They left, but the attraction was inescapable. Within an hour of their chauffeur driving them away, they returned to further investigate the property, toying with the idea of staying in a tropical paradise for an entire winter. Although they were not impressed with McBryde's house, they snapped many photographs to study later in Illinois.

Within a month, they wired an offer to Mr. Rice for the estate,[6] agreeing to pay $50,000 for the original 83 acres.[7]

Prior to McBryde, Queen Emma Kalanikaumakaamano Kaleleonalani Naea Rooke owned the property. She had been married to King Kamehameha IV from 1856 until he died in 1863. A devout promoter of Hawaiian heritage, she also tended to be pro-English. She belonged to the Anglican church, enjoyed tea, and, similar to Queen Victoria (whom she had met once), she dressed in widow's mourning. Her traditional Hawaiian cottage-style house, patterned after New England missionary homes and painted green, originally sat atop a cliff overlooking Lawai Beach. From the house site that she named "Maunakilohana," she would often ride on horseback down to the beachfront. An avid gardener, she planted shade trees by the beach and three bougainvillea vines[8] near her cottage. To this day, the lavish purple and red bougainvillea vines cascade color down the cliffs behind the Allerton house.

The McBryde family purchased certain portions of her property after her death in 1886, paying $5,000 at auction. Soon they were cultivating the land in sugar cane, taro, and rice. By 1899, Alexander McBryde, the eldest son, owned the lower valley portion known as Lawai Beach. The family's business, McBryde Sugar Company, occupied the rest of her property. McBryde rescued Queen Emma's cottage from destruction when the company expanded their sugarcane fields, lowering the house in sections from the high bluff to the valley floor. For sixteen years he lived in her cottage until he built his own larger bungalow, known as *Hale Pua*.

A HOME IN PARADISE

When Robert bought the Lawai Beach property, they renamed it "Lawai-Kai." The name comes from *lava a'i* which means "valley of plenty."[9] The property itself merited years of attention, but the first and most important priority was a new residence. They planned to stay in McBryde's bungalow while salvaging pieces from it for extra buildings. John deemed that "the living room was only fit for a photographic dark room and the roof should have been on Hansel and Gretel's pan-cake house."[10] They kept only a few items, donating McBryde's roll-top desk to a local doctor and giving his upright piano with attached brass candlesticks to a Koloa church.[11]

Hawaiian homes are typically perched at least three feet above ground on small wooden supports. John deviated from this tradition, designing their new home to be the first on the island placed flat on the ground. Situated next to Queen Emma's cottage, the new house would represent a happy marriage of the old and the modern.

Working from Illinois, John took a cue from Robert's childhood memories. Queen Emma's unadorned rectangular, clapboard cottage must have reminded Robert of the simple colonial houses surrounding his New Hampshire prep school. John said he used the headmaster's house at St. Paul's School as his inspiration for the new home, basically a one-story rambler. However, it appears the patterned building may have been Shute Cottage, a St. Paul's landmark once occupied by a blacksmith, purchased by the school in 1865. Similar in its modest size to Queen Emma's cottage, the building had a set-back porch covered by a main roof. The roof of the new house—built around a large Chinese banyan tree[12]—protected a broad, screened lanai instead of an open porch. John called their Hawaii home "a cage for ourselves,"[13] allowing indoor/outdoor living while keeping the critters and birds at bay.

By the time they arrived back on Kauai in time for Thanksgiving 1938, their plans and supplies were ready. Contending with a scarcity of building material on the island, they purchased and shipped all their hardware and plumbing supplies from Crane Company's Chicago office. To clear the site for their new home, they sawed McBryde's bungalow in two, living on one side as they recycled materials from the other half.

Robert and John planned to rent out the Astor Street apartment[14] and incorporate its Biedermier furniture and assorted pieces from The Farms into the interior design of Lawai-Kai. They commissioned customized moldings for every room from a mill on the island at Port Allen. With a new electric stove and a Chinese-American novice cook/housekeeper, they were finally gaining a sense of completion. In December John wrote to their Chicago bookkeeper, Helen Murphy:

> *I can't start telling you about the joys of this place. We hardly exist we're so happy and gay. The new house is starting and there are so many other things to do that we're fairly tongue-tied and just sort of look at each other like Cheshire cats. Don't expect too much... in the way of description. It is beyond words."*[15]

CONSTRUCTION COMMENCES

Their Japanese contractor, Hironaka,[16] dug the foundation after Christmas. Their furniture and horticulture books[17] arrived in perfect shape in mid-February, and they took movies of everything being unpacked on the lawn. The contractor finished by March 1. Simply constructed with plywood, the L-shaped house certainly required less attention than his Illinois mansion. The most intricate effort involved the molding, John's area of expertise when he had been employed with David Adler. Two bedrooms (each with a private bathroom), closets, a dining room, and a kitchen comprised the floor plan—its entirety edged with a screened-in lanai separating the house from the patio.

Within a few weeks they razed the rest of the McBryde cottage and burned the debris—much to the consternation of many islanders, who felt they were squandering precious commodities.

Immediately after finishing the main house, and using some of the materials from McBryde's home, the contractor started building a guesthouse where McBryde's washhouse had been located, facing the river that ran west of Robert's house.[18] Originally Robert wanted no guest rooms, insisting his visitors could stay at the Lihue Inn. But he quickly decided that a guest cottage would be more appropriate. Queen Emma's cottage, next to the new residence, served at various times as a guest house, or as rooms for the cook, houseboy, or gardeners.[19] Eventually Robert had the cottage painted white to match their new home.

During construction, John ordered bedding for the house and guests: top grade cotton (not linen), with dark blue embroidered block letters spelling LAWAI-KAI, specifying the distance between the fold and the letters. Helen Murphy expedited the requests.

Helen handled special duties and requests for both properties. She even helped John locate a Siamese cat to replace their farm cat, Pete, after it fell into a vat of lime. When they needed unusual items or gifts for friends, Helen contacted Marshall Field & Co.'s personal shopping service. Her duties ranged from managing their investments and invoices, obtaining opera tickets, scheduling doctor appointments in Chicago, arranging transportation for Monticello visitors, to buying Robert's hearing aid supplies, yarn, embroidery thread, and shaving cream. She sent boxes of pens, sauces, canned goods, Gillette razor blades, shower curtains, blankets, powdered eggs, Keds tennis shoes, different types of cheeses, and other items unavailable on Kauai. She salted her letters with Illinois weather details, referring to Robert as either "Mr. Allerton" or "our boss." In his replies to Helen, John also called him "our boss," and on very rare occasions, "Robert."[20]

THE GROUNDS

As at The Farms, Robert and John wanted their privacy. Alexander McBryde, an openly gay man, had encouraged local citizens to visit the beach for swimming and picnics. It had been said about the McBryde brothers (Walter and Alexander): for business issues, contact Walter; for parties, contact Alexander.

Alexander McBryde built a public boardwalk, privy, and bathing facilities, but regretted his decision when the bathers' parties became too loud and frequent. They brought "Victrolas and... made whoopee on the beach."[21] During their property purchase, Robert and John requested that the lawyer place a notice in the newspaper, announcing that Lawai Beach was closed to the public. Chained gates made the message clear. But even today, wanderers make their way from the overhanging cliffs down to the beach below, much to the frustration of the estate's security staff.

With the exception of McBryde's improvements to the beach, the rest of Lawai-Kai had received little attention during the previous few years. In Illinois Robert had begun sketching preliminary garden designs, planning to transfer extra statuary from The Farms.

On their first New Year's Day (1939) at Lawai-Kai, they made their foray into tropical gardening, planting a breadfruit tree. For good luck, their friend and visitor, Mrs. Walter Brewster of Lake Forest, tossed a dime into the hole.[22] From this ceremonial beginning, the careful restructuring of the grounds took decades. John said:

> *My father... started organizing that part of the land which had at one time belonged to Queen Emma. We discovered old walls and house sites and many burial caves. We found fine springs in what seemed like mere mud-holes. Areas thick with haole koa and lantana were cleared to make way for more sophisticated tropical plants, all without the use of a bulldozer that would have changed the contour or turned over moss-covered rocks.*[23]

Robert eventually transformed Lawai-Kai into a stunning botanical garden, preserving the disappearing natural beauty. They created meandering trails throughout the property, and with the help of an expert "stone man," Mr. Yamamoto, they designed countless stone walls. Robert loved exploring unknown areas and creating new views.[24] As with his Illinois property, he created garden rooms, each specializing in vegetation and sculpture, opening like pages in a book. "Whenever an act of nature came along," John Allerton said, "he used it as part of the design, rather than... inflict[ing] his own design on it. He always made his plan subservient to nature."[25]

The growing habits of Lawai-Kai's flora often confounded them. Robert tried cultivating certain plants for distinctive borders, but some grew much taller than their siblings. He labored for years to create a formal avenue of hibiscus[26] but finally gave up trying to corral them. Some of the more precious ones were even stolen. Finding it impossible to create straight avenues and borders, he eventually broke free from the European tradition, developing a new respect for the island environment.

On the other hand, his agricultural expertise translated quickly and easily to the new "Farms." His Hawaiian friends and staff provided advice and manual labor for new crops of bananas, guavas, papayas, sweet potatoes, oranges, and limes.

Grateful for the life he and John enjoyed at Lawai-Kai, Robert wanted to enhance the island with new and exciting plants.[27] They brought back many exotic ones from their travels to Fiji, Sri Lanka, the Philippines, and Australia. As Rick Hanna, of the Allerton Gardens, wrote, these plants "supplied a living palette for Robert and John to create a masterpiece."[28] Harnessing the estate's abundant water supply, they created pools and water falls, strategically placing gazebos, fountains, and statuary (some new, some sent from The Farms). Ficus, monkey pod trees, bamboo, giant anthuriums, coconut palms, philodendrons, aralia, frangipani, plumeria, heliconias, ginger, calatheas, night-blooming Cereus—they fill the estate with their beauty and aroma. Although some of their imports might have proven more detrimental to the island's ecology than they realized,[29] Robert and John's artistic endeavors created a rain-forested museum that never ceases to delight the casual wanderer.

Michael Holtz

Cupid fountains near the Thanksgiving Pavilion.

ART AT THE ISLAND HOME

Similar to The Farms, one unexpectedly encounters statues positioned in niches and gardens in Robert's tropical paradise. Years earlier, he had commissioned a stoneworker named Yamanaka to duplicate fish statues that he had seen on the grounds of a Kyoto museum. The artisan created bronze casts and gilded the completed statues, but by the time Robert wanted to install additional copies at Lawai-Kai, the casts had been destroyed. Fortunately, the sculptor was still alive and he was able to create another set for Lawai-Kai.[30] Near the fish sculptures, Robert later installed a bronze copy of the statue he had given the Art Institute of Chicago in 1911, *Young Sophocles Leading the Chorus of Victory after the Battle of Salamis,* by John Donoghue.

As a visitor walks from the valley floor toward the house, the first surprise is the Thanksgiving Pavilion garden with its natural green walls of trees. Two *Cupid* fountains sent from The Farms—copies of statutes from Herculaneum[31]—stand opposite each other in a small rectangular pool. One *Cupid* fountain holds a dolphin over its shoulder, and the other clasps a goose. Beyond the pool stands a small Asian-inspired pavilion, much like the Lost Garden's pavilion, also designed by John Gregg Allerton.[32] The name "Thanksgiving Garden" originated from the surprise party that they gave one year on that holiday.[33]

Michael Holtz

Each *Gazelle* sculpture is approximately three feet high and two feet long. One looks to the left and the other to the right. "Chiurazzi, Naples, Italy" is inscribed on one of the bases. This foundry specialized in reproducing ancient art, work considered by art historians to be among the world's best.

In a small area behind the Pavilion, two bronze *Gazelle* statues (sometimes referred to as *Deer*) stand on small columns, guarding side entrances to the garden. Robert brought them from The Farms in the 1940s. The sculptures are based on original Herculaneum designs.[34]

In 1942 Robert and John awaited the arrival of *Flora,* a sculpture sent from The Farms. But the head gardener sent them the wrong one—a copy of *Diana of Gabies*—and they were at a loss where to install it.[35] They finally chose a location just beyond the Thanksgiving Pavilion, at the end of a rectangular

Michael Holtz

The *Diana* Pavilion sits on a small rise between the Thanksgiving Pavilion and the *Mermaid* statues. The statue of *Diana* faces the Pavilion.

pool on a raised area of land. *Diana* faces a gazebo[36] decorated with marble statues. At an earlier date, some of the decorations in the gazebo included heads copied from originals found in the ashes of Mount Vesuvius and housed in a Naples museum.[37] Several of the heads also appear scattered through other Lawai-Kai gardens. Behind *Diana,* lava boulders create a small waterfall, and lava steps on both sides lead down to the riverside path. Philodendrons and mother-in-law tongue plants abound.

Earlier, during the 1939-1940 World's Fair in Flushing Meadows, New York, Robert and John were intrigued by Art Deco statues at a restaurant in the Italian Pavilion.[38] The popular second-floor restaurant, designed like the salon of an Italian line steamship, was one of the most elegant and expensive at the fair.[39] A pair of plaster *Mermaid* statues were exhibited at the entrance's interior. Over their heads, the *Mermaids* held vases wired with bulbs to provide indirect up-lighting. The Italian consul agreed to Robert's request to copy the statues in bronze and ship him the finished product. After placing a down payment, he awaited shipment. When the war broke out overseas, he gave up hope, assuming the bronze had been melted down to make bullets. But early in 1940, the statues arrived in the port of Baltimore. They were shipped to Lawai-Kai via The Farms, arriving in July.

Michael Holtz

Diana is based on *Diana of Gabies*. Behind the statue, lava steps lead to the Lawai River.

For a time the *Mermaids* functioned as front-gate posts. Later they were moved to face each other at opposite ends of a water garden.[40] Two rows of wave-like concrete structures feed a thin runway of water starting from one *Mermaid* toward the other. Tiny concrete dams inside the waterway cause the liquid to spill into the next section, creating mild waves, until it falls into the bowl at the end. A giant half shell sits under one *Mermaid,* with bubbling water running underground until it spurts up a few feet away into the wavy structure. John copied the shell from one at the Stockholm capitol building. His contractor, Hironaka, and staff member, Wataro, created the shell from a mold. Using the shell and the runway, John duplicated, as best as possible, the waterway at Villa Farnese at Caprarola, Italy, home to the Italian president.[41] (Incidentally, John Borie produced work for the gardens at the Farnese Palace.)[42]

The *Mermaids* and waterway are situated in one of the most charming areas of the estate. Slender moats border its length, separating it on the south from a grove of bamboo which shelters a statue of *Buddha.* When rain pummels the island's famous red soil, the Lawai river, in front of the *Buddha,* turns a shade of orange—like melted milk chocolate in tomato soup. Carved steps rise from the lava rocks to the opposite cliff. One can almost imagine Hawaiian royalty descending those steps, with clucking chickens and competing roosters at their feet, free from harm by Kauai law. Coconuts lie under the trees, ready for the taking.

Robert and John built a lookout across the valley, a hut they called Phoenix House. Adapted from a Georgian building in England, it provided shelter from sudden rain storms.

Michael Holtz

Waterway constructed between the two *Mermaid* statues.

One of their joys was to sit there, with or without guests, having drinks and watching the sun set.

WORLD WAR II ON THE ISLAND

At seven o'clock p.m. on December 7, 1941, Robert and John received a phone call from a neighbor who wanted to make sure they had turned out their lights. As infrequent radio listeners, it was only through that phone call that Robert and John learned the shocking news—that morning the Japanese had attacked Pearl Harbor, 85 miles from Lawai-Kai.

John's letter to Helen two days later calmed her fears. Robert and John wanted to help out as much as possible on the island. They loaned their Ford station wagon to a local doctor to use as an ambulance, retaining one car for their own use.

Michael Holtz

The *Mermaid* statue farther away from the river uses both hands to hold a base atop her head. The one closest to the Lawai River uses only her left hand to hold the vase. The inscription "L. Andreotti, Firenze, 1931" appears at the base of that statue. Master sculptor Libero Andreotti created the original set of *Mermaids* in plaster for the Italian Pavilion of the 1931 exposition Coloniale Internationale (World's Fair) in Paris. That pair was sold to an Italian cruise ship company (for the ballroom of the steamship Columbus) before being displayed at the World's Fair in New York in 1939-1940, where Robert and John first saw them.

They chose to remain at Lawai-Kai for the duration of the war and signed over powers of attorney to Helen Murphy in case of emergency. John served as a First Lieutenant in the Kauai Volunteers, drilling a platoon of 100 Filipino soldiers. The draft's age limit of thirty-eight years exempted John from service, much to the relief of "the boss." But John carried the pistol he had been issued, spent much of his time at the Lihue Intelligence Office, and served as assistant to the sheriff.

John was permitted to use gasoline above the ration of three gallons per week, but Robert scrupulously monitored his own usage to ensure that he would have four gallons per month for mowing. With goods scarce and mail infrequent, sometimes Robert didn't leave the property for several weeks at a time. However, he assisted the war effort by hosting Red Cross picnics honoring convalescent troops. One such party included one hundred people (troops, nurses, and motor corps personnel), two Hawaii orchestras, and hula dancers—but all parties ended before seven o'clock to comply with black-outs.[43]

The Army rolled yards of barbed wire across the beach to hinder Japanese attack. In the intense tropical climate, vines immediately climbed over the wire. Floods filled the wire with logs and floating debris, obscuring a view of the ocean from the residence. Robert finally convinced the troops to cut an opening so everyone could swim.[44] For years afterward they picked remnants of rusty barbed wire from the sand.

By 1942 the island had become an Army camp. Robert had lost all his gardeners (he usually needed between six and nine) either to the draft or the pineapple and cane sugar fields. All construction projects on the premises halted except for those that Robert and John could complete on their own. Robert, at age sixty-nine, worked as much of his property as he could. Everyone grew victory gardens, and to assist the local Office of Food Production, he planted fifteen acres in sweet potatoes and suggested that soldiers grow their own crops in his gardens.

With no eggs, chickens, onions, or liquor available, they relied on Helen for care packages of cheese, powdered eggs, graham crackers, and canned breakfast sausages to augment small rations of ham and bacon. They made ice cream from Eagle Brand condensed milk. Helen sent "soya-beans," and strawberry and chard seeds as experimental crops for Kauai. One package—very welcome—included chocolate. One of John's letters mentioned his relief at obtaining flour again. They hoarded their shortening and cooking oil, but John squeezed three pounds of butter from seventeen coconuts, some of which he used to bake a batch of corn bread and some brownies.

Every evening after John returned from his defense work, he and Robert retreated to their windowless pantry and storeroom to eat dinner and read until bedtime. As the war ramped up, John hired and trained teenaged boys and girls, some as young as twelve, to cook and clean house. The cook would experiment with different meals, as noted in letters home to Helen. One created a stew and stuffed a chicken with opihis (limpets) gathered from the beach rocks. Although many people might gag at the menu, Robert and John found both dishes delicious. But the cook/maid didn't always clean according to the Allerton standard. Periodically Robert left dimes under the beds to test their thoroughness, and he would be satisfied if the money was gone.

Robert served on the Executive Committee of Kauai's Red Cross. During the war and after, he typically gave $500 to the Chicago Red Cross and $500 to Piatt County's Red Cross. The island's Red Cross benefited with $6,000 in 1945 alone.

They returned to The Farms after a two-year absence, flying back on empty troop transport planes. After some months, they returned to Lawai-Kai in a convoy with civilian workers and other personnel—a fourteen-day journey across the ocean, running zig-zag to confound the enemy.[45] They visited Illinois again for six months during the spring and summer of 1944, but returned to Kauai in time for Thanksgiving. They continued their Red Cross duties, with John chairing the 1945 Easter Red Cross drive.

Shortly after the attack on Pearl Harbor, Robert learned that Ellen Emmet—the woman to whom he had been devoted—had died in a New York hospital. On December 18, 1941 she had suffered a heart attack and passed away at the age of sixty-six. Decades later, Ellen's granddaughter found a cache of letters—tied with a ribbon—that Robert had written to Ellen in 1901.

CHAPTER EIGHTEEN
Robert's Legacy

Real generosity toward the future lies in giving all to the present.

Albert Camus (1913-1960)

LIMITATIONS

Robert may have considered seeking a permanent retreat from the harsh Illinois winters when he found his new home. The island, distant from European and Asian fighting, would have seemed to be safe. When he learned, shortly after setting up household on Kauai, that Hitler had invaded Poland and later destroyed Czechoslovakia, he must have felt even more confident in his decision.

After a few years, managing The Farms from Kauai had become a challenge. Robert and John—and the Illinois staff—were aging. Soon they would need to hire and train a new group of trustworthy employees.

And life at The Farms didn't come cheap. In 1940 the estate yielded an income of approximately $25,000, but expenses were almost double that amount. Of the expenses, $8,000 went for alterations and decorating, with $2,600 for household furnishings.[1] The Hawaii expenses came in at only $10,000 (2007 purchasing power of $148,000).

As early as April 1941, in a letter to Helen, John broached the subject of living in Hawaii full-time:

> *The time here is getting much too short and it seems awful to leave this beautiful place. It is going to be an awful wrench to do it. One has to remember how beautiful it is in Monticello and concentrate on tulips and apple blossoms and all that to be able to renounce this life for another. I think now that we ought to move the office and the farms out here and never live any other place.*

By the time the war commenced, Robert and John were seriously discussing giving The

Farms to the University of Illinois. Lawai-Kai offered them more freedom to be themselves than they had in Illinois. While they called themselves "father and son," their homosexual relationship was accepted as a matter of fact on Kauai.

NEW WORK IN MONTICELLO

Even though Robert contemplated divesting himself of The Farms, he still did not neglect Monticello nor his patronage of Illinois artists. A park north of town was named after Robert's friend, William F. Lodge, and Robert wanted to honor him further. He asked John to design the stone columns that still stand at the entrance of Lodge Park today.

Michael Holtz

The subject of Lili Auer's 1941 concrete sculpture, *Girl with a Scarf* is a nude woman of elongated proportion who sits on the ground, pulling a long scarf to her head. The fabric, as if blown by the breeze into a stylized arc, forms the shape of a crescent moon behind her.

Girl with a Scarf, a sculpture by Lili Auer, finalized Robert's acquisitions for The Farms. The Brick Wall Garden had never housed a proper sculpture; the only centerpiece had been a cistern pool that was removed in the 1930s because it leaked. As if to bring closure to the space (it was, after all, the first garden Robert created, forty years earlier), he reached to his early art experience in Munich, to his association with the Art Institute of Chicago, and to his patronage of lesser-known artists. His selection of Lili Auer's *Girl with a Scarf* in 1942 related to each of those aspects of his own career.

Lili Auer was born in Munich in 1904.[2] After completing her art training there, she came to Chicago in the early 1930s.[3] Her sculpture was well-received at ten different exhibitions at the Art Institute of Chicago. Having seen *Girl with a Scarf* at the Art Institute's 1941-42 Exhibition of American Paintings and Sculpture,[4] Robert purchased it for the sum of $300.

The concrete sculpture is not cast, but formed by troweling a stiff mixture over an armature of iron bars and chicken wire. Auer rubbed crushed rock into the surface, finishing with a dusting of powdered white silica to unify the color and add a low luster.[5]

THE GIFT

The war delayed decisions on exactly what land to give, what roles John and Robert would take after the gift, and other details. On June 30, 1946 the newspapers announced the final agreement—Robert would give the house and grounds to the University of Illinois on October 24, along with the 1946 corn crop estimated at $51,000. The acreage plus eight farms, comprising approximately 5,500 acres, appraised at approximately $1.3 million. At that time, it constituted the most generous gift extended to the University. The deed of gift stated that the property "be used by the University as an educational and research center, as a forest and wild-life and plant-life reserve, as an example of landscape gardening, and as a public park." The non-farmland property was to be named "The Robert Allerton Park," and the farmland was to be used to maintain and develop the Park. For the sake of practicality,

Robert and John reversed one clause that prohibited moving the statuary.[6] In addition to the gift, Robert also designated the adjacent 250 acres across the road from the mansion for an Illinois 4-H Memorial Camp.

In a letter to University of Illinois president, Dr. George Stoddard, Robert itemized his concerns regarding the gardeners at The Farms. He listed their salaries and privileges, confirming that nothing would change. He specified that one man might need to occupy his farmhouse for five more months until his pension, paid by Robert, would commence. The head gardener was to keep his utility-paid apartment. Another man lived in a house with his utilities and coal covered, plus a daily allowance of milk and cream. Additional notes clearly outlined Robert's concerns that the University would continue to care for his staff as he had.[7]

Robert had squirreled away books, art, costumes, and jewelry at The Farms. In preparation for the move, they constructed additional rooms at Lawai-Kai, including a room for a possible future care-giver, a library, and a dish cupboard for Robert's porcelain collection.[8] Determining which of their many books to take, John chose the architectural and decorative arts books, while Robert kept the art and theater volumes. Together they picked over the travel books. But the library was still packed with volumes, and included many first editions. Robert allowed a Chicago bookstore, Hamell and Barker, to review the remaining books and sell those of value. After deducting their commission, the bookstore forwarded the proceeds to the Art Institute of Chicago. Books of lesser interest stayed in the mansion. (Unfortunately, after the house opened to the public, books with Robert's signature disappeared.[9])

After Robert and John culled the household furnishings, art, and books, Robert offered his friends first pick from his costume collection. He gave some to the Art Institute and moved the rest to Lawai-Kai. There they would be stored in a newly-built room on the top floor of the Lawai-Kai guest cottage, in cedar closets salvaged from McBryde's house.[10]

They moved their few belongings remaining in Illinois into a small frame house that Robert owned, where they planned to stay during their summer visits. Donated to the University as part of the total property, it was located on Allerton Road near the main entrance to The Farms. The house, only a bit larger than Robert's original pre-mansion cottage, stood behind the farm manager's house where Elmer Priebe lived. The wives of some of the gardeners would clean it before Robert and John returned each year.[11]

University of Illinois

John, Robert, and Elmer Priebe on a visit to Allerton Park and Retreat Center in 1962.

As packing continued, they asked eight different antique dealers to examine the remaining furnishings. The collection included an ebony commode with gilt drawer pulls, Chinese and Japanese art, old paintings, and eighteenth-century English furniture.

The highest bidder, Chicago furniture dealer John A. Colby & Sons, obtained the entire lot to sell, with the Art Institute of Chicago again receiving the proceeds. Robert and John sailed for Kauai on October 15, and the sale ran until November 11, 1946, with many Allerton friends purchasing favorite pieces.[12] The newspaper listed some of the prices: a Korean lacquer chest inlaid with mother of pearl at $650, chests at $500, a Sheraton mahogany bookcase at $3,250, and antique mahogany chairs with red Moroccan leather seats at $375 a pair.

Robert and John arrived at Lawai-Kai[13] and in February 1947 their shipment of furniture, books, and artwork arrived. All they had to do was squeeze decades of life in a mansion into a one-story Kauai home.

PUTTING DOWN ROOTS

Once they settled into Lawai-Kai, their friends and acquaintances had to travel farther to see them. But who wouldn't want to idle in Hawaii, especially in winter? An early visitor in 1939 was Georgia O'Keeffe, the acclaimed artist. The Dole Pineapple Corporation offered to pay her travel expenses in exchange for paintings of pineapples. She painted heliconia, hibiscus, lotus, plumeria, papaya, and red ginger, but not a single pineapple. After her return to New York, she produced paintings for Dole—a papaya (the product of their main competitor) and several others before she finally delivered one of the promised fruit.[14] She later wrote a note to Robert, thanking him for letting her stay at Lawai-Kai.

National Tropical Botanical Garden of Hawaii

Robert and John in Hawaii.

Frederic and Evelyn Bartlett also visited. During their 1948 sojourn, Evelyn picked up some monkey ear pods dropped from a nearby tree and stashed them in her purse. When she reached their Florida estate, seven seeds remained inside the pods. She planted them in pots and watched them grow quickly in the Florida heat. After giving one young sapling to Catherine Beveridge, she gave several away to others, and kept three, planting them on the Bonnet House property. Eventually the roots of one encroached too closely to the foundation of the house and had to be removed, but two of them still grow there.

Frederic's visits to Lawai-Kai halted when he suffered a debilitating stroke around 1949. He died on June 25, 1953 at his Whitehall home in Beverly, Massachusetts. Robert stayed friends with Evelyn Bartlett, but it was not the same. Eighty years of closeness had died with Frederic. But Robert still had John.

Kauai was their private paradise. With only the two of them in the house, they saw no need for doors on the bedrooms or bathrooms. A sense of freedom also extended to clothing, in particular on Wednesdays—the gardeners' day off. One particular Wednesday an accountant visited from their bank, dressed in his business suit and carrying his briefcase. Robert and John spent the entire three-hour visit au naturel on the porch, discussing their investments with him.[15]

Robert still participated on the Board of Trustees of Chicago Memorial Hospital as well as other organizations he loved.[16] He continued sponsoring favorite artists. In 1951 he commissioned Chicago artist Rainey Bennett* to create four paintings to be placed within the panelings in The Farm's Oak Room where portraits of Robert's grandparents had been displayed. Even though he no longer owned the mansion, he wanted to be a patron to Bennett and let visitors see the artist's vision of The Farms.[17] Impressions of estate statuary appear behind the urns of flowers in the paintings. Robert undoubtedly knew Bennett at least as early as the 1940s when Bennett began teaching at the Art Institute of Chicago.

Robert and John returned to Monticello, Chicago, and occasionally New York, usually during May or June. John needed to keep an Illinois residence in order to eventually function as executor of Robert's will,[18] and they also wanted to ensure that the University of Illinois followed through on Robert's wishes regarding The Farms. Robert cared less about the house than the pavilions and art scattered around the property, but even so, he and John did not take kindly to the manner in which the house was treated after they left. The few rugs and used furniture from University storage filled only some of the mansion's empty space, making it appear bleak and institutional. The University asked for more funds to maintain the mansion, but Robert declined. He simply wanted to preserve the natural beauty of the grounds; he did not want the University to build classrooms or convert the mansion to a hotel.

During his summer visits to The Farms, he enjoyed spending hours chatting with the gardeners. One former employee mentioned that when Robert still lived in the mansion, he once fired a gardener because the man wouldn't talk with him.[19]

In 1960 Robert and John finally celebrated a milestone in their lives. During their forty years together, Robert had regularly called John Gregg his "adopted" son, and many times the newspapers even referred to John as such. But the state of Illinois prohibited adoption of an adult by another adult. They had contemplated going to Missouri where such adoption was allowed, but Robert never wanted to give up his Illinois residence. They waited, and finally in 1959 the Illinois state legislature changed the law.[20] On March 4, 1960 Judge Henry Timmons Dighton of Monticello decreed John Wyatt Gregg, at the age of sixty, to be the legal son of eighty-seven-year-old Robert Allerton.

LAWAI-KAI GOES HOLLYWOOD

Kauai attracts movie and television studios. Hula dancers entertained John Wayne and his co-stars on the lawn of the Allerton estate in the 1963 film, *Donovan's Reef*,[21] and the characters in *Jurassic Park* found a raptor egg and dinosaur bones among the raised roots of a Morton Bay Fig tree on the estate.[22]

Michael Holtz

Roots of the Moreton Bay Fig trees where a scene from *Jurassic Park* was filmed.

Other movies with scenes filmed on the property include *South Pacific* with Mitzi Gaynor (1958), *Lt. Robin Crusoe* with Dick Van Dyke (1966), *Islands in the Stream* with George C.

Scott (1977), *Last Flight of Noah's Ark* with Eliot Gould (1980), *Island of the Alive* with Michael Moriarty (1987), and *Honeymoon in Vegas* with Nicholas Cage (1992). In the romantic miniseries, "The Thorn Birds," the small house where Richard Chamberlain and Rachel Ward met for their beach trysts was also Allerton property. The house, located at Ke'e Beach in Ha'ena, burned down in the 1990s.[23]

ROBERT'S LEGACY TO HAWAII AND ILLINOIS

In the early 1960s Robert had joined with several other philanthropists to petition Congress to establish a botanical garden, and donated $75,000 to the garden foundation toward initial expenses. Finally in 1964 Congress recognized the need to conserve and protect the tropical plant resources of the world, especially threatened and endangered species. Public Law 88-449 was passed on August 19, 1964, chartering the Pacific Tropical Botanical Gardens as a non-profit corporation to provide an educational and scientific center. As a founding trustee, Robert donated $1 million to kick-start the project and purchase adjoining land, known today as the McBryde Garden.

On December 20, 1964, Robert fell at home and fractured his hip.[24] While trying to recover in Lihue's Wilcox Hospital, he succumbed to coronary thrombosis at noon on December 22—forty years and two days after the death of Agnes, his beloved stepmother. Robert was ninety-one. John followed his adopted father's final wishes, holding no funeral services. Robert's body was cremated, and John scattered his ashes over the bay at Lawai-Kai.

Robert's estate was valued at approximately $21.5 million in 1964 (2007 purchasing power of approximately $144 million). John Gregg Allerton inherited most of it, including personal effects and real estate, both in Hawaii and Illinois. Robert left $100,000 to the Visiting Nurses Association of Chicago[25] for establishment and maintenance of three fellowships: the Kate Allerton Johnstone Nurse, the Agnes Allerton Nurse, and the Robert Allerton Nurse. Additionally, he bequeathed to the Art Institute of Chicago a sum of $500,000 for the upkeep and maintenance of the Art Institute's Allerton Wing. Fifty-five smaller bequests went to Illinois and Kauai staff members, friends, relatives, and John Gregg's sister and brother-in-law (Frank and Katherine Courtenay). He also left a trust for Vanderburgh Johnstone, Kate's son.

Prior to his death, when newspapers reported Robert's intent to bequeath a half-million dollars to the Art Institute of Chicago, he joked in an interview about the effect of the publicity: "a crank contacted me and said he'd like to emulate my generosity. He asked me to give him $50,000 so he could begin his benevolence."[26]

During the interview, the same reporter mentioned that Robert had become the Art Institute's greatest living benefactor. Robert said, "That can't be true. Why, Mrs. Sterling Morton just gave one million dollars for the Morton wing." When the reporter told him he had donated double that amount, Robert said, "I have? Have you checked that fact with the Art Institute?"[27] The reporter's details were correct. In fact, over his lifetime, Robert donated more than 6,000 pieces of art to the museum. In 1968, to honor him, the Art Institute named the original 1893 building The Robert Allerton Building.

From the 1940s onward he had donated at least 200 works of art to the Honolulu Academy of Art. His gifts had included works by Degas, Picasso, Disney, Cezanne, Matisse, Tiepolo, Dufy, and Utrillo. Some of the many Asian works included a seventh-century Buddha from the T'ang dynasty, a Shinto deity from the twelfth-thirteenth century, and a thirteenth-century Japanese hanging scroll. In 1955 he funded the museum's art library construction. Later they honored him by naming it the Robert Allerton Art Research Library. It was no surprise that the Academy was a beneficiary. His perpetual trust benefited the Art Institute of Chicago and the Honolulu Academy, with two-thirds of the trust's annual income going to the Art Institute, and one-third to the Honolulu Academy of Art. The First National Bank of Chicago and John Gregg served as executors and trustees.

JOHN'S STEWARDSHIP

In 1965 John Gregg legally changed his name to John Wyatt Gregg Allerton.[28] He wanted to carry on Robert's donations under the name of "Allerton," not "Gregg." He spent the next two decades as Robert would have wished, enhancing Lawai-Kai and giving generously to pet projects, including the Art Institute of Chicago, where he became a life trustee in 1970.[29] He continued to travel to faraway places, even managing—with six broken ribs—to accompany Andre Kostelanetz and classical pianist Leonard Pennario to New Zealand in November 1970.[30] John visited Monticello annually with his staff member and companion, Toshio Kaneko. Together they roamed The Farms, monitoring the University work, not always telling the new owners what they wanted to hear.

In May 1972 John found a pile of ashes where the Lost Garden Pavilion once stood. Angry, he learned that in February the sculptures had been relocated, the Pavilion torn down, and the debris burned. Only the copper roof was salvaged. A lawsuit had prompted the University's drastic action. The flooring of the roof sundeck had deteriorated, and instead of replacing it, they had simply sealed off the spiral stairway access. However, a young boy was not deterred. He made his way up the stairs, but fell through a rotten roof, suffering a broken leg.[31]

A series of miscommunications occurred between John and the Director regarding whether to rebuild the Pavilion. The University agreed to John's suggestion to install hedges outlining the original Pavilion foundation. Nowadays, a new entry off Allerton Road invites hikers, but the Lost Garden's name has sealed its fate. Along the overgrown path, only vacant concrete slabs—and perhaps the whispering ghosts of Robert's long-gone friends—suggest the site ever harbored a special retreat.

Over the years, the University's attention ebbed and flowed. John persisted, visiting each year, keeping Robert's spirit and intent fresh in the minds of the new stewards.

Even after Robert's death, John continued to explore and find new wonders at Lawai-Kai. Until 1965, he had not gone beyond a small road, called the "cane-haul road." Soon he discovered waterfalls, a dam, a canyon, and caves deep in the jungle valley ("Harry's Valley") behind the gardens—land owned by the McBrydes and known today as the McBryde Garden.[32]

John traveled, continued to develop the Lawai-Kai gardens, helped with the McBryde Garden, and entertained visitors. Although his property was private, the beach itself was public. He encouraged male beachgoers and surfers to enjoy the beach, but asked that women stay away.

Richard Nixon was photographed at Lawai-Kai in September, 1979, returning after a swim in the bay. Otherwise, most guests were simply old friends from Illinois.

The End of an Era

John was eighty-six when he was hospitalized in early April 1986, undergoing heart surgery shortly afterward. He died at six a.m. on Thursday, May 1, 1986 at the Kauai Veterans Memorial Hospital. As with Robert, there was no funeral service and his body, like Robert's, was cremated, and his ashes spread over Lawai Bay.

John's will left bequests to a few family members and many friends. To Toshio Kaneko, he left a cottage, land, and personal property in Ha'ena, Kauai. The Honolulu Academy of Art inherited his art and art literature. He bequeathed Lawai-Kai in trust to the Pacific Tropical Botanical Garden, with The First National Bank of Chicago as trustee. He left an endowment to maintain the property, as well as funds for research and educational purposes.

The rest of his estate was combined with Robert's trust to benefit The Honolulu Academy of Art, the Pacific Tropical Botanical Garden, and the Art Institute of Chicago. The National Tropical Botanical Garden (as it is known today) features more than 5,000 species of flora, with over 75 types of fruit trees, much of this the result of Robert's and John's devotion to the island. Botanists from around the world flock to Kauai to study and research at the facility there. The National Tropical Botanical Garden publishes a periodic series of papers called *Allertonia,* comprised of contributions by botanists and horticulturists. One might imagine that both Robert and John could have penned lay-person articles for it if they were still with us.

* * *

In a 1980 interview, John Gregg Allerton said about their Monticello home, "I feel closer to my father here than in Hawaii because he created all of this and his love and connection is here... I feel my father's spirit is more alive here than it is back there."[33]

Rightfully so, considering Robert spent nearly forty years creating what we know today as Allerton Park and Retreat Center. His decades in Chicago and Lawai-Kai represent substantial bookends to his life, but what remains at Monticello represents his true soul.

Early in his life, when Robert had emotionally finished with something, he tended to destroy it—his early paintings in Europe, The Folly, his family home on Prairie Avenue. But after he transferred his private sanctuary to Lawai-Kai, he wanted to see The Farms live on. At the time of his gift to the University of Illinois, he didn't care whether they left the mansion standing.[34] He only wished for the gardens to be opened to the public. Now each visitor receives Robert's most personal gift—a bit of privacy within its boundaries, in any number of secret hideaways.

What if Robert had been born to a poor farming family? Separating the wealth from Robert's identity leaves us with an even more curious creature. A hearing-impaired boy, without the tutors. An artist, without the training. An adventurer, without the price of a steamer ticket. An experimental agrarian, without the acreage. He might have been the neighboring bachelor farmer, a bit eccentric, proud of his ornamental birdbath and a patch of flowers that he refused to replace with corn. That man might have revealed an equally compelling story, but not the reality. Robert was wealthy, and his wealth defined the path of his life.

Money allowed him to extend his creative intellect to its ultimate conclusion. The world is full of starving artists, but collectors and patrons are always in short supply. Art is always a two-sided proposition: one side makes what is seen, the other side sees what has been made. The gifts that Robert Allerton left behind inspire both possibilities in us.

EPILOGUE
What Would Robert Do?

In collaboration with Jessica Elena Hampson and Hilary T. Holbrook

With any gift comes an obligation to honor the donor's intent—an uneasy obligation in the case of an especially generous gift that was not on the wish list. When Robert Allerton deeded almost 6,000 acres to the University of Illinois, he specified that the land be used as an educational and research center, a nature reserve, an example of landscape gardening, and a public park. Those objectives represented variations of his own achievements, but not necessarily the University's most pressing needs. And the gift came tied in a snarl of ribbons—the dilemma of how to manage it. The organizational chart evolved as a patchwork of split appointments and partial directorships, much of it centered on campus, twenty-five miles from the site.

Samuel Allerton was content to be an absentee landlord. Robert (or as John Gregg Allerton called him, the "benevolent dictator") rejected that notion. Although he employed a farm manager, he watched over every aspect of his farms, saving extended travels for the winters, after the harvests. Meanwhile, he sat on countless boards of directors and actively engaged in Chicago's cultural growth. Extraordinary results come from extraordinary passion—and empowerment.

Robert's diverse interests relate to every academic area, not just to agriculture, the natural sciences, and architecture, whose researchers have most actively claimed the land as laboratories. The Allerton Scholars Program targets specific, on-site academic initiatives, but Allerton, both as a place and as the hub of a cross-disciplinary concept, has yet to be fully exploited. The Retreat Center is frequently the setting of scholarly gatherings, but much less frequently the subject itself. However, drawing conferences from a variety of corporate, nonprofit, and educational institutions raises Allerton's profile and helps sustain it financially.

The farms, intended to support Allerton Park and Retreat Center, have historically generated inadequate funding. As citizens respond with donations of time and money, they expect to be heard. During Robert's reign, local residents danced carefully around the gates of the Allerton Empire. But when Robert Allerton Park (as it was first named) opened in 1947, curious Monticello residents dressed in their Sunday best to stroll the gardens and tour the mansion. Their pride in the Allerton legacy extends well beyond what would be merited by that family's early philanthropy to the town. Many townspeople feel a *de facto* ownership in the actual Allerton estate, three miles from their city limits.

Men with deep Piatt County roots—Joseph C. Llewellyn (husband of Emma Piatt), William F. Lodge, Lew Wagy, and Francis J. Brooks—literally built much of what we experience today as Allerton Park and Retreat Center. Local farmers have always plowed the Allerton fields. Monticello citizens groomed Robert's gardens and laundered, cooked, and served at The Farms. Even today, many Allerton employees, volunteers, visitors, and donors reside in Monticello.

Issues of University land sale and usage have erupted over the years. The most heated and sustained battle arose in the 1960s and 1970s when the Army Corps of Engineers proposed building a dam on the Sangamon that likely would have flooded the precious Allerton bottomlands. (In 1970 the National Park Service granted National Natural Landmark status to 1,000 acres of Allerton Park in recognition of its stream valley ecosystem and its bottomland and upland forests.) Oakley Dam was initially supported by the University of Illinois administration, the governor, and high-profile state legislators,[1] but the plan was ultimately defeated by an unlikely coalition of professors, students, area farmers, and Piatt County citizens. As separate factions with complementary agendas, the diverse concerns of the opposition reflected aspects of Robert's personal interests—nature, art, and agriculture—all potentially threatened by the proposed dam. As if to answer the question, "What would Robert do?" the opposition honored what they assumed to be his wishes.

However, in 1977 the late William Lodge (son of William F. Lodge and once John Gregg Allerton's college roommate) recalled a revealing conversation that took place around 1929 near the site of *The Death of the Last Centaur* sculpture on Allerton's estate:

> *I worked with father on the Allerton building projects including the formal gardens for about 15 summers and on weekends. One day, after we had finished the wide brick stairs that lead from the gardens down to near the bottomlands level, father, Mr. Allerton and I were standing at the top of the steps and Mr. Allerton said, with a sweep of his arm out toward the bottomlands, "wouldn't it be wonderful if those bottomlands were a lake!"*[2]

We can never know what Robert would have wanted. Still, as we listen for his answers, it is worth remembering that he rarely hesitated to alter the landscape to suit his fancy.

Oakley Dam is now water under the proverbial bridge. But the word "bridge" brings even soft-spoken Monticello residents to their feet. For safety reasons, in 2001 the University closed the Park's south entrance from Allerton Road, declaring the severely deteriorated bridge off-limits.

Some say that Samuel Allerton cautioned Robert that the bridge would be a waste of money. Whether or not the account is true, Robert waited until after his father's death in 1914 to commission Joseph C. Llewellyn's design for the concrete bridge that withstood over eight decades of use. Many respect its beauty and historic character. Others care only that they must now use the Park's secondary, unadorned entrance off Interstate 72 instead of the direct and tree-lined, formal drive from town. Once again, if only symbolically, many Monticello citizens feel locked out. In a further affront, the closing redirects desirable tourist traffic around, rather than through, Monticello's business district.

With the bridge as its main talking point, the University acknowledges that Monticello considers the University to be a poor steward of Allerton. In response, it works to educate city leaders on the complexity of University finances, propose joint tourism initiatives, solicit private donations and endowments, and enlist local volunteers. There is still no bridge, but those dedicated to finding solutions have contributed generously to other recent successes. Recently most major sculptures have been restored, gardens replanted, architectural garden features repaired, the pond rebuilt and replenished, and road newly paved. None of this would have been possible without the generous support of Allerton donors and the tireless efforts of the Allerton staff and volunteers.

Fresh energy for these accomplishments resulted from consolidated and streamlined on-site management, and has helped put Allerton on the map. Both the National Register of Historic Places and the American Institute of Architects' list of "150 Great

Places in Illinois" include Allerton Park and Retreat Center among their recognized sites. In 2007 the Illinois Bureau of Tourism named Allerton Park one of its "7 Wonders of Illinois," the result of a spirited Internet poll.

The rustic setting and isolation of Allerton Park and Retreat Center has always held appeal. Robert did not want to see the mansion converted to a hotel, but opening it to private guests and special events generates revenue and raises public appreciation. Ironically, the estate of a confirmed bachelor is now a popular wedding location for both indoor and outdoor events. Together, the mansion, Evergreen Lodge, Gate House, and House in the Woods accommodate between 50 and 100 overnight guests in newly refurbished rooms. Recently added televisions and wireless Internet service at the mansion have updated the nineteenth-century domicile.

The Schroth Interpretive Trail, south of the Sangamon River, winds for three miles through a tapestry of natural areas. Here reside more than 1,000 species of vascular plants, 60 species of birds, 30 species of mammals, and 28 species of reptiles and amphibians. The trail, with 12 interpretive stations, encompasses bottomland forests, bluffs along the Sangamon River, and a 30-acre restored prairie. Its name honors Eugene "Buck" Schroth (1905-1993), an educator, coach, scoutmaster, Facilities Manager of Allerton Park, and volunteer trail guide. Supportive families provided signs and benches, and the trail is endowed for maintenance and improvements.

A two-story, Dutch-style hay barn on the southern Allerton farmland had previously been used for storage. Undergoing continuous renovation, it has become a unique concert hall. The Allerton Music Barn Festival concert series, now in its third year, represents a successful collaboration between Allerton Park and Retreat Center and the University's School of Music. Robert, a life-long music lover, would be amused and surprised.

Restorations at Allerton

Robert declared that artwork should be routinely moved to refresh the view. Yet when he gave the property to the University, his deed initially prohibited it from following his philosophy. He soon changed his mind. By necessity, several sculptures have found new homes within the Park's landscape, and some are faithful replacements. Gifts, private endowments, and individual tribute donations fund most of these restorations.

Avenue of the *Chinese Musicians*

Annual income generated from a generous endowment established by the Hilfinger family has provided for upgrades to the Avenue of the *Chinese Musicians*. Paving an upper level parallel to the pea gravel path has improved accessibility, and Canadian hemlock trees and groundcover have restored the backdrop. In 2007 stone carver Timothy Doyle[3] re-carved a lute player and restored two other damaged pieces.

A gift from the Illinois Prairie Hosta Society of Champaign, Illinois transformed a formerly vacant area between the Avenue of the *Chinese Musicians* and the Chinese Maze Garden into a hosta garden. This garden will expand into an adjoining, previously neglected, space now redesigned as a tribute area with trees, flowering shrubs, fieldstone retaining walls, and groundcovers.

The *Fu Dog* Garden

In 1970 one of the twenty-two *Fu Dog* sculptures disappeared, and thieves soon managed to make off with five more. Three were recovered, but one was stolen twice.[4] In 1981 the University commissioned University of Illinois Professor Donald Frith to recreate the four missing ones and two others that were damaged. After extensive study and testing over 100 glazes, he managed to capture the spontaneous, hand-built quality of the originals. Fred Manthei, a tile and marble setter, repaired others,[5] and volunteer Ed Bondurant continues to preserve the *Fu Dogs* today. In a 2009 landscape restoration, forty-four white firs replaced overgrown and missing trees, native grasses and flowers were replanted, and the adjacent tree canopy was thinned dramatically.

At the head of the *Fu Dog* Garden stands the House of the *Golden Buddhas*. Over the years, the gilding of the two *Siamese Buddhas* inside the pagoda had worn away. After vandals broke and defaced the statues, workers glued them back together and "restored" them with gold radiator spray paint.[6] Fortunately, the mother-of-pearl inlaid eyes remained intact. In 1989 Professor Robert Youngman of the University of Illinois properly restored the two sculptures by replacing ten missing toes and the damaged parts of the carved robes, stripping the gold paint, and resurfacing the sculptures with bronzing powders, liquids, and wax.[7]

As part of the 2009 garden restoration, shingles on the roof of the House of *Golden Buddhas* were replaced with eco-shakes, a recycled product. Staff repaired and repainted the underside of the roof and the ornamental wrought iron. Dozens of new trees and shrubs have revived the landscaping.

Venus

In 1995 conservator Sharon Koehler restored the Park's Carrara marble copy of Canova's *Venus Italica.* She thoroughly cleaned the statue, filled cracks, replaced a missing little finger of the right hand, and stabilized an ankle, severed from the base. The marble has been sealed to prevent further damage, and *Venus* now resides in the mansion's Conservatory, protected from the elements.[8]

The Brick Wall Garden

Over the decades, much of the brickwork in the Brick Wall Garden—the estate's oldest garden—suffered from weather and other elements. Attempts to repair the damage revealed underlying age-related structural problems. The wall is being rebuilt and repaired in the summer of 2009, and new garden material will be installed in 2010.

By the spring of 1993, the Brick Wall Garden centerpiece, Lili Auer's *Girl with a Scarf* required extensive repair.[9] The armature had corroded, and the base had been eaten away by squirrels. Wasps, birds, and mice had made their homes inside the sculpture itself. Carol Forsythe of Conservation Services Laboratory at the Detroit Institute of Arts[10] completed the sculpture's restoration in 1995.[11] An endowment gift from Thomas and Jessica McCraw in memory of Erwin Arkell McCraw provided plantings in the surrounding garden's four quadrants.

The Sun Singer

Over the decades, Carl Milles' *The Sun Singer* suffered from weather and vandalism. In 2007 a crane hoisted the gigantic sculpture from its pedestal, moving it to ground level so that Chicago sculptor Barry Tinsley[12] could restore it. Tinsley thoroughly cleaned the sculpture down to bare bronze, and found it to have remarkable structural integrity. He then applied new patina and sealed, waxed, and buffed the surface to a soft luster. *The Sun Singer,* returned to its location, once again looks out over the vista. The limestone base was cleaned of graffiti, and the circular plaza was resealed and encircled by new native plantings. Monetary gifts for this restoration came from as far away as Mississippi and Washington State.

The Three Graces

Robert Allerton's replica of Germain Pilon's sixteenth century sculpture, *The Three Graces,* also suffered severe erosion from the weather. In 2008 stone carver Timothy Doyle masterfully restored it. In his opinion, the original craftsman was trained with Gothic skills, the highest certification in stone carving in the early 1900s. *The Three Graces,* once showcased in the Lost Garden, now resides in the Peony Garden.[13] *Friends of Allerton,* the large group of Allerton Park donors, funded the project.

The Death of the Last Centaur

As of 2009 the concrete pillars at the site of Émile-Antoine Bourdelle's *The Death of the Last Centaur* await restoration. The Swedish cast-iron urns that normally top them have been stored until two of them can be replaced. Other proposed work includes resurfacing the eight pillars, trimming the woodland canopy, and preserving the sculpture.

Gorilla Carrying off a Woman and *Bear and Man of the Stone Age*

When the University of Illinois first acquired two Emmanuel Frémiet bronze castings, *Gorilla Carrying off a Woman* and *Bear and Man of the Stone Age,* it had no place to house them. The sculptures stood for years on secluded spots of a riverside woodland pathway at Allerton Park—much to the surprise of unsuspecting hikers. Eventually, the two sculptures were removed and placed in storage at Allerton Park. The National Gallery of Art in Washington, D.C. requested a loan of them in 2006 to include in an art show entitled *Henri Rousseau: Jungle in Paris.* In exchange, the National Gallery cleaned and waxed the statues and paid transportation costs. The sculptures now reside at the University's Krannert Art Museum's Kinkead Pavilion.

The Sunken Garden

A summer storm in 2006 dumped eleven inches of rain in the area, damaging tiles and outlets that serve the Sunken Garden. Later that year, extensive work rectified the problem. In 2007 the crumbling concrete pylons were rebuilt and refreshed to gleaming white, adding to the Sunken Garden's appeal as a site for weddings. The sixteen *Japanese Guardian Fish* atop the pylons were temporarily removed in 2008 for repairs. They were skillfully bronze-welded, using excess U.S. Mint material from production of the Susan B. Anthony dollars. Protective mesh was added to reinforce their undersides, and a clear, weather-resistant finish was applied before the sculptures were repositioned in spring 2009. Once again, loyal donors funded this important restoration.

* * *

What was once the private oasis for one influential man and his circle of friends is now a vibrant learning, recreational, and celebratory sanctuary for more than 100,000 visitors and guests every year. The century-old mansion lives on as a distinctive retreat and conference facility, enjoyed by guests from around the world. Indoor and outdoor areas of the estate serve as unforgettable settings for weddings and special events. The public enjoys the Park's natural areas, formal gardens, sculptures, and hiking trails, and various organizations use the area for environmental study. Allerton Park and Retreat Center is a unique cultural and environmental asset to the University of Illinois, and its treasured landscape is deeply rooted in the history of the region.

Allerton Park and Retreat Center will always be a work-in-progress, but all who experience it—whether as a visitor, volunteer, or donor—participate in the enduring fascination it offers. Long after Robert Allerton's departure, his gift continues to touch, amaze, and inspire in ways even he could not have imagined.

FAMILY AND FRIENDS

THE ALLERTON ANCESTORS

Isaac Allerton (1585-1659) – At age thirty-seven in 1620, Isaac was one of the wealthiest of the *Mayflower* Pilgrims, from whom Samuel Waters Allerton was an eighth-generation direct descendant. A tailor by trade, Isaac arrived at Plymouth Plantation with his wife and children, and was widowed shortly thereafter. Isaac then married William Brewster's daughter, named Fear. Five years after Isaac's arrival, Governor Bradford appointed Isaac to replace the colony's financial agent in London. By 1630 Isaac's financial chicanery prompted Bradford to remove him from his position. Between 1633 and 1644, Isaac established a fishing fleet in Salem. He then moved to New Amsterdam (present-day New York), and finally to New Haven, Connecticut, where he died in poverty. His house on a two-acre lot (at the northwest corner of Union and Fair Streets) is long gone. A plaque in New Haven's Grove Street Cemetery honors his contributions.

Isaac Allerton II (1630-1702) – First-born son of Isaac and Fear (Brewster) Allerton. Served in 1675 as second-in-command to Colonel John Washington (George Washington's great-grandfather) in the Virginia forces against the Indians.

Dr. Reuben Allerton (1753-1808) – Samuel Allerton's grandfather. Served the Continental cause as a surgeon in the Sixth Dutchess County New York Militia during the American Revolution. Robert donated two family portraits to the Art Institute. One depicts Reuben's wife, Lois Atherton Allerton; the other shows Cornelius Allerton, Lois' and Reuben's son. Both portraits were painted by New England artist Ammi Phillips.

Samuel Waters Allerton (1828-1914) – Chicago agriculture, meat-packing, and banking tycoon. Father of Kate Reinette Allerton and Robert Henry Allerton.

Pamilla Wigdon (Thompson) Allerton (1840-1880) – First wife of Samuel Waters Allerton (married in 1860). Mother of Kate Reinette Allerton and Robert Henry Allerton.

THE FAMILY OF ROBERT'S MOTHER

(The Thompsons and Dightons)

Agnes Catharine (Thompson) Allerton (1858-1924) – Youngest sister of Pamilla Wigdon (Thompson) Allerton. Second wife of Samuel Waters Allerton (married in 1882).

Jessie (Thompson) Dighton – Robert Allerton's cousin. Jessie's father, Charles Thompson, was a brother of Agnes and Pamilla (Thompson) Allerton. Jessie married William Dighton of Monticello, Illinois.

Asler Carr Dighton (1904-1940) – Son of William and Jessie (Thompson) Dighton. Roommate and Zeta Psi fraternity brother of John Wyatt Gregg Allerton (Robert's adopted son) at the University of Illinois.

THE FAMILY OF ROBERT'S SISTER, KATE

Katharine "Kate" Reinette (Allerton) Papin Johnstone (1863-1937) – Robert Allerton's sister. In 1885 Kate married Dr. Francis Sidney Papin of Keokuk, Iowa at a ceremony in the Allerton's Prairie Avenue home. Dr. Papin died in 1889 in Mexico. In 1898 she married Hugo Richards Johnstone. (Originally from Keokuk, Hugo was a friend of Dr. Papin and had attended Papin's wedding to Kate.) Kate and Hugo had two sons, Allerton and Vanderburgh. To ensure that they excelled in baseball, she purchased the lot next to her Pasadena home and turned it into a regulation baseball field. She divorced Hugo in 1931, two years after the death of her elder son, Allerton.

Hugo Richards Johnstone (March 25, 1872-June 22, 1947) – Kate Allerton's second husband (married in 1898). Hugo was one of four children born to Judge Edward Johnstone and Elizabeth Vanderburgh Richards of Keokuk, Iowa. He was a member of the New York Stock Exchange, president of the Jersey City Stock Yards Company, and president of the Pasadena Dredging Company.

Hugo and Kate were listed in the Social Register of New York. An avid sportsman, Hugo belonged to several elite athletic clubs on the East Coast and in Pasadena as well as the Royal Thames Yacht Club of London. They were both members of the exclusive Jekyll Island Club off the coast of Georgia. Kate became the club's first female member.

In August 1903 Kate sued Hugo for divorce, naming a burlesque actress, Nina Farrington, as correspondent. (Farrington's real name was Minerva Cool Love.) Nina's second husband, Sidney C. Love, was Hugo's best friend and cousin. (Sidney Love and Hugo had both attended Kate's first wedding to Dr. Papin.) When Sidney Love discovered letters from Nina addressed to Hugo, he filed for divorce from Nina, who had previously been linked with millionaires Augustus Pfizer and Joseph Leiter (son of Marshall Field's partner, Levi Leiter).

Hugo and Kate did not officially divorce until 1931. Hugo then married Olive Mitchel, widow of former New York City Mayor John Purroy Mitchel. Hugo had been living at the Racquet and Tennis Club at the time of their wedding at Olive's Fifth Avenue residence. He died of colon cancer in 1947 in San Diego and was buried in Keokuk.

Allerton Johnstone (December 25, 1900-June 9, 1929) – First-born son of Kate Allerton Johnstone and Hugo R. Johnstone. Weighing over 300 pounds, he died after a fall from the window of Hotel Hayward in Los Angeles, assumed to be a suicide.

Vanderburgh Johnstone (January 6, 1903-1987) – Second-born son of Kate and Hugo Johnstone. As a teenager at Phillips Academy (Andover, Massachusetts), Vanderburgh captained the baseball and football teams, and later played for Princeton. Like many wealthy students of the times, he wore a raccoon coat and drove a Stutz Bearcat. He became a businessman and owner of the Diamond K ranch near San Jose, New Mexico.

He and his first wife, Ardith Crane, became parents of twin boys: Crane Allerton Johnstone and Vanderburgh Johnstone II. Ardith left him, and he sued for divorce on September 16, 1938. Later he married a woman named Elizabeth ("Liza"). They lived in Santa Barbara, California. He married a third wife, Nancy.

Vanderburgh didn't speak to his father, Hugo, for years. When Hugo was diagnosed with cancer, Vanderburgh finally journeyed to California to see him, but Hugo died before Vanderburgh could reach him.

Vanderburgh Johnstone II (April 1931-September 1970) and **Crane Allerton Johnstone** (April 1931-February 2009) – Twin sons of Vanderburgh and Ardith Johnstone. Vanderburgh II was the first born.

During delivery of the twins, forceps crushed Crane's skull and he never progressed mentally beyond age five. When Vanderburgh and Ardith Johnstone separated, Ardith took young "Van" with her, leaving Crane in the care of his father and his grandmother, Kate Allerton Johnstone. Vanderburgh and his next wife, Liza, cared for Crane until early 1942. At that time Vanderburgh joined the armed forces and admitted Crane into a Southern California facility.

After her divorce in 1938, Ardith married Jack McKinley. She and Vanderburgh II, renamed as Robin McKinley, lived at McKinley's New Mexico ranch. An elderly ranch hand cared for the child during the couple's extensive travels. Vanderburgh II (Robin) had three sons and one daughter: Crane, Sean, Vanderburgh III (originally named Adam McKinley), and Heather. In 1970 Vanderburgh II died of esophageal cancer, most probably the result of exposure to toxins during his career as a botanist in California.

ROBERT'S ADOPTED SON

John Wyatt Gregg Allerton (November 7, 1899-May 1, 1986) – Robert Allerton's adopted son and heir. John Gregg's maternal grandmother was related to Cyrus Field, the man who, in 1858, laid the first telegraph cable across the Atlantic Ocean. Gregg was also distantly related to Noah Webster.

ROBERT'S FRIENDS

David Adler (1882-1949) – Noted residential architect, once employed by Howard Van Doren Shaw's architectural firm in Chicago. Later his own firm (at one time in partnership with Henry Dangler), set the standard for restrained elegance during the period. Many of his clients were Robert's friends: Mrs. C. Morse Ely, Mr. and Mrs. Richard T. Crane, and Mr. and Mrs. Stanley Field. He employed John Wyatt Gregg during the 1920s.

Adler was a trustee of the Art Institute of Chicago from 1925 until 1949. Prior to that, he worked with Robert Allerton on the Art Institute's Committee on Decorative Arts. His friendship with Robert grew through their mutual involvement both at the Art Institute and through the Arts Club of Chicago and the Cliff Dwellers Club.

In 1916 Adler married Katherine Keith (from the Edson Keith family, who lived two houses away from the Allertons on Prairie Avenue). Katherine, a novelist, was killed in an automobile accident in France in 1930. Adler's grief and the financial challenges of the Great Depression forced him to close his practice in the 1930s. He died on September 27, 1949 in Libertyville and is buried along with his wife at Graceland Cemetery.

Theodora "Dodo" (Winterbotham) Badger Brown (1902-1990) – Daughter of John H. and Anne R. Winterbotham, niece of Rue (Winterbotham) Carpenter, and sister of Rue (Winterbotham) Shaw. Dodo's grandfather, Joseph Humphrey Winterbotham, gave $50,000 in 1921 to the Art Institute for European painting purchases. The resulting Winterbotham Collection includes many important Impressionist works. Dodo and her first husband, Shreve Cowles Badger, visited The Farms in the 1930s. They divorced, and in the 1940s she married Amos Howard Calef Brown (1894-1981).

Adolphus Bartlett (1844-1922) – Frederic Clay Bartlett's father. The Bartletts once lived at 2222 Calumet Avenue near the Allertons, later moving to 2720 Prairie Avenue. Adolphus began his career with a job as a janitor in the Chicago wholesale hardware firm of Tuttle, Hibbard and eventually became a partner in the company. The renamed Hibbard, Spencer, Bartlett & Co. was sold in 1962 and is known today as *True Value*.

Frederic Clay Bartlett (1873-1953) – Robert's best friend since childhood. He married Dora Tripp Schmid in 1898, Helen Birch in 1919, and Evelyn Fortune Lilly in 1931. He raised a son, Clay, Jr. from his marriage with Dora. He died in 1953.

Dora (Tripp Schmid) Bartlett (1879-1917) – Married Frederic Bartlett in October 1898, just days before her nineteenth birthday. Mother of Clay Bartlett, Jr., she died in 1917 at the age of 37.

Helen (Birch) Bartlett (1883-1925) – Frederic Bartlett's second wife. Helen was a talented poet and shared Frederic's passion for collecting art. Helen's father, Hugh Taylor Birch (1848-1943) was a partner in Galt, Birch and Galt and the first State's Attorney of Cook County, Illinois (1872). In 1876 he married Maria "Mollie" Root. (Mollie was the daughter of Delia Spencer and Francis H. Root. Delia was Catherine Eddy Beveridge's great-aunt.) The Birch family lived at 1912 Michigan Avenue, several blocks away from the Spencers and Eddys in the Prairie Avenue district. One of the Birch sons, Carlton, died in infancy; the other son, Hugh, Jr., died in 1907. Helen was their only other child.

Hugh Birch gave Helen and Frederic 40 acres along the Atlantic coast in Fort Lauderdale as a wedding present. The couple built a spectacular home on the land, naming it Bonnet House for the bonnet lilies that grow there. After Helen died from breast cancer in 1925, Hugh donated 250 acres (the Glen Helen Nature Preserves) to Yellow Springs, Ohio in honor of her memory.

Evelyn (Fortune) Lilly Bartlett (1887-1997) – Frederic Bartlett's third wife. Having divorced Eli Lilly (grandson of the pharmaceutical founder) around 1927, she married Frederic Bartlett in 1931. After Frederic's death in 1953, she married Daniel Huger. He died in 1967, and she returned to using the Bartlett name. She outlived Frederic by more than four decades, dying at the age of 109 at her home in Beverly, Massachusetts.

Rainey Bennett (1907-1998) – Painter, muralist, and illustrator. While Rainey was a student at the School of the Art Institute of Chicago, he met Robert Allerton. During the 1930s, he supervised Works Progress Administration and Federal Art Project artists at the University of Illinois medical school. An 8 x 12 foot mural of his design (executed by other artists) featuring the Champaign-Urbana campus is displayed there. Bennett joined the faculty of the School of the Art Institute in the 1960s, freelancing as a writer and illustrator of children's books. Over the years, Robert purchased a number of Rainey's paintings for both The Farms and his Kauai estate, many of which were later donated to the Honolulu Academy of Art.

Catherine (Eddy) Beveridge (1881-1970) – Daughter of Augustus and Abigail Spencer Eddy. Her maternal grandfather, Franklin Spencer, was a partner in Hibbard, Spencer, Bartlett & Co. Catherine's aunt (her mother's sister) was Delia (Caton) Field. Catherine's brother, Spencer, was the same age as Frederic Bartlett and Robert Allerton. She grew to be close friends with both Frederic and his first wife, Dora. Her cousin,

Helen Birch, became Frederic's second wife. Catherine married Indiana Senator Albert J. Beveridge in 1907. She had homes in Beverly, Massachusetts and Fort Lauderdale, near the Bartletts.

Margaret Day Blake and Tiffany Blake – Friends and guests of Robert. Margaret had been a childhood friend. Her husband, Tiffany, was once the *Chicago Tribune's* chief editorial writer. Both were involved with the Arts Club and donated a number of paintings to the Art Institute's collections. Margaret served with Robert on the University of Illinois Campus Plan Commission in the 1920s.

John Joseph "Dickey" Borie III (1869-1925) – Architect of Robert Allerton's Monticello mansion. Borie was descended from an influential Philadelphia family of French ancestry. His uncle, Adolphe Borie, served as Secretary of War under President Grant. His sister, Emily, married Arthur Ryerson, who was drowned in 1912 with the sinking of the *Titanic*.

John "Dickey" Borie attended the University of Pennsylvania. He did not graduate, but continued his studies at the École des Beaux-Arts in Paris. He then worked for the Philadelphia architectural firm of Cope and Stewardson. Around 1897 Thomas Eakins painted a portrait of Dickey entitled *The Architect,* now at the Hood Museum of Dartmouth College.

In 1906-07 Borie moved to London, living on Gloucester Road in South Kensington. His last work involved the remodeling of his Tudor cottage in Glatton, Huntingdonshire. Until his death on November 29, 1925, he lived with his friend, musician Victor Beigel. Beverley Nichols (a friend of Dickey's sister, Emily) purchased the home and wrote a book describing it. The novel, *A Thatched Roof,* is illustrated by Rex Whistler and dedicated to John Borie, "who is still at Allways" ("Allways" being the fictional name of the village of Glatton). Borie is buried in the Glatton fifteenth-century church cemetery. His tombstone inscription reads: "An American Who Loved England." In 1992 art historian Etta Arntzen wrote that the grave was hidden under mounds of ivy planted there by Beverly Nichols.

John Alden Carpenter (1876-1951) – One of America's top composers in the early and mid-1900s. He studied briefly under Edward Elgar. His music typically accompanied ballets and operas. He directed musical events at the Chicago Arts Club, with accompanying dances occasionally choreographed by Ruth Page. Walt Disney planned to use Carpenter's compositions in a sequel to his film, *Fantasia,* but the project fell through. Carpenter's other friends included Picasso, Irene Castle, Cole Porter, Igor Stravinsky, John Philip Sousa, John Barrymore, and others.

Carpenter traced his roots to John Alden, the *Mayflower* pilgrim. John's first wife, Rue Winterbotham Carpenter, died in 1931. In February 1933 he married his mistress, Ellen Borden. (Ellen divorced stockbroker/oilman John Borden in 1925. Her affair with Carpenter began around 1914.) Ellen's and Borden's daughter, also named Ellen, married Adlai Stevenson II.

Rue (Winterbotham) Carpenter (1879-1931) – Daughter of Joseph Winterbotham, who established a fund for the purchase of modern art at the Art Institute of Chicago in 1921-24. Rue married John Alden Carpenter in 1900, raising a daughter, Genevieve (Mrs. Patrick Hill). Rue became the second president of the two-year old Arts Club of Chicago in 1918, serving until her 1931 death from a cerebral hemorrhage at age 55. Rue Winterbotham Carpenter's niece was Rue Winterbotham Shaw.

Elizabeth "Bobsy" (Fuller) Goodspeed Chapman (1893-1980) – A vibrant force in Chicago society and charity events from the 1920s through the 1940s. Bobsy's first husband, Charles Goodspeed, was a trustee of the University of Chicago and served on the board of the Art Institute. Bobsy succeeded Rue Winterbotham Carpenter as President of the Arts Club in 1932, serving until 1940. In 1927 Bobsy and her husband moved to a David Adler-designed apartment in Lincoln Park, entertaining such friends as John T. McCutcheon, Thornton Wilder, Gertrude Stein, and Alice B. Toklas. In a 1954 cookbook, Toklas included Bobsy's recipe for turtle soup. Charles Goodspeed died in 1947. Three years later, Bobsy married widower Gilbert Whipple Chapman.

Ambrose Coghill Cramer (1891-1970) – One-time employee of David Adler. Cramer was first married to Arthur Meeker's sister, Grace (1895-1983). Their son, also named Ambrose Coghill Cramer, was born in 1917. Grace divorced Ambrose in 1927 on grounds of desertion. He then married Grace's sister, Mary Meeker, in March 1929. Cramer was most proud of his design for Brushwood, a summer home for Ryerson Steel chairman Edward L. Ryerson.

Richard T. Crane, Jr. (1873-1931) – Son of the founder of Crane Co. (plumbing fixtures), a great-nephew of Martin Ryerson, and husband to Florence Higinbotham (daughter of Harlow Higinbotham). Castle Hill, their Ipswich, Massachusetts summer home designed by David Adler in 1928, bears a striking resemblance to Robert Allerton's Monticello mansion. Their son, Cornelius Vanderbilt Crane, married opera singer Cathalene Browning Parker and adopted her daughter (also named Cathalene) from her first marriage. That daughter married writer and editor, Edward Tinsley "Ned" Chase, in 1941. In 1943, three years after her mother's divorce from Crane, she bore a son she named Cornelius Crane Chase—the actor-comedian known as "Chevy" Chase.

Katherine Dudley (born 1884) – Poet and portrait painter. Daughter of a prominent gynecologist (Dr. E. C. Dudley) from the Prairie Avenue area. Her sisters were Dorothy (biographer of Theodore Dreiser), Helen (Bertrand Russell's lover), and Caroline (wife to French writer Joseph Delteil). Katherine had been living in France on the Rue de Seine when the Germans took control of the country during World War II. At one point, she and a Mme. Tartière helped shelter American flyers. She was eventually imprisoned in a concentration camp in Vittel (the mineral springs park). She was a close friend of Gertrude Stein and Sylvia Beach, founder of an English bookstore in Paris, Shakespeare and Company (unaffiliated with the current one in Paris).

Spencer Fayette Eddy (1874-1939) – Older brother of Catherine Eddy Beveridge; childhood friend of Robert and Frederic. Spencer served in various diplomatic positions worldwide and was employed as private secretary to U.S. Ambassador to the Court of St. James, John Hay. He married Lurline Elizabeth Spreckels in 1906, and they had a son in 1907. They were divorced around 1923; she charged desertion. He was often considered the "best dressed American" in London.

Ellen Gertrude "Bay" (Emmet) Rand (1875-1941) – Painter to whom Robert Allerton was romantically linked. Born in San Francisco to Christopher Temple Emmet and Ellen Temple, who were distantly related. When her father died in 1884, her mother moved with her children to New York. Her mother later married George Hunter. By age twelve, Ellen was studying art in Boston under Dennis Miller Bunker, attending the Art Students League from 1889 to 1893. There Ellen studied with William Merritt Chase, Kenyon Cox, and Robert Reid.

Ellen's sister, (Edith) Leslie, was also a painter. The extended family boasted even more artists. Ellen's aunt,

Julia Colt (Pierson) Emmet, worked as an illustrator. Julia's son-in-law, Wilfred von Glehn, and her three daughters—Rosina (nicknamed "Posie"), Lydia Field Emmet, and Jane Erin von Glehn—were all successful painters. Cousin Rosina's son, Robert Sherwood, became a playwright.

Ellen married William Blanchard Rand and they raised three sons: Christopher, William, Jr., and John. Christopher became an author and foreign correspondent. Ellen's granddaughter, Ellen Rand, is a painter and art gallery owner in New York City.

"La Estrellita" (Stella Davenport) (1879-1973) – Dancer. Stella Davenport was born in Cincinnati, Ohio, daughter of Millie Davenport, an actress. She began dancing at the age of four with her sister, touring as "Stella and Edna Davenport." As "La Estrellita," she headlined with the Keith and Orpheum vaudeville circuits. In addition to designing her own costumes, she collected and lectured on art. In 1906 "La Estrellita" performed at a Panama Pacific International Exhibition commemoration of San Francisco's rise from the terrible earthquake. The celebration ran for ten months. She married Paul R. Jones, an entomologist.

Ethel Field (1873-1932) – Daughter of Chicago retailer Marshall Field and Nannie Douglas Scott Field. Prairie Avenue childhood friend of Robert Allerton. In 1891 Ethel married real estate developer Arthur Magie Tree (son of Lambert Tree, a Chicago judge and minister to Belgium, then to Russia). As newlyweds, the couple lived in England at Compton Varney, near Warwick. Two children, Gladys and Lambert, died in infancy. She gave birth to Ronald Lambert Tree on September 26, 1897. Arthur filed for divorce, claiming that Ethel deserted the family; the divorce became final on May 12, 1901. Ten days later, Ethel married David Beatty (1871-1936). Ethel and David had two children: David Field Beatty, 2nd Earl Beatty (1905-1972) and Hon. Peter Randolph Louis Beatty (1910-1949). Ethel became Countess Beatty on September 27, 1919. On July 17, 1932 she died at Dingley Hall, Leicestershire, England, after years of treatment for severe depression.

(Charles) Russell Hewlett (1872-1913) – Son of James Augustus Hewlett. The town of Hewlett, on Long Island, is named for his family. Their home was known as Rock Hall. After graduating from Columbia University, Russell studied art in Paris for three years, following in the steps of his older brother, James Monroe Hewlett. (An architect, James had studied at the École des Beaux Arts in 1891-92. James worked at McKim, Mead, & White before and after his Paris studies.) After Russell's Parisian stay, he spent a year in Japan studying art before returning to New York. Later he joined his brother's architectural firm, Lord & Hewlett. Russell may have met Robert in Paris or through his brother. In 1908 Russell joined the Carnegie Institute of Technology (known then as the Carnegie School) where he became of Dean of the School of Applied Design. He was President of the Pittsburgh Art Society, winning recognition for his work in art and music. He fell ill with pneumonia in early November 1913, dying in West Pennsylvania Hospital on November 12, 1913. One of his brother's ten children, Anne, married the futurist architect and visionary designer R. Buckminster Fuller.

Charles L. Hutchinson (1854-1924) – Banker and philanthropist. As the first President of the Art Institute of Chicago, Hutchinson played a strong role in its formative years. In addition to his many other titled positions, he was among the original Trustees of the University of Chicago. He and his wife, Frances Kinsley Hutchinson, named their Lake Geneva summer home Wychwood for the wych-hazel that grew on the property. Her books reflect the couple's devotion to nature—*Our Country Home* in 1907, *Our Country*

Life in 1912, and *Wychwood: The History of an Idea* in 1928.

Caroline Kirkland (1865-1930) – *Chicago Tribune* society columnist, "Madame X." As a frequent visitor to Robert Allerton's Piatt County estate, she wrote many gushing columns about him. She was born in Syracuse, New York, daughter of Major and Mrs. Joseph Kirkland. They later lived at 719 Rush Street, and she grew up among prominent Chicago families. She joined the *Chicago Tribune* staff in 1909. With her membership in the Arts Club and other Chicago music and art societies, she socialized with Robert and their mutual friends. She lived at 25 E. Walton Place and had a summer home in Westminster Road in Lake Forest. In addition to being a columnist, she authored two books and spearheaded the preservation of the Chicago Water Tower, a remnant from the Great Chicago Fire of 1871. She died on August 10, 1930 from a cerebral hemorrhage. Robert was an honorary pallbearer, along with John T. McCutcheon and Colonel Robert McCormick, owner of the *Chicago Tribune*.

George T. Langhorne (1867-1962) – Decorated veteran of the Spanish-American War and assistant to Major Leonard Wood. In 1916 he commanded a squadron in pursuit of Pancho Villa, leading his troops (among them, the young George S. Patton) from his Cadillac touring car. Langhorne lived briefly with the Patton family during this time. Later he worked in the office of the Chief of Staff in Washington and served as a military attaché in Berlin and at The Hague. In 1928 he married Mary Kirk Waller (daughter of Edward Carson Waller, Sr. and Mary Kirk) of Chicago at the England home of his cousin, Viscountess Nancy Witcher Langhorne Astor. His wife's best friend and cousin was Ellen Borden Carpenter, second wife to John Alden Carpenter. Colonel and Mrs. Langhorne were photographed at The Farms around 1940. Mary Langhorne was a contributor to the Art Institute of Chicago.

Joseph Corson Llewellyn (1855-1932) – Architect for several projects at The Farms, including the entrance bridge to Robert's estate. On May 17, 1883 Llewellyn married Emma Clarinda Piatt (b. 1857). Emma was the daughter of William Hart Piatt and Clarinda Marquiss Piatt, descendents of the founder of Piatt County, Illinois. During the first year of her marriage, Emma Piatt Llewellyn wrote *The History of Piatt County*. Joseph Corson Llewellyn designed numerous schools and office buildings throughout Illinois and figured prominently in founding the Architectural League of America. The Piatt County work of his firm included: the 1919 Pepsin Syrup building in Monticello, Deland Township High School, Bement High School, Monticello High School, restoration of the William H. Kratz store and office building, and the residences for W. E. Smith and Charles W. Piatt.

William F. Lodge (1868-1935) – Monticello lawyer, contractor, businessman, and local authority on wildflowers and trees. His friendship with Robert propelled John Gregg into Robert's world. Lodge's son, William T. Lodge, was a fraternity brother of John Gregg. William F. Lodge was active in many clubs, such as Rotary, Boy Scouts, and the University of Illinois Dad's Association. He helped initiate the Piatt County Forest Preserve District. Lodge Park, originally part of his 470-acre estate on the outskirts of Monticello, was sold to the Forest Preserve in 1938 after he died. John Gregg designed the entrance gates to Lodge Park; Robert Allerton funded their construction.

Hazel Martyn (1880-1935) – Daughter of Edward Jenner Martyn, who was Vice President of the Union Stock Yards and confidential associate of Philip D. Armour. Her father died in April 1897, leaving only a small estate. During the summer of 1898, as American artists flocked to Europe to study, she visited France.

The red-haired young woman debuted into society in 1899. Her friends Ethel Hooper, Marie Truesdale, and Rue Winterbotham numbered among the twenty-eight girls attending her at the ball. After that, her name appeared regularly in society columns. Only five-foot-two with almond-shaped hazel eyes, she was considered a beauty.

As the family fortune dwindled, by 1900 they sold the family home on Astor Street. Her mother borrowed money from Armour & Co., allowing them to live in Europe during much of 1901 and 1902. She returned to Paris in the summer of 1902 to study etching. Meanwhile, Mrs. Martyn searched for a suitable husband for Hazel.

Hazel had fallen in love with famous Irish painter and patriot John Lavery, but Mrs. Martyn forced her into a marriage on December 28, 1903 to Dr. Edward Livingston Trudeau, Jr. of New York. Miss Ethel Hooper, daughter of Chicago physician Dr. Henry Hooper, was a bridesmaid (probably the same "Miss Hooper" who attended a play in 1901 with Hazel and Robert Allerton). Instead of the customary pearls or diamonds, Hazel's fiancé gave her an etching press as a wedding gift. Trudeau also provided her an art studio in New York in addition to their elaborate apartment at 772 Park Avenue. After only five months of marriage, Dr. Trudeau died from a pulmonary embolism.

Three years later, on the eve of her wedding to Leonard Moorhead Thomas, her fiancé jilted her. Eventually she married John Lavery. During World War I, Lavery was knighted, elevating Hazel to the title of Lady Lavery. Until the 1970s, Lavery's portrait of Hazel appeared on Irish banknotes, and it was used as a watermark on Republic of Ireland banknotes until the introduction of the Euro. While married to Lavery, rumors circulated that she had an affair with Irish revolutionary leader Michael Collins, who died with a letter to her in his pocket.

William Mavor (1848-1904) – Masonry contractor for Robert's mansion. William and his brother, John, worked together at the William Mavor Co. The firm constructed the Architectural Building at the 1893 Columbian Exposition, portions of the Masonic Temple, Marshall Field & Co.'s building, the Armour residence, Harold McCormick's residence, and other Chicago projects. With his office at 636 First National Bank Building, Mavor likely would have known Sam Allerton. Mavor married Mary Eadie Strang in 1872, and they raised five children. As a Chicago Alderman for the 32nd Ward, he led the city council for almost six years. A Chicago bathhouse at 4645 Gross (later McDowell) Avenue was constructed in 1900 and named after him.

John T. McCutcheon (1870-1949) – Cartoonist. One of Robert's frequent visitors, John McCutcheon is best remembered today for his "Indian Summer" cartoon that appeared each autumn in the *Chicago Tribune*. A political cartoonist for the *Chicago Tribune* for forty-three years, he was awarded a Pulitzer Prize in 1932. McCutcheon and Frederic Clay Bartlett had studios next to each other on the tenth floor of the Fine Arts Building, along with another illustrious tenant, Lorado Taft. Like Robert and Frederic, McCutcheon was an active member of the Cliff Dwellers and the other arts organizations.

Joseph Medill McCormick (1877-1925) – Honeymooned in 1903 with his wife, Ruth Hanna, at The Farms. At the time, McCormick held one of the editor positions at the *Chicago Tribune*. He was the son of Robert S. McCormick (Ambassador to Russia); nephew of Cyrus McCormick (inventor of the reaper and founder of International Harvester); and grandson of Joseph Medill (owner and managing editor of the *Chicago Tribune* and one-time Chicago mayor). Eventually owning the *Chicago Tribune* himself, McCormick later served Illinois first as a congressman, then as a senator. McCormick committed suicide in 1925.

Arthur Meeker (1902–1971) – Son of Arthur Meeker and Grace Murray Meeker. His father worked at Armour & Co., and they lived on Prairie Avenue. When the neighborhood changed, they moved to the sparsely populated north side, settling first at 3030 Lake Shore Drive and later in Lake Forest. He wrote *Prairie Avenue,* a thinly-veiled novel about life in his childhood neighborhood, and a more direct memoir and commentary, *To Chicago with Love.*

Ruth Page (1899-1991) – American ballerina and choreographer. In 1920 she danced in *Birthday of the Infanta,* John Carpenter's ballet based on a play written by Oscar Wilde. She visited The Farms.

Pauline (Kohlsaat) Palmer (1882-1956) – Wife of Potter Palmer II, who was Director of the First National Bank of Chicago and President of the Art Institute. She and her husband, along with his parents, Berthe and Potter Palmer, were significant donators to the Art Institute.

Glyn Warren Philpot (1884-1937) – English Symbolist painter and portraitist who visited The Farms on two occasions. While staying with Robert, he completed a portrait of his host, now in the Tate Collection. He also designed the *Primitive Man* statues located near the mansion. Philpot served with the Royal Fusiliers in World War I. Recuperating from a health crisis, he supported the war effort, as did many artists, by illustrating propaganda for the British government and donating artwork to benefit the Red Cross. His artistic achievements were honored by admission to the Royal Academy in 1923. In later years, his artwork became increasingly erotic and met with negative criticism. Glyn had a long-term homosexual relationship with artist Vivian Forbes (1891-1937), who committed suicide four days after Philpot's funeral.

Charles Burrall Pike (1871-1941) – Son of prominent Chicago banker, Eugene S. Pike. Charles became a Chicago lawyer, financier, founding President of the Hamilton Bank, and President of Merchants Safe Deposit Company. Pike was a member of the Chicago Club, University Club, Chicago Athletic Club, Onwentsia Club, and Saddle and Cycle Club, and founder of the Racquet Club. He also served as President of the Chicago Historical Society during its 1932 move to Lincoln Park. In 1898 he married Frances Aura Alger, the youngest daughter of Russell A. Alger (financier, Governor and U. S. Senator from Michigan, and Secretary of War under President McKinley). President McKinley and Vice President Hobart attended their wedding. David Adler designed the Pike home in Lake Forest, Illinois. Robert's *Diana* and *Ephebe* statues were gifts from the Pikes.

Roger Quilter (1877-1953) – Prolific English composer known for his light orchestral music. He became friends with Robert through mutual acquaintances, Jane von Glehn (Ellen Emmet's cousin) and Victor Beigel. Robert, four years older, was devoted to Roger and wanted him to come to America to compose, staying as long as possible at The Farms. Fearing travel to an unfamiliar country and the possibility of becoming ill, Roger never made the trip. He found it difficult to deal with his homosexuality, and deteriorated into mental illness after his nephew died in World War II. Roger admitted to only one homosexual relationship: with Robert.

Anna Rathbone – Wife of Mortimer Rathbone. She lived at 307 Henry Street, Grand Rapids, Michigan at the time of Agnes Allerton's death. As Robert's godmother, she chaperoned Ellen Emmet's visits to The Farms. Mrs. Rathbone's portrait hangs in the mansion's Oak Room, previously Robert's office. She was a close friend of Sam's sister, Lois Allerton.

James Gamble Rogers (1867-1946) – Architect who worked for William LeBaron Jenney and Burnham and Root before establishing his own practice in Chicago in 1891. He then studied at the École des Beaux-Arts in Paris, where he attained his architectural certification. Rogers graduated in 1898, just as Allerton and Borie were searching Europe for home designs. He returned to Chicago and opened a firm with his brother, John Arthur Rogers. Because Rogers, but not Borie, had obtained his Illinois architect license, he reviewed and stamped Borie's designs.

Eleanor Roosevelt (1884-1962) – At the time of her debutante ball in 1902, Eleanor Roosevelt became friends with Ellen Emmet. Eleanor would frequently visit Bay in her Greenwich Village studio. Ellen's connections to the Roosevelt family continued for decades. In 1920 Franklin D. Roosevelt joined the law firm of Ellen's cousin, Grenville Temple Emmet, Jr., and Ellen painted Roosevelt's presidential portrait in 1936. The Allertons had their own connection to the Roosevelts—Franklin D. Roosevelt was also a direct descendant of Isaac Allerton.

Alice Roullier (1883-1963) – Arts Club's Exhibition Chairman from 1918-41. During that time, she influenced the Chicago art world by introducing works by Marcel Duchamp, Picasso, Modigliani and Braque. After the death in 1920 of her father, Albert Roullier, she took over as director of the Albert Roullier Art Galleries located in Chicago's Fine Arts Building. Robert frequently acquired artwork from Roullier Galleries, to be donated to the Art Institute. The French government named her to the Legion of Honor in 1923 for outstanding contributions to French art in America. She is considered, along with Rue Carpenter and Rue Shaw, one of top leaders of the Arts Club.

Emily Maria (Borie) Ryerson (1863-1939) – John J. Borie III's sister, and wife of Arthur Larned Ryerson. The Ryersons and their children had been visiting Europe in 1912 when they learned of the death of their son, Arthur, Jr. in an automobile accident. The group, which included their son (John Borie Ryerson, age 13), two daughters (Emily Borie Ryerson, age 18 and Suzette Parker Ryerson, age 21), maid (Miss Victorine Chaudanson), and John's governess, Grace Scott Bowen, hurried back to America on board the *Titanic*. Emily and her children were rescued from a lifeboat (along with Mrs. John Jacob Astor IV), but Arthur went down with the ship. His body, if recovered, was never identified. (In the movie *Titanic,* it is Arthur Ryerson's coat that "Jack Dawson" borrowed, and into its pocket that his rival slipped the diamond necklace to frame him.)

Emily worked tirelessly after the First World War, raising money to help France with their orphans and wounded citizens. At the age of 62, during a trip to China, she married 45-year-old Forsythe Sherfesee, an advisor to the Chinese Government. In 1909 Arthur's brother, Joseph T. Ryerson, married another Prairie Avenue neighbor, Annie Lawrie McBirney (daughter of Hugh McBirney).

Martin A. Ryerson (1856-1932) – Lawyer and lumber magnate. In 1881 he married Carrie Hutchinson, cousin of Charles Hutchinson, who was then President of the Art Institute. Martin A. Ryerson was a founding trustee of the Art Institute and one of its largest donors of artwork. He endowed the Ryerson Library at the Art Institute and helped incorporate Chicago's Field Museum of Natural History.

Paul and Dorothy Schweiker – Friends of Robert from the Arts Club. Early in his career, Paul Schweiker (1903-1997) worked as an employee of David Adler. Later he became Chairman of the Yale School of Architecture, and head of the Department of Architecture at Carnegie Institute of Technology (now Carnegie-Mellon).

Rue (Winterbotham) Shaw (1905-1979) – Rue Winterbotham Carpenter's niece, sister to Theodora Winterbotham Badger Brown, and a visitor to The Farms. In 1932 she married Boston architect Alfred P. Shaw who designed the Merchandise Mart, the Field Building, and the Morton Wing of the Art Institute. As a member of the Arts Club, she was elected president in 1940 after Bobsy Goodspeed stepped down. She held the position until her death in 1979. Rue and her husband are buried in Graceland Cemetery, Chicago.

Carleton Smith (1908-1984) – A 1924 graduate of Bement High School in Bement, Illinois, a small town seven miles south of The Farms in Monticello. A journalist and music critic for *Esquire Magazine,* he also founded the National Arts Foundation (of New York) around 1947-48. He interviewed Hitler, Mussolini, Stalin, Trotsky, Molotov, the Shah of Iran, and George Bernard Shaw. He became friends with President Harry Truman, Jean Sibelius and Ignaz Paderewski. After World War II he worked to locate lost manuscripts of composers such as Mozart, Beethoven, and Wagner. (He is featured in the 1981 book *Paperchase: Mozart, Beethoven, Bach–: the Search for their Lost Music,* by Nigel Lewis.) Smith was a key force in establishing the Pritzker Prize for Architecture. He taught music appreciation at the University of Illinois from 1926-29, economics and foreign trade at DePaul University from 1928-34, and music history at Oxford University from 1931-39.

Carleton Smith is best remembered in Central Illinois for bringing Marilyn Monroe and Carl Sandburg to the 1955 Bement Centennial Celebration. Smith had offered to pay Monroe's large hotel bill when they met in New York—but only if she agreed to attend the Bement Centennial Celebration.

Adlai Stevenson (1900-1965) – Governor of Illinois from 1948-1953. Defeated as candidate for President in 1952 and 1956. In 1928 he married Ellen Borden, daughter of millionaires John and Ellen Wallace (Waller) Borden, and stepdaughter of John Alden Carpenter. Allerton and Ellen were part of the same social circle, and the Stevensons visited The Farms. While still married to Ellen, Adlai began an affair with Marietta Tree (wife of Ronald Tree, the son of Ethel Field Tree Beatty). Shortly after being sworn in as Illinois governor, Adlai and Ellen divorced. He continued seeing Marietta, dying of a heart attack while walking with her in London.

Melville Elijah "Ned" Stone, Jr. (1874-1918) – The son of Melville Elijah Stone, founder of the *Chicago Daily News* and manager of the Associated Press, Ned Stone worked with the publishing company Stone & Kimball. His wife of eight months, Lucretia Hosmer, died in early August 1901. Shortly thereafter, he stayed for several weeks with Allerton, trying to ease his grief. He never married again. His brother Herbert died in the sinking of the *Lusitania*. Later he moved to Pasadena and passed away in 1918, after suffering from lung problems for years.

(Arthur) Ronald Lambert Field Tree (1897-1976) – Son of Ethel Field and Ethel's first husband, Arthur Tree. Ronald lived in England most of his life, working as a journalist, eventually editing the *New York Journal,* and *Forum Magazine,* starting around 1922, before turning to investing. After returning to England in 1927 with his wife, Nancy Keene Perkins, he was elected to Parliament in 1933. His friend, Winston Churchill, used Tree's home, Ditchley, as headquarters during World War II because its dense foliage provided security from air strikes. Churchill gave him a position in the Ministry of Information, where he met and carried on an affair with Marietta Peabody FitzGerald. They divorced their spouses and, although he was twenty years older than Marietta and bisexual, they married in 1947. By then, they were living in the United States where Marietta became involved with director John Huston and, later, Adlai Stevenson. Marietta's and Ronald's daughter, Penelope Tree, was born in 1949 and achieved fame as a fashion model in the 1960s.

Anne (Reynolds) Winterbotham (born ~1877) – Wife of John H. Winterbotham (whose family fortune came from barrel-making) and mother to Theodora "Dodo" Winterbotham. She and her husband donated many pieces of artwork to the Art Institute and visited The Farms.

BIBLIOGRAPHY

Abbreviations for Sources Cited in Endnotes

INTERVIEWS

Buckingham, interview – Myrlin Buckingham, June 2008.

Gale, interview – Juanita Gale, September 2008.

Johnstone, interview – Sean Johnstone (great-grandson of Kate Allerton Papin Johnstone), December 2008.

Marlin, interview – John Marlin (conducted by Hilary Holbrook), December 2007.

Piatt, interview – Donn Piatt, July 2008.

Rand, interview – Ellen Emmet Rand, January 2009.

Shonkwiler, interview – Pauline Shonkwiler (daughter of Emma Priebe Ashby), September 2007.

Vaughn, interview – Ecus Vaughn, July 2008.

PUBLISHED AND UNPUBLISHED MATERIALS

Allerton Legacy, Blair – Blair, Lachlan F., "Allerton the Politician and Civic Leader," Proceedings of The Allerton Legacy Symposium, (Monticello, IL: May 22, 1981).

Allerton Legacy, Bowman – Bowman, David, "Samuel W. Allerton (1828-1914)," Proceedings of The Allerton Legacy Symposium, (Monticello, IL: May 22, 1981).

Allerton Legacy, JGA – Allerton, John Gregg, "Development of the House and Gardens," Proceedings of The Allerton Legacy Symposium, (Monticello, IL: May 22, 1981).

Allerton Legacy, Priebe – Priebe, Irene, "Robert Allerton - The Man," Proceedings of The Allerton Legacy Symposium, (Monticello, IL: May 22, 1981).

Allerton Lib., Author Unknown – Unknown author of notes in Allerton Miscellaneous notebooks at Allerton Public Library, Monticello. Assumed to be from Irene Priebe or Jessie Morgan.

Allerton, Walter – Allerton, Walter S., *A History of the Allerton Family in the United States 1585-1885* (Rev. and enl. By Horace True Currier. Samuel Waters Allerton, Chicago: 1900).

Andreas (Cook County) – Andreas, A. T., *History of Cook County, Illinois,* (Chicago: The A.T. Andreas Company, 1884).

Andreas (Chicago) – Andreas, A. T., *History of Chicago From 1857 Until the Fire of 1871, Vol. II,* (Chicago: The A.T. Andreas Company, 1885).

Azzam and Anderson – Azzam, Azzeddine M. and Dale G. Anderson, "Assessing Competition in Meatpacking: Economic History, Theory, and Evidence," (U.S. Dept of Agriculture, May 1996).

Baker – Baker, Paul R., Stanny, *The Gilded Life of Stanford White,* (New York: The Free Press, A Division of Macmillan, Inc., 1989).

Bartlett – Bartlett, Frederic Clay, *Sortofa Kindofa Journal of My Own,* (Chicago: The Lakeside Press, R.R. Donnelly & Sons Co., 1965). Courtesy of Elisabeth Bartlett Sturges and Eric Bartlett Wentworth, children of Clay Bartlett.

Bartlett graves – www.cemeterysurveysinc.com/index.php?s=bartlett&paged=2

Bateman, Selby and Shonkwiler – Bateman, Newton, Paul Selby, and Francis M. Shonkwiler, *Historical Encyclopedia of Illinois: Piatt County, Volume II* (Chicago: Munsell Publishing Co., 1917).

Battle for Sangamon – *Battle for the Sangamon, The Struggle to Save Allerton Park,* The Committee on Allerton Park, 1971.

Becker, interview – "John Gregg Allerton Memoir," interview conducted by Nancy M. Becker, May 9, 1984, (Springfield, IL: Sangamon State University).

Beveridge and Radomsky – Beveridge III, Albert J. and Susan Radomsky, *The Chronicle of Catherine Eddy Beveridge,* (Maryland: Hamilton Books, 2005).

Bock – Bock, Kay J., *Majestic Allerton,* (Urbana, IL: University of Illinois Foundation, 1998).

Cackett – UIUC Archives, notes and tapes by Cyril Cackett.

Cook – Cook, Chris, *The Kauai Movie Book,* (Honolulu, Hawaii: Mutual Publishing, 1996).

Dedmon – Dedmon, Emmett, *Fabulous Chicago,* (New York: Random House, 1953).

Delaney – Delaney, J. G. P., *Glyn Philpot: His Life and Art,* (Aldershot, England: Ashgate Publishing Co., 1999).

Donnell – Donnell, Courtney Graham, "Frederic Clay and Helen Birch Bartlett: The Collectors," *Art Institute of Chicago Museum Studies Volume 12,* No. 2 (1986).

EE to Leslie – Letter from Ellen Emmet to her sister, (Edith) Leslie Emmet. Courtesy of granddaughter, Ellen Emmet Rand.

Falk and Bien – Falk, Peter H. and Andrea Ansell Bien, Art Institute of Chicago, *The Annual Exhibition Record of the Art Institute of Chicago, 1888-1950,* (Madison, CT: Sound View Press, 1990).

Gates – Gates, Paul Wallace, "Frontier Landlords and Pioneer Tenants," (*Journal of the Illinois State Historical Society,* Springfield, Illinois: The Illinois State Historical Society, June 1945).

Gelernter – Gelernter, David, *1939 The Lost World of the Fair,* (New York: The Free Press, 1995).

Gilbert and Bryson – Gilbert, Paul and Charles Lee Bryson, *Chicago and Its Makers,* (Chicago: Felix Mendelsohn, Publisher, 1929).

Goodspeed – Goodspeed, Thomas Wakefield, *The University of Chicago Biographical Sketches, Volume II,* (Chicago: University of Chicago Press, 1925).

Gordon – Gordon, Lyndall, *A Private Life of Henry James: Two Women and His Art,* (New York: W. W. Norton & Co., 1998).

Hall – Hall, Allan N., "St. Paul's School: Its First Hundred Years," *The Classical Journal,* Vol. 51, No. 5 (The Classical Association of the Middle West and South, Inc., Northfield, MN, Feb. 1956).

Hanna – Hanna, Richard E., "National Tropical Botanical Garden Master Plan for Lawai-Kai," Draft Version 2/15/2008.

Harris – Harris, Britta B., *The Oakley Reservoir Mirage: A Case Study in Water Resource Decision Making,* (University of Illinois, Institute of Government and Public Affairs; Institute for Environmental Studies, 1978).

Harrison – Harrison, Mitchell C., *Prominent and Progressive Americans, An Encyclopaedia of Contemporaneous Biography, Volume I,* (*New York Tribune,* The Tribune Association, 1902).

Herbert – Herbert, Robert L., ed., *Modern Artist On Art, Ten Unabridged Essays,* (Prentice-Hall, Inc., Englewood Cliffs, NJ, 1964). Excerpts cited are translations from a 1913 article by Wassily Kandinsky entitled "Reminiscences," published in the Berlin expressionist magazine, *Der Sturm (The Storm).*

HM to JG – Letter from Helen Murphy to John Gregg, (Urbana, IL: University of Illinois Archives).

HM to RA – Letter from Helen Murphy to Robert Allerton, (Urbana, IL: University of Illinois Archives).

Horowitz – Horowitz, Helen Lefkowitz, *Culture & The City, Cultural Philanthropy in Chicago from the 1880s to 1917,* (University Press of Kentucky, 1976).

Host, interview – Transcript of Betty Blackwood Host interview conducted by David Bowman, Anthony Rubano, and Connie Fairchild, Lake Geneva, IL., August 7, 1996,

(Urbana, IL: University of Illinois Archives).

Hoyt – Hoyt, Austin, *Chicago, City of the Century* (WGBH Educational Foundation and Window to the World Communications, Inc., 2003). From transcript of televised program.

JG to HM – Letter from John Gregg (Allerton) to Helen Murphy, (Urbana, IL: University of Illinois Archives).

JG to WK – Letter from John Gregg (Allerton) to Walter Keith, (Urbana, IL: University of Illinois Archives).

JGA Speech – John Gregg Allerton, Speech given to the Honolulu Social Science Association on January 2, 1971, (Urbana, IL: University of Illinois Archives).

Kanter – Kanter, Rob, "Eastern Massasauga Rattlesnakes at Allerton Park," (www.environmentalalmanac.blogspot.com/2005_07_01_archive.html) of July 7, 2005.

Langfield – Langfield, Valerie, *Roger Quilter,* (Suffolk, UK: The Boydell Press, 2002).

Lindsley – Lindsley, George A., "The Allerton Legacy, The Farm Memorial to Samuel W. Allerton and John Phalen," February 1, 1996.

London – London, Jack, "The Kanaka Surf," *Hearst's Magazine,* (New York City), Vol. 31, February 1917, 11, 130-134.

Madsen – Madsen, Axel, *The Marshall Fields,* (Hoboken, NJ: John Wiley & Sons, Inc., 2002).

Marquiss – *Marquiss Community Handbook of Monticello,* (Monticello, IL 1921-22).

McCoole – McCoole, Sinead, *Hazel: A Life of Lady Lavery, 1880-1935,* (The Lilliput Press, Ltd., Dublin, Ireland, 1996).

Mehaffey – Mehaffey, Scott, "The Lost Garden: An Historical Perspective, A Working History Documenting the Chronological Development of a Missing Landmark," (Robert Allerton Park, University of Illinois, 1987, revised, 1988).

Morgan, interview – Jessie Morgan's oral history conducted by Susan Gortner for WILL Radio/Television, Urbana, IL, January 24, 1983 (Monticello, IL: Allerton Public Library Oral History Collection).

Notz – Notz, John K., Jr., "Did 'Success' Spoil Theodore Dreiser or From Dreiser to Yerkes to Cowperwood – a Triple Play," (The Chicago Literary Club, March 13, 2006 – The Cliff Dwellers Club).

Piatt Co. Hwy. Dept. – Piatt County Highway Department records.

Pier – Pier, Arthur Stanwood, *St. Paul's School 1855-1934,* (New York: Charles Scribner's Sons, 1934).

Priebe, Elmer, interview – Transcript of Elmer Priebe oral history conducted by Susan Gortner for WILL Radio/Television, Urbana, IL, February 21, 1983 (Monticello, IL: Allerton Public Library Oral History Collection).

Priebe, Irene, interview – Transcript of Irene Priebe interview conducted by Jessie Morgan, undated, (Urbana, IL: University of Illinois Archives).

Prince – Prince, Sue Ann, *The Old Guard and the Avant-Garde, Modernism in Chicago, 1910-1940,* (Chicago: University of Chicago Press, 1990).

RA to EE – Letter from Robert Allerton to Ellen Emmet.

RA to HM – Letter from Robert Allerton to Helen Murphy, (Urbana, IL: University of Illinois Archives).

RA to GS – Letter from Robert Allerton to Dr. George Stoddard, University President, (Urbana, IL: University of Illinois Archives).

Rand – Rand, Ellen E., *Dear Females,* published by Ellen E. Rand, (New York, 2009).

Rotenstein – Rotenstein, David S. "Hudson River Cowboys: The Origins of Modern Livestock Shipping," *The Hudson Valley Regional Review,* (Poughkeepsie, NY: Volume 19, Number 1).

Rubano – Rubano, Anthony, "Lili Auer's *Girl with the Scarf:* Conservation of a Sculpture at Allerton Park," (Krannert Art Museum and Kinkead Pavilion, University of Illinois at Urbana-Champaign, 1996).

Sasaki Associates and Berg – Sasaki Associates, Inc. and Shary Page Berg, *Cultural Landscape Treatment Plan, Robert Allerton Park, Monticello, Illinois,* (Study prepared for the University of Illinois, 2001, Urbana, IL: University of Illinois Archives).

Scheinman – Scheinman, Muriel, *A Guide to Art at The University of Illinois,* (Urbana IL: University of Illinois Press, 1995).

Sculpture Tour – "Sculpture Tour," undated. Prepared for Robert Allerton Park, University of Illinois at Urbana-Champaign, Library archives.

Shaw – Shaw, Sophia (editor), *The Arts Club of Chicago, The Collection 1916-1996,* (Chicago: The Arts Club of Chicago, 1997).

Small and Smith – Small, Kathleen Edwards and J. Larry Smith, *History of Tulare County and Kings County, California, Vol. II,* (Chicago: The S. J. Clarke Publishing Company, 1926).

Smithsonian – Emmet family papers, 1792-1989 (bulk 1851-1989). Archives of American Art, Smithsonian Institution, Washington, D.C.

Soruika, interview – Transcript of John Gregg Allerton interview conducted by Georgia Soruika, University of Illinois, Champaign, IL, 1971, (Urbana, IL: University of Illinois Archives).

Sparks – Sparks, Dr. Esther, doctoral dissertation: "A Biographic Dictionary of Painters and Sculptors of Illinois, 1808-1945," (Evanston, IL: Northwestern University).

St. Paul's – "St. Paul's School Sesquicentennial Exhibition," Ohrstrom Library and St. Paul's School, Concord NH, 2005.

SWA to RA, KA – Letter from Samuel W. Allerton to his children, May 25, 1878, (Urbana, IL: University of Illinois Archives).

Swinth – Swinth, Kirsten, *Painting Professionals Women Artists and the Development of Modern American Art, 1870-1930,* (Chapel Hill, NC: University of North Carolina Press, 2001).

Tappert – Tappert, Tara Leigh, *The Emmets: A Generation of Gifted Women,* (New York: Borghi & Co., 1993).

Theobald, interview – Transcript of John Gregg Allerton interviews conducted by Dr. William L. Theobald, between June 23 and August 16, 1978, (Urbana, IL: University of Illinois Archives).

Tripp Diary – Entry from diary of Dora Tripp Bartlett. Provided by Bonnet House Museum & Gardens. courtesy of Elisabeth Bartlett Sturges and Eric Bartlett Wentworth, children of Clay Bartlett.

Trowbridge – "Trowbridge & Beals Collection," Drawings and Documents Archive, Ball State University, Muncie Indiana.

UIUC Archives – Archives of the University of Illinois Urbana Champaign.

Walton – Walton, Clyde C., *An Illinois Reader* (DeKalb, IL, Northern Illinois University Press, 1970).

Waterman – Waterman, A. N., ed., *Historical Review of Chicago and Cook County, Vol. 1,* (Chicago: The Lewis Publishing Company, 1908), 471-2.

Wolfmeyer and Gage – Wolfmeyer, Ann and Mary Burns Gage, *Lake Geneva—Newport of the West 1870-1920,* Volume 1, (Lake Geneva, IL: Lake Geneva Historical Society, Inc., 1976).

Young – Young, James E., *The Texture of Memory: Holocaust Memorials and Meaning,* (New Haven, Yale University Press, 1993).

PERIODICALS

American – *The Chicago Daily American,* (Chicago, IL)

Bulletin – *The Monticello Bulletin,* (Monticello, IL)

Courier – *Champaign-Urbana Courier,* (Champaign, IL)

Daily News – *The Chicago Daily News,* (Chicago, IL)

Gazette – *The Champaign News-Gazette,* (Champaign, IL)

Herald-Examiner – *Chicago Herald-Examiner,* (Chicago, IL)

Herald Review – *Herald & Review,* (Decatur, IL)

HBGF Newsletter – Newsletter from Hawaiian Botanical Garden Foundation, Inc, Honolulu, Hawaii

House Beautiful – *House Beautiful,* (Chicago, IL)

IL Magazine – *Illinois Magazine,* (Benton, IL).

IL Steward – *The Illinois Steward Magazine,* University of Illinois at Urbana-Champaign.

Illini – *The Daily Illini,* (Champaign, IL)

Journal-Republican – *Piatt County Journal-Republican,* (Monticello, IL)

LA Times – *Los Angeles Times,* (Los Angeles, CA)

Nature – *Nature of Allerton* newsletter, Allerton Park and Retreat Center, University of Illinois at Urbana-Champaign

NY Times – *The New York Times,* (New York, NY)

Pantagraph – *The Daily Pantagraph,* (Bloomington, IL)

Pilot – *The Piatt County Pilot,* (Monticello, IL)

Republican – *The Piatt County Republican,* (Monticello, IL)

Tribune – *The Chicago Daily Tribune,* (Chicago, IL)

***Tribune*, Mme. X** – *The Chicago Daily Tribune* articles by Madame X (Caroline Kirkland)

Washington Post – *The Washington Post,* (Washington, DC)

ENDNOTES

Chapter One.
The Allertons Help Build America

1 *Tribune*, "Richest Bachelor in Chicago," February 18, 1906, D1.
2 Ibid.
3 Ibid.
4 Ibid.
5 Ibid.
6 Walton, 195. By 1901, Samuel Allerton owned 11,492 acres in Piatt County, Illinois. By 1918 he had purchased an additional 892 acres for a total of 12,384 acres.
7 Allerton, Walter, 13-27.
8 Ibid., 59-62. The nine children were, in order, Cornelia, Amaryllis, Henry, Orville, Amanda, Byron, Rebecca, Lois, Samuel.
9 SWA to RA, KA.
10 Bock, 4.
11 SWA to RA, KA.
12 Allerton, Walter, 84.
13 Allerton Legacy, Bowman, 1-2.
14 *Republican*, "A Successful Farmer," May 17, 1900, 2.
15 *Tribune*, "Samuel Allerton, Pioneer Packer, Taken By Death," February 23, 1914, 4.
16 *Pantagraph*, "Sam Allerton," January 8, 1894, 7.
17 SWA to RA, KA.
18 Allerton, Walter, 85.
19 *Pantagraph*, "Sam Allerton," January 8, 1894, 7.
20 The National Bank Act established a system of national bank charters and encouraged development of a national currency.
21 Gates, 174.
22 Allerton, Walter, 87.
23 Andreas (Cook County), 671.
24 East St. Louis Action Research Project, The IBEX Archive: (www.eslarp.uiuc.edu/ibex/archive/IDOT/idot22.htm).
25 Andreas (Chicago), 704.
26 Ibid.
27 After renumbering the streets, the old address of 644 Michigan Avenue became part of the South 1800 block.
28 Andreas (Chicago), 628.
29 *Piatt County Herald*, "Local Brevities," December 4, 1878, 5.
30 Rotenstein, 12.
31 Robert would later drop usage of "Henry."
32 Azzam and Anderson, 15-16.
33 Ibid., 15.
34 SWA to RA, KA.
35 Ibid.
36 Ibid.
37 Soruika, interview.
38 Politzer Society website, www.politzersociety.org/Adam/Adam4.htm. In 1863 Dr. Adam Politzer (1835-1920) established a clinic in Vienna, the first clinic strictly for treatment of ear diseases. Ten years later he led the University of Vienna's otological clinic at the Wiener Allgemeines Krankenhaus.
39 Soruika, interview.
40 Ibid.
41 Gates, 173-5.
42 *Samuel W. Allerton and His Family*, (Allerton, Illinois Historical Society), 2.
43 *Republican*, "Allerton County, Illinois," August 31, 1899, 3.
44 *Bulletin*, "Wild Cat," April 21, 1893, 4.
45 *Allerton Legacy*, Blair, 3.
46 *Tribune*, "Chicago Farmers Give Tips on Corn," October 4, 1907, 3.
47 Bateman, Selby and Shonkwiler, 695.
48 Lisa Winters, Director of Allerton Library.
49 Notz, 13.
50 *Allerton Legacy*, Blair, 3-4.
51 Dedmon, 136.
52 *Allerton Legacy*, Blair, 3-4.
53 *Republican, April 6, 1893*, 4.
54 *Tribune*, "Real Estate," April 13, 1879, 16. Sam sold the property for $28,000.
55 *Tribune*, "A Private Palace," October 30, 1869, 3. The Allerton's Prairie Avenue home (66x94 feet) was designed by Lavall B. Dixon for Daniel Thompson and built at a cost of $100,000. Rooms included: a library, reception room, parlor, dining room, butler's pantry, china closet, kitchen, laundry room, basement billiard-room, upstairs ballroom, bathrooms, dressing room, four

chambers and three bedrooms with "closets and wash-stands to each," storeroom, attic, and tower. A two-story barn (89x90 feet) with horse stalls, carriage stalls, other rooms, and water-closets cost an estimated $18,000.

56 *Tribune*, Herma Clark, "After 50 Years Prairie Avenue Stirs Again," December 12, 1937, H3.
57 Wolfmeyer, and Gage, 64.
58 Ibid., 65. Henry Lord Gay of San Diego founded the American Institute of Architects.
59 Host, interview.
60 Ibid.
61 Bock, 9.
62 *Republican*, April 20, 1893, 2.
63 *Tribune*, "Matrimonial: Papin-Allerton," November 12, 1885, 8. The First Universalist Church's Rev. J. Coleman Adams performed the ceremony. Kate had no bridesmaids, but approximately twenty-five people attended the wedding at Prairie Avenue. They embarked afterwards on a six-month honeymoon tour of California.
64 *Tribune*, "Dr. Papin's Remains Sent Home," January 7, 1889, 3.
65 Soruika, interview.
66 *Republican*, "S. W. Allerton's Mansion," February 26, 1903, 3, reprinted from the *Los Angeles Times*.
67 Priebe, Elmer, interview.
68 The fact that the wines were highly regarded by experts seems to dispute claims that Agnes didn't tolerate wine being served at the table. But a staff member said that if Robert wanted wine, the butler would have to leave a tray with a bottle and a glass outside Robert's bedroom door.
69 *Daily News*, "Thieves Guests of S. W. Allerton," June 6, 1912, 1.
70 Ibid.
71 *Tribune*, "Women See Robber Held," August 10, 1912, 2.
72 *Tribune*, "Plunder of Chicago's $200,000 Society Burglar," August 5, 1912, 6.
73 Mary ("May") E. Lester was Reinette's step-daughter from her marriage to John T. Lester.
74 A probate affidavit filed by Agnes and Robert estimated Sam's personal estate at $2.5 million and real estate at $1.5 million.

Chapter Two. Robert, Growing Up on Prairie Avenue

1 Priebe, Irene, interview.
2 Bartlett, 4-5.
3 *Tribune*, "Gorgeous Receptions," January 2, 1886, 6.
4 Ibid.
5 *Tribune*, "The Mikado Ball," February 14, 1886, 9.
6 JGA Speech.
7 Soruika, interview.
8 Ibid.
9 JGA Speech.
10 UIUC Archives.
11 Ibid.
12 School of the Art Institute of Chicago. Robert's transcript shows these dates: December 15, 1891, January 19, 1892, March 16, 1892, February 16, 1893 and April 1, 1893. The class was labeled as "E" (Elementary), and the department "AC" (Antique Class). Robert's marks fell between 60-70.
13 Pier, 213.
14 *NY Times*, "What It Costs to Go to Yale," February 4, 1900, 1.
15 Pier, 172-3. The December 1889 issue of *Harper's Young People*, featured an article about the "Vacation Special of St. Paul's School," along with a full-page cartoon.
16 "St. Paul's School Sesquicentennial Exhibition," Ohrstrom Library and St. Paul's School, Concord NH, 2005.
17 Arthur Stanwood Pier (1874-1966) entered St. Paul's School as a third-former (corresponding to ninth grade) in 1887 and graduated in 1890 at age 16.
18 Pier, 11-12.
19 Ibid., 6.
20 Ibid., 19.
21 Priebe, Elmer, interview.
22 Pier, 295-312.
23 Ibid., 98-99.
24 Andover-Harvard Theological Library, Harvard Divinity School website (www.hds.harvard.edu), "Timeline of Significant Events in the Merger of the Unitarian and Universalist Churches During the 1800s."
25 Hall, 203.
26 *Tribune*, "Beware of the Kodak", December 28, 1890, 17.
27 *Tribune*, "Mrs. Mary Pitkin Bartlett," December 20, 1890, 3.
28 *Tribune*, "All Sorts of Equipages There," June 21, 1891, 2.
29 Ibid.
30 *NY Times*, "Opened by the President," May 2, 1893, 1.
31 Illinois Institute of Technology, Paul V. Galvin Library Digital History Collection website (http://columbus.gl.iit.edu/index.html), Paul Barrett, "Introductory Essay: Chicago's Quest for World Status," 1999.
32 Among the architects for the 1893 World's Columbian Exposition were Henry Ives Cobb, Richard Morris Hunt, Charles McKim, George B. Post, Stanford White, and Louis Sullivan. For the landscape design, Burnham enlisted Frederick Law Olmsted of New York City's Central Park fame—a symbolic victory for Chicago.
33 The World's Congresses building, now the Art Institute of Chicago, was designed by Shepley, Rutan, and Coolidge.
34 In 1968 the Art Institute of Chicago renamed its main original building The Robert Allerton Building in honor of his

long-time trusteeship.
35 Bartlett, 4.
36 Dedmon, 222. "Demand for roulette wheels became so great that the ordinary source of supply was inadequate and a new factory was started."
37 Bartlett, 4.

Chapter Three. The Artist's Life

1 *NY Times*, "A Crowded Profession," April 2, 1883, 8. (This article was cited by Kirsten Swinth in *Painting Professionals*.)
2 *NY Times*, Henry I. Kawalsky, "Need of a National Conservatory," August 19, 1900, 8.
3 *NY Times*, "A Crowded Profession," April 2, 1883, 8.
4 Soruika, interview.
5 School of the Art Institute of Chicago.
6 Soruika, interview.
7 Swinth, 40. $1,000 at that time was equivalent in 2007 to $24,000.
8 Bartlett, 7. Frederic's journal was published after his death by his wife, Evelyn Fortune Bartlett. Apparently, the original manuscript from 1932 no longer exists. It is unclear whether Frederic or Evelyn omitted specific names.
9 Soruika, interview and Bartlett, 10. In the Soruika interview, John Gregg Allerton said that the man with whom Robert and Frederic stayed collected armor. Bartlett's journal states that the man's father was an architect. A note found on one of Bartlett's portfolios (with his 1898 Paris address) noted a Herr Rud Kuppelmayr at Schellingstre R.K.B. in Munich. Rudolph Kuppelmayr (1843-1918) fits the description. His father, Max Kuppelmayr, who died 1888, was both a noted collector of armor and an architect.
10 Bartlett, 13.
11 Bartlett, 17.
12 Wassily Kandinsky, "Reminiscences," *Der Sturm*, Berlin, 1913. Excerpts and translations from Robert L. Herbert, *Modern Artist On Art, Ten Unabridged Essays*, (Prentice-Hall, Inc., Englewood Cliffs, NJ, 1964), 36-38.
13 Dora Tripp Bartlett was born October 7, 1879. Her mother, Lucie, was the daughter of New York State Senator Edmund Sutherland.
14 Bartlett, 23.
15 Ibid., 24. Bartlett misspelled Aman-Jean and Colarossi as "Amer Jean" and "Carlo Rossi."
16 *NY Times*, "Special to *The New York Times*," May 25, 1901, 1.
17 Soruika, interview.
18 Ibid.
19 Beatty later earned the title Admiral Sir David Beatty, First Sea Lord, Earl of Brooksby and of the North Sea.
20 Madsen, 126.
21 Ibid., 203-204. Ethel Field was treated by noted psychiatrists Émile Coué and Frank Dengler.
22 Soruika, interview.
23 Ibid.

Chapter Four. Getting in Touch with a Farm Somewhere

1 *Tribune*, Hollis W. Field, "The Multimillionaires of Chicago. IV. Samuel W. Allerton," June 30, 1907, E1.
2 Soruika, interview.
3 Ibid.
4 Ibid.
5 *Tribune*, Hollis W. Field, "The Multimillionaires of Chicago. IV. Samuel W. Allerton," June 30, 1907, E1. Samuel Allerton's timeline of "two or three years" is not completely in accord with Frederic Clay Bartlett's chronology. The year that Robert Allerton destroyed his artwork and returned to America differs in various sources.
6 Waterman, 471-2.
7 Gates, 195.
8 *Journal Republican*, "A Look into the Past," April 8, 1998, 4.
9 UIUC Archives, copy of statement by Adolphe Borie (cousin of John Borie III) to the Hood Museum, Dartmouth College, 1933, and research of Etta Arntzen.
10 *Tribune*, Mme. X, "News of Chicago Society," December 6, 1925, H1.
11 The firm of Walter Cope and John Stewardson is best known for its architecture on the campuses of the University of Pennsylvania, Princeton, and Washington University in St. Louis. Borie is recognized as their sculptor of gargoyles, notably those on the facade of the men's dormitory on the University of Pennsylvania campus.
12 Kent Planck, Bonnet House Museum and Gardens, Fort Lauderdale, FL. Frederic and Dora Tripp were married at Grace Episcopal Church. Frederic's brother, Frank, served as an usher and his sister, Florence, was a bridesmaid. Frederic's father, Adolphus Bartlett, had refused to give Frederic a generous allowance until he could support himself and Dora. He also disapproved of Dora attending art school.
13 In 1898 Frederic lived at 38 Rue Boileau in Paris.
14 Falk and Bien.
15 *Tribune*, Mrs. Papin Wedded in New York," October 22, 1898, 5. (The Rev. Dr. G. C. Houghton of the Church of the Transfiguration officiated at the wedding.)
16 *Bulletin*, "Personal and Social," April 14, 1899, 1.
17 *Bulletin*, "Plain Facts," April 21, 1899, 1. A prominent

paragraph mentioned the groundbreaking for Robert's new "summer resort."

18 *Tribune,* "Among Architects and Builders," May 28, 1899, 38.

19 *Republican,* June 15, 1899, 5.

20 Bedford limestone, found in many buildings such as the Pentagon, the Empire State Building, and the National Cathedral, is prized for its beauty and durability. The town is known as "Limestone Capital of the World."

21 Priebe, Irene, interview. Irene Priebe also said the cornerstone was laid in September, 1899.

22 *Bulletin,* "Narrow Escape," October 20, 1899, page unknown.

23 *Pilot,* "Local Laconics," October 25, 1899, 1.

24 *Republican,* "Wild Cat," November 2, 1899, 8.

25 *Bulletin,* "Nineteen Years Ago," September 13, 1918, 3.

26 *Republican,* "Wild Cat," April 22, 1900, page unknown.

27 *Republican,* "Allerton Summer Resort," April 5, 1900, 3.

28 *Republican,* May 17, 1900, page unknown.

29 *IL Magazine,* David Jeffery Fletcher, "The Building of Allerton Park," May 1979, 11.

30 UIUC Archives, copy of a card announcing "Mr John Borie, Architect, begs to inform you that he has taken an office in the St. James Building, 1133 Broadway. May first 1902."

31 *Bulletin,* "Fine Barn," March 22, 1901, 7.

32 RA to EE, letter of August 27, 1901.

33 Nels Larson's barn, built in 1910, rivaled Robert's stable. He topped it with a 68-foot tower housing a 1.5-ton, four-sided Seth Thomas clock, each face measuring 6 feet. The tower was destroyed in a 1976 storm. The home is listed on the National Register of Historic Places and is rumored to be haunted.

34 RA to EE, 1901 undated letter.

35 JGA, Speech.

Chapter Five.
Interlude: A Visit to "The Farms"

1 *House Beautiful,* "A Modern Farmhouse," April 1904, 260.

2 Charles Nelson Thompson married Caroline Putnam. Their son, Asler Carr Thompson, was Robert's cousin.

3 In 1916 Jessie and William Dighton rebuilt a home at 712 N. State Street into an impressive English Tudor-styled home, complete with a carriage house.

4 *House Beautiful,* "A Modern Farmhouse," April 1904, 260.

5 Soruika, interview.

6 *Republican,* April 11, 1901, page unknown.

7 *Tribune,* Mme. X, " 'The Farms' is Typical of the Larger American Country Estates," October 8, 1911, 9.

8 Scheinman, 105.

9 Trowbridge. 2. Robert Work was an associate of David Adler from 1917-1928.

10 The University of Illinois later removed stone columns from the conservatory to make it more suitable for conferences.

11 *Tribune,* Mme. X, " 'The Farms' is Typical of the Larger American Country Estates," October 8, 1911, 9.

12 Becker, interview, 21.

13 *Gazette,* Lex Peterson, "Adopted Son Says Park Looking Better," March 30, 1980, A6.

14 Becker, interview, 5.

15 In 1895 Oscar Wilde was convicted of having committed "acts of gross indecency." He died in 1900 after serving two years in prison. His neighborhood in Chelsea was home to many artists associated with Robert's circle of friends: James McNeill Whistler, John Singer Sargent, Glyn Philpot, Roger Quilter, and Jane and Wilfred de Glehn.

16 Sasaki Associates and Berg, III-24.

17 Ibid., III-32.

18 Made of a soft material and damaged by weather, the sculptures are in storage as of 2009 with no immediate plans for their restoration.

19 Scheinman, 120. Scheinman dates the sculptures according to the opinion of John Gregg Allerton.

20 Ibid., 103.

21 Ibid., 113. John Gregg could not say where the prototypes were acquired.

22 Sasaki Associates and Berg, III-40.

23 Soruika, interview.

24 Sasaki Associates and Berg, III-37.

25 Scheinman, 98.

26 Sasaki Associates and Berg, III-57.

27 Soruika, interview.

28 Sasaki Associates and Berg, III-66.

29 Scheinman, 122.

30 Sasaki Associates and Berg, III-64.

31 Ibid., III-13, III-14.

Chapter Six.
A Time for Romance

1 *Tribune,* "In the Society World, Lent Leaves Little But the Theater to Supply Gayety," March 17, 1901, 38.

2 Marshall Field, Jr. died of a gunshot wound in November 1905, supposedly as he cleaned his weapon at home. Others claim it occurred during a night at the famous Everleigh bordello in Chicago.

3 *Tribune,* "In the Society World, Mr. and Mrs. A. N. Eddy Give a Unique Entertainment," March 20, 1901, 16.

4 *Tribune,* "In the Society World,

Prospect of Easter Gayety Brightens the Season," March 24, 1901, 38.

5 Beveridge and Radomsky, 68.

6 *Tribune*, "Calm After the Social Storm - Weekend Parties at Lake Geneva - Allerton's Rare Costumes," May 10, 1914, F1.

7 We assume "Mrs. Birch" to have been Maria Root Birch, wife of Hugh Birch. Their daughter, Helen Birch, would eventually become Frederic Clay Bartlett's second wife.

8 *Tribune*, "In the Society World, Prospect of Easter Gayety Brightens the Season," March 24, 1901, 38.

9 Becker, interview, 14.

10 Tappert, 38. *Harper's Bazar* was the original spelling of the magazine's name, later changed to *Harper's Bazaar*.

11 Rand.

12 Ibid., 40.

13 Ellen's address was 96 Boulevard Montparnasse in Montmartre. In her letters she refers to the street as Mt. Parnasse.

14 Gordon, 298-300. Gordon postulated that Henry James, thirty-two years Ellen's senior, saw great resemblance between Ellen Emmet and her aunt, Minny Temple, who died in 1847. Minny Temple inspired the character "Milly" in James' *The Wings of the Dove*, published in 1902.

15 Tappert, 40.

16 Ibid., 41. Tappert locates Ellen Emmet's apartment at the corner of South Washington Square and West Broadway, #64. Another apartment, as of 1909, is listed at #62, according to *NY Times*, "In the Real Estate Field," October 22, 1909, 12.

17 Soruika, interview.

18 EE to Leslie, date unknown.

19 RA to EE, letter of May 11, 1901.

20 RA to EE, letter of June 23, 1901.

21 RA to EE, letter of July 15, 1901.

22 RA to EE, letter of September 26, 1901.

23 RA to EE, letter of July 31, 1901.

24 RA to EE, letter of August 26, 1901.

25 RA to EE, letter of July 31, 1901.

26 RA to EE, letter of August 24, 1901.

27 Anecdote provided by Peter Rand, Ellen Emmet Rand's grandson on January 21, 2009.

28 EE to Leslie, date unknown.

29 Becker, interview, 13. A third portrait has sometimes been attributed to her, that of Mrs. Anna Rathbone. However, John Gregg Allerton thought that a friend or sister of Ellen's (who also visited at that time) may have painted Mrs. Rathbone's portrait. Ellen Emmet's granddaughter stated that the painting did not appear to be Ellen Emmet's work.

30 Rand, interview.

31 *NY Times*, "Miss Hanna a Bride," June 11, 1903, 9.

32 *Washington Post*, "Actress Causes Discord," August 16, 1903, 1.

33 *Tribune*, "Brilliant Array of People in Boxes at the Coliseum," October 24, 1905, 2.

34 Smithsonian, Julia Emmet (mother) to Jane Emmet von Glehn, November 8, 1905.

35 Smithsonian, Julia Emmet (mother) to Jane Emmet von Glehn, November 27, 1905.

36 The family changed their name to a non-Germanic sounding "de Glehn" after World War I commenced.

37 Smithsonian, Russell Hewlett to Jane Emmet von Glehn, December 1, 1905.

38 Becker, interview, 10. They came away with many pieces of very high quality. Some went to furnish the house; others were eventually either donated to the Art Institute or auctioned with the mansion contents.

39 Smithsonian, Julia Emmet (mother) to Jane Emmet von Glehn, November 29, 1905.

40 *Tribune*, "Richest Bachelor in Chicago," February 18, 1906, D1.

41 Ibid.

42 *Tribune*, "Matrimonial Chances for Chicago Girls," April 14, 1907, F3.

43 Frederic Clay Bartlett, Jr. was born on November 21, 1907, the result of a second pregnancy. Dora and Frederic first became parents to twins in 1906, but both children died and are buried at Chicago's Graceland Cemetery: a boy named Clay and a girl named Mary.

44 Smithsonian, Julia Emmet (mother) to Jane Emmet von Glehn, January 2, 1907.

45 Smithsonian, Jane Emmet von Glehn to Mrs. W. J. (Julia) Emmet (mother), January (undated) 1907.

46 Smithsonian, Jane Emmet von Glehn to Mrs. W. J. (Julia) Emmet (mother), February 2, 1907.

47 Smithsonian, Julia Emmet (mother) to Jane Emmet von Glehn, February 8, 1907.

Chapter Seven. Love and Loss

1 Thoreau, Henry David and Jeffrey S. Cramer, *I to Myself: An Annotated Selection from the Journal of Henry D. Thoreau*, (Yale University Press, 2007), 12.

2 Becker, interview, 17.

3 *NY Times*, "Costume Carnival in Artist's Studio," January 19, 1908, 11.

4 Soruika, interview.

5 Ibid.

6 Ibid.

7 Ibid.

8 Allerton Legacy, Priebe.

9 Becker, interview, 13. According to the Theobald interview, each guestbook covered two years.

10 Bock, 9.
11 *Tribune*, Mme. X, "News of the Society World," August 28, 1910, B9.
12 *NY Times*, "In the World of Fashion," January 15, 1911, X7.
13 *Tribune*, "Society, Clubs, Entertainments," January 11, 1911, 8. Henrietta Alice McCrea, daughter of Mr. and Mrs. W. S. McCrea (Reinette Thompson Lester McCrea), married the day before.
14 Passenger records of The Statue of Liberty-Ellis Island Foundation, Inc. (The *Lusitania* was torpedoed on May 7, 1915 by a German submarine during the First World War. It sank off the Irish coast, killing almost 1200 of the almost 2000 people aboard. This helped turn many people against Germany.)
15 *NY Times*, "Miss Ellen Emmet a Bride," May 7, 1911, 11.
16 *Tribune*, Mme. X, "Recent Activities in the Society World," May 7, 1911, 9.
17 Bock, 22.
18 Soruika, interview.
19 Langfield, 35. Letter from Roger Quilter to Percy Grainger, February 25, 1911.
20 Robert Allerton to Roger Quilter, February 23, 1911, Roger Quilter Papers, British Library, London. Add MS 70602 f85. Transcription provided by Valerie Langfield, author of *Roger Quilter*. Three years later the "Susie Metcalf" mentioned in this letter married Pablo Casals.
21 Langfield, 36. In email between Ms. Langfield and this book's author, Ms. Langfield mentioned the name of Mark Raphael as the acquaintance and Roger Raphael as the son.
22 *NY Times*, "Big Crowd Sails To-Day," January 24, 1912, 8.
23 *Bulletin*, January 19, 1912, 3.
24 *Tribune*, "Society and Entertainments," July 9, 1912, 10.
25 *Tribune*, Mme. X, "Events in Society Circles," December 24, 1911, 12.
26 He returned home on the *Mauretania* on April 19.
27 *Tribune*, Mme. X, "News of the Society World," September 21, 1913, E2.
28 Delaney, 19.
29 Ibid., 1. Glyn's mother was Jesse Carpenter. After her death, her husband, John Philpot, married her half-sister, Julia Carpenter.
30 Ibid., 36. Citing correspondence from Glyn Philpot to his sister, Daisy Philpot, dated August 26, 1913.
31 Ibid., 36. Citing correspondence from Glyn Philpot to his sister, Daisy Philpot, dated August, 1913.
32 Ibid., 36. Citing correspondence from Glyn Philpot to his sister, Daisy Philpot, dated August, 1913.
33 Ibid., 36. Citing correspondence from Glyn Philpot to his sister, Daisy Philpot, dated September 16, 1913.
34 *Tribune*, Mme. X, "News of the Society World," September 21, 1913, E2.
35 Delaney, 37. Delaney quotes correspondence from Glyn Philpot to his sister, Daisy Philpot, dated October 8, 1913. The gag gifts included " 'a most gaudy artificial buttonhole,' a nearly empty packet of Lavasol for the bath, and a 'pencil in a sort of hygienic ventilated case'."
36 Ibid., 37. Citing correspondence from Glyn Philpot to his sister, Daisy Philpot, dated c. October 22, 1913.
37 Ibid., 37.
38 *Tribune*, Cinderella, "Winter Wanderers Drift Chicagowards," May 17, 1916, 19. Tate Gallery was constructed as a branch of the National Gallery in 1890, originally called the National Gallery, Millbank. In 1954 Tate Gallery became an independent institution, where Philpot's *The Man in Black* is included in the permanent collection. It was purchased for presentation to Tate in the autumn of 1914.
39 Delaney, 38. Delaney incorrectly said the portrait was most likely of Annie Lawrie McBirney.
40 John Borie's sister Emily was married to Arthur Ryserson, who died on the *Titanic*. Isabelle's sister, Annie Lawrie McBirney, was married to Arthur Ryerson's brother, Joseph T. Ryerson.
41 *NY Times*, "C. Russell Hewlett Dies," November 12, 1913, 9.
42 Tripp diary, entry of Friday, November 14, 1913.
43 Tripp diary, entry of Friday, November 29, 1913.
44 According to a statement to the authors from John P. Delaney.
45 Soruika, interview. Author's note: Robert avoided cold weather in the winter and would hardly have chosen Moscow as a vacation spot in February. Tahiti was more his style.
46 Robert Allerton to Roger Quilter, February (undated) 1914, Roger Quilter Papers, British Library, London. Add MS 70602 f146. Transcription provided by Valerie Langfield, author of *Roger Quilter*.
47 *Tribune*, Mme. X, "Comment by Mme. X," March 1, 1914, D2.
48 Tripp diary, entry of Sunday, March 8, 1914.
49 Tripp diary, entry for March 10, 1914.
50 *Tribune*, "S.W. Allerton Funeral Held," March 15, 1914, 8. According to Sam's will, the Imperial Quartet was paid $30 to sing at the burial. Other payments listed in the will included $128 to the undertaker, J. W. Buffum, and

$25 to Rev. White for the funeral service. Kate's address listed in the will was 703 S. Pasadena Avenue, Pasadena. California.

Chapter Eight. Wealth and Responsibility

1 *Tribune*, "Samuel W. Allerton Will Disposes of $4,000,000 Estate," April 23, 1913, 15. The article stated that the total included two and one half million dollars worth of personal property. C. A. Martyn was paid five thousand dollars for settling the estate. (It is unclear whether he was related to Hazel Martyn's family.)
2 Soruika, interview.
3 Julia Moynihan received twenty shares in the Omaha Union Stockyards.
4 *Tribune*, "Raze Old South Side Home to Make Room for Factory," September 16, 1915, 3. The factory was designed by Alfred S. Alschuler. With the sale of the property, the address changed to 1918 Prairie Avenue. Years later, condos replaced the razed hairpin factory.
5 Gilbert and Bryson, 915.
6 *Bulletin*, "Board of Supervisors," May 15, 1903, 1. The pledges were to be collected only after a sum of $25,000 had been expended upon the courthouse's construction.
7 Marquiss, 49. The Community House, located at 200 South Charter Street, officially opened on August 12, 1921. Robert Allerton purchased it from the family of Dr. W. B. Caldwell.
8 Before Allerton Public Library became tax-supported in 1919, it was funded by income from an 800-seat opera house located within Township Hall. After the opera house closed, the building was renovated to allow the Library to move into that space. Robert paid to refurnish the original Library space, renaming it the Garden Room.
9 Priebe, Elmer, interview.
10 Allerton Legacy, Priebe.
11 Piatt County Highway Department. Ownership of the western section of the road was transferred from the State of Illinois to Piatt County in 1981, at which time the brick paving was resurfaced. The eastern section was transferred to the City of Monticello in 1988.
12 JG to WK. Date of construction noted in June 12, 1978.
13 Bateman, Selby, and Shonkwiler, 705.
14 *Gazette*, Tom Kacich, "Lodge Family," July 13, 2003, B-3. Other prominent Piatt County citizens (with names such as England, Dilatush, Burgess, Kratz, Lodge, Phalen, Kirby, Moore, Hott, Mackey, Bumstead, Noecker, and Knott) also helped cover the cost, giving between $100 to $1,000.
15 Soruika, interview.
16 "Robert Allerton Trust Fund," (after Dr. Chislett's death in 1931, the fund name was changed to "Howard R. Chislett Memorial Fund"), Northwestern Memorial Hospital. Information provided by Susan Sacharski, Archivist.
17 Hahnemann's Executive Committee named him honorary trustee in 1953. Later the hospital became known as Chicago Memorial Hospital. In 1954 that hospital closed and its medical staff and endowments merged with Wesley Memorial, becoming Chicago Wesley Memorial Hospital, eventually becoming Northwestern Memorial.
18 *Tribune*, "Allerton Gift is Accepted by Piatt County, August 3, 1919, 15.
19 *Tribune*, "Phthisis Foe," July 31, 1919, 8.
20 Lindsley, 1, 2.
21 Ibid. The agreement required a five-person Board, comprised of Robert and four others whom he appointed: William Dighton, William F. Lodge. Elizabeth Phalen, and Farm Advisor for the Piatt County Farm Bureau (Arthur E. Burwash). The 1,200 acres were to be conveyed to the Trustees (not to Piatt County itself), with much of the land to be farmed following the most approved methods, and managed by the Farm Advisor. Farm income would support the farm, and surplus would be used for the Old Peoples' Home.
22 In April 2009 the Goose Creek Township Carnegie Library announced plans to relocate to another building in Deland.
23 *Bulletin*, October 4, 1928, page unknown.
24 Allerton Lib., author unknown.
25 *Tribune*, "Red Cross Contributions," June 25, 1917, 2.
26 *Republican*, "Allerton Gives Crops," May 10, 1917, 1.
27 *Republican*, "Red Cross War Fund," July 5, 1917, 1.
28 UIUC Archives. Undated, unsigned notes, possibly by Jessie Morgan.
29 *Tribune*, "Charity Bazaar Swells Tobacco Fund for Troops," October 14, 1917, 5.
30 *Tribune*, "Robert Allerton Gives Ambulance to the Army," January 28, 1918, 14.
31 *Tribune*, "Less than $250 Needed Now for the First Ambulance," October 19, 1917, 12.
32 *Tribune*, "Hospital in France to Commemorate 'Coty' Campbell," February 3, 1918, C4.
33 *Bulletin*, September 13, 1918, page unknown.
34 *Tribune*, "Robert Allerton Quits

Hospital; Poison Denied," October 24, 1918, 13.

35 *Bulletin,* October 25, 1918, page unknown.
36 It is unclear whether his first name may actually have been Reinhardt, and misspelled by the census-taker.
37 Becker, interview, 19. Robert fired Gollop in 1921, the same year that Glyn Philpot made his second visit to the Farms, accompanied by Vivian Forbes. Robert paid Gollop a "salary" (Gollop's family members speculated it was hush money) until Gollop died.
38 Cackett.
39 Gale, interview.
40 Becker, interview, 19.
41 Priebe, Elmer, interview. Also, Becker, interview, 19.
42 Gale, interview.
43 Allerton Legacy, Priebe.
44 Shonkwiler, interview.
45 Priebe, Elmer, interview.
46 Ibid.
47 Irene Priebe married Elmer on December 23, 1947 and died in an automobile accident on December 18, 1966.
48 Allerton Legacy, Priebe.
49 Ibid.
50 Gale, interview.
51 Vaughn, interview and Shonkwiler, interview.
52 Becker, interview, 20.
53 Ibid.
54 Note signed by E. Taflan, October, 12, 1989.
55 *Bulletin,* "Wild Cat," August 26, 1904, 8.
56 Gale, interview, follow-up conversation.

Chapter Nine. Myths and Misperceptions

1 *Tribune,* "Beast Seen 200 Miles from Point of Attack Last Friday," July 15, 1917, 1.
2 The two commanders were Captain Herbert Walsh and Lieutenant J. M. Donahue.
3 *Tribune,* "Lion Hunter Fires at Auto's Gleaming Eyes," July 16, 1917, 1.
4 *Republican,* "Lioness Brings Monticello Much Publicity," July 19, 1917, 1.
5 *Tribune,* "T. R. Urged to Aid Lion Hunt,", July 18, 1917, 13.
6 *Tribune,* "A Line O' Type or Two," July 19, 1917, 6.
7 *LA Times,* "Lure of the Mate," July 17, 1917, 12.
8 *Washington Post,* "An Illinois Lion Hunt," July 24, 1917, 6.
9 *Tribune,* "Allerton's Lion and Dog Fight Until Both Die," July 21, 1917, 1.
10 Buckingham, interview.
11 Vaughn, interview.
12 Allerton Lib., author unknown. Archive files mention that Stanley Gollop, while well-liked and reserved, had been fired for stealing money from Robert. No substantiation can be found other than an email from a distant relation of another servant.
13 Allerton Legacy, Priebe.
14 *Bulletin,* "Poking Fun at Our Lion," July 27, 1917, 1.
15 Vaughn, interview. An article in *The Monticello Bulletin* of August 1, 1935 also noted that the caretaker, Charles Fulk, had captured a two-and-a-half-foot long rattler, with six rattles. This had been his second snake capture in the month.
16 Vaughn, interview.
17 Kanter.
18 Shonkwiler, interview.
19 Small and Smith, 401-2.
20 Priebe, Elmer, interview.
21 Small and Smith, 402.
22 London, page unknown.
23 Becker, interview, 21. Robert wasn't home at the time of the Pons and Smith visit.
24 Baker, 375.
25 Becker, interview, 18.
26 Priebe, Elmer, interview. Page 1 of *The Monticello Bulletin* of Friday, August 26, 1904 reported that Mr. Bryan spoke at the "Twin City" Chautauqua on the previous Sunday.

Chapter Ten. The Arts Go Hog Wild

1 Hoyt.
2 The original Columbian Museum of Chicago in Jackson Park changed its name to the Field Museum of Natural History in 1905. For sixteen more years the Field Museum remained in the Palace of Fine Arts, but finally relocated to its present building near downtown in 1921. After the Field Museum moved out, the Palace of Fine Arts fell into decline, but was renovated from 1926-1933 as a home for the Museum of Science and Industry.
3 The John Crerar Library was opened to the public in 1897.
4 The Newberry Library was founded in 1887, but moved to its location across the street from Washington Square Park in 1893.
5 Organized in 1890, Orchestra Hall was dedicated in 1904.
6 The University of Chicago formally opened in 1892.
7 Hoyt.
8 Joel S. Dryer, "The Story You Don't Know About a Place We All Love," speech delivered to the Chicago Literary Club, May 14, 2001. The once promising Chicago Academy of Fine Art never fully recovered from the Chicago Fire of 1871. Housed in leased quarters, a new board of trustees was appointed, comprised of businessmen rather than artists. Through questionable and circuitous financial transactions, the Academy and its tax-free charter were transferred to what would become the Art Institute of Chicago.
9 Prince, 173.
10 Donnell, 1. Quoted from a 1902 interview of Frederic

Clay Bartlett by an unnamed reporter.

11 Frederic built Dorfred House—since torn down—two doors down from his father's house on Prairie Avenue. *House Beautiful* magazine featured it in a 1902 issue.

12 *Tribune*, "The Most Wonderful House in Chicago," March 11, 1906, F1.

13 Adolphus Bartlett is best known for his donation of the Frank Dickinson Bartlett Gymnasium to the University of Chicago, a memorial to his son who died in 1900. Frederic decorated the interior of the building with his murals. Adolphus Bartlett's other donations to Chicago institutions are quite extensive.

14 Piatt, interview. The story was told to him by Elmer Priebe, Robert Allerton's chauffeur.

15 Horowitz, 52. Horowitz described Benjamin Hutchinson: "Hard driving, hard-drinking, he was an extreme example of the aggressive, single-minded businessman of the Gilded Age." Benjamin Hutchinson served as director of the First National Bank for four years.

16 Horowitz, 53.

17 Goodspeed, 31.

18 Ibid., 33. Hutchinson served as president of St. Paul's Universalist Church and presided four times at the Universalist National Convention. Through his efforts and influence, St. Paul's relocated "from the heart of what had become the colored district at Thirteenth Street and Prairie Avenue to Dorchester Avenue and Sixtieth Street, and became St. Paul's on the Midway."

19 Adolphus Bartlett's Lake Geneva summer home, named "The House in the Woods," was built in 1906. Frederic worked with architect Howard Van Doren Shaw on its design.

20 Bock, 16. Bock lists John Muir, who founded the Sierra Club in 1892, among Robert Allerton's visitors to The Farms. Theodore Roosevelt doubled the number of national parks from five to ten.

21 Horowitz, 51.

22 Goodspeed, 38. Among his many positions, Hutchinson served an original trustee of the University of Chicago, trustee of the Chicago Symphony Orchestra, and treasurer of Rush Medical College.

23 Prince, 199.

24 Ibid., 188. Prince cites a letter from Bartlett to Robert B. Harshe, July 12, 1933, Archives of the Art Institute of Chicago.

25 *Tribune*, "Cliff Dwellers in Chicago," November 7, 1907, 8. First called The Attic Club, the group renamed itself in 1909.

26 Horowitz, 171.

27 Daniel Chester French, James Whitcomb Riley, and Otis Skinner were honorary Cliff Dwellers members.

28 Shaw, "A Collection to Remember," 21-30. The Arts Club's first headquartered on the fifth floor of the Fine Arts Building at 410-12 S. Michigan Avenue. It moved to several other locations on Michigan Avenue until 1951, when Ludwig Mies van der Rohe designed a new headquarters at 109 E. Ontario Street. That building was crumbling by the 1990s, so the Arts Club moved temporarily to 222 W. Superior Street. Finally in 1996, they purchased 201 E. Ontario St.

29 *Tribune*, Mme. X, "New Year Greeted by Gay Parties at Home and Club," January 5, 1919, C4.

30 *Tribune*, "Mrs. George E. Marcy Hostess at Tea for Members of W.A.C.," May 16, 1924, 23.

31 Shaw, "A Collection to Remember," 22.

32 *Tribune*, Jeff Lyon, "State of the Art," October 12, 1986, 110.

33 John K. Notz, Jr., " 'The Ineffective Hand of the Dead' or 'The Crane Siblings' Support of The Arts'," (http://www.chilit.org/, The Chicago Literary Club, February 23, 2004); Rudolf A. Bernatschke and Cathalene Crane Bernatschke v. the United States, United States Court of Claims. - 364 F.2d 400; and *NYT*, "Deaths, Cathalene Crane," January 6, 2005.

34 *Tribune*, Mme. X, "Warmer Climes Begin to Lure the Snow Bound," January 6, 1918, C4; and *Tribune*, Mme. X, "News of Chicago Society," January 13, 1918, C4.

35 *Tribune*, Eleanor Jewett, "Flaxman Drawings Shown in Setting of Period They Depict," January 16, 1919, 14.

36 *Tribune*, "Directors' Board is Named for the Opera," December 11, 1918, 18.

37 *Tribune*, Mme. X, "Comment," March 30, 1919, C2.

38 *Tribune*, Mme. X, "News of Chicago Society," December 2, 1912, G1.

39 *Tribune*, Mme. X, "News of Chicago Society," September 12, 1926, G1.

40 *Tribune*, Mme. X, "News of Chicago Society," October 19, 1924, F1.

41 Robert also belonged to two New York City clubs, The Racquet and the Coffee House.

Chapter Eleven.
One for Me, One for You

1 Yeats, William B., *The Wild Swans at Coole*, (New York: The Macmillan Company, 1919), 14.

2 Reinette Thompson (1855-1916) first married Frank Bruce, then John T. Lester, and finally Wiley S. McCrea.

3 Soruika, interview.

4 Scheinman, 123.
5 Mehaffey, 3.
6 Ibid.
7 Becker, interview, 18.
8 Soruika, interview.
9 "Sculpture Tour," undated. Prepared for Robert Allerton Park, UIUC. UIUC Library archives. The *Shepherd* is a 1985 replacement from the original molds.
10 Wolfmeyer and Gage, 62-63. Frederic used his father's Lake Geneva house, complete with a heated studio for Frederic, whenever he chose. The house was sold in 1923 to a Chicago realtor named—by very odd coincidence—Frederick H. Bartlett. They were not related.
11 Tripp diary, entry for June 3, 1916.
12 Their new home was an apartment at 131 East 66th Street.
13 Tripp diary, entry for January 12, 1917.
14 *Tribune*, Mme. X, "Comment by Mme. X.," February 18, 1917, C2.
15 *Tribune*, "Mrs. F. C. Bartlett," March 4, 1917, 15.
16 *Tribune*, "Obituary," July 28, 1900, 8.
17 Helen's address in Boston was 22 Marlborough St.
18 *Tribune*, Mme. X, "Comment by Mme. X," January 26, 1919, E5.
19 Horowitz, 67.
20 Unknown newspaper clipping dated June 13, 1922. Art Institute of Chicago, *Scrapbook, Volume 43*, 113.
21 Today run by the Florida Trust for Historic Preservation, Bonnet House is open to the public for a fee.
22 Gale, interview. The $5 is equivalent in 2007 money to $63.
23 In February 4, 1990 letter to Mr. William Laing, Etta Arntzen identified the sculptor as Charles Laing. She identified the *Obelisks*, the *Hari-Hara*, the first copy of *Adam*, and the *Assyrian Lions* also as his work. Laing came to Chicago from Scotland in 1905 and started the Laing and Lind Monument Co., which later became the Laing & Sons Granite Co. He also produced work for the Art Institute of Chicago and the Chicago Park District.
24 Gale, interview. This comment was recalled by Ted Page's son-in-law, Robert Gale.
25 Delaney, 70.
26 *Tribune*, Eleanor Jewett, "Institute Reports Largest Physical Growth of Record," January 20, 1924, E10.
27 Soruika, interview.
28 Scheinman, 119.
29 *Tribune*, "Mrs. Allerton in Auto Crash," May 12, 1910, 3.
30 *Tribune*, "S. W. Allerton's Widow Victim of Long Illness," December 20, 1924, 12.
31 *LA Times*, "Rich Widow Remember Pasadenans," December 28, 1924, F6.
32 *Tribune*, "Mrs. Allerton's Will Disposes of $2,000,000," December 28, 1924, 17; Agnes Allerton's will, UIUC Archives.
33 Soruika, interview.
34 Ibid.
35 Ibid.

Chapter Twelve. Father and Son

1 JGA Speech.
2 Illinois Field was constrained by its location along Wright Street between University and Springfield Avenues.
3 Another Zeta Psi fraternity brother, a year behind Gregg, was the famous Harold "Red" Grange, also known as "The Galloping Ghost."
4 Becker, interview, 17.
5 Accounts differ whether John Wyatt Gregg was 16 or 18 when his mother died.
6 Becker, interview, 2.
7 Ibid., 3.
8 Soruika, interview. Gregg and Asler shared apartments together over several years.
9 Becker, interview, 1.
10 JGA Speech.
11 *Illini*, "Arch Society Elects Gregg Vice-President," October 9, 1924, 2.
12 *Illini*, "Arch Fete Brings Bit of Russia to Campus," March 20, 1926, 1.
13 Soruika, interview.
14 John Gregg's license, number 2058, cost an initial $5, with a $1 per year renewal fee.
15 Soruika, interview.
16 John Gregg's professor was Professor Pickering.
17 Soruika, interview.
18 Becker, interview, 3.
19 Ibid.
20 Ibid.
21 *Gazette*, Lex Peterson, "Adopted Son Says Park Looking Better," March 30, 1980, A6.
22 Soruika, interview.

Chapter Thirteen. Through Art, Life Endures

1 The title of Quilter's song was taken from the title of a Shelley poem.
2 Dwight, Eleanor, *The Letters of Pauline Palmer: A Great Lady of Chicago's First Family*, (Chicago: M. T. Train/Scala Books, 2005), 241-242. Letter from Pauline Palmer to her mother, dated October 26, 1925.
3 www.bonnethouse.org/pdf/LifeGift.pdf
4 Helen Birch Bartlett, *Capricious Winds*, (Boston and New York: Houghton Mifflin Company, 1927), xviii. Quoted from the introductory appreciation entitled "The Poetry of Helen Birch Bartlett," by Harriet Monroe.
5 Donnell, 14.
6 Robert Allerton served as Vice President of the Art Institute of Chicago from 1925-1949.

7 *Tribune*, "Days's News in Society," March 16, 1925, 23.
8 *Herald-Examiner*, The Dowager, "Honors His Mother in Needle Art," January 16, 1928, page unknown.
9 *Tribune*, Edith Weigle, "Art Institute to Pay Tribute to Allerton; Patron to be Named Honorary President," October 22, 1956.
10 Becker, interview, 6.
11 *Tribune*, Mme. X, "News of Chicago Society," May 29, 1927, H1.
12 Becker, interview, 6.
13 *Bulletin*, "Miss Allerton Dies," April 15, 1926, 1.

Chapter Fourteen. Feathering His Nests

1 Soruika, interview.
2 Sasaki Associates and Berg, III-89.
3 Art Institute of Chicago, *General Catalogue of Sculpture, Paintings & Other Objects*, (Art Institute of Chicago, 1910), 31.
4 Becker, interview, 5.
5 Scheinman, 125.
6 Becker, interview, 5.
7 Sasaki Associates and Berg, III-72.
8 *Tribune*, Mme. X, "Age of Large Mansions is Passing Away: Plan New Co-Op," December 16, 1928, 12.
9 *Tribune*, Mme. X, "Chicagoans Engage in Interchange of Domiciles," October 13, 1929, I1. Also *Tribune*, Mme. X, "News of Chicago Society," February 29, 1929, H1.
10 Frederic's apartment on the entire second floor covered 3300 square feet. He painted a trompe-l'oeil mural, an homage to painter Giorgio De Chirico, on the dining room walls where it can still be seen. In the 1980s the film critic, Gene Siskel, owned the apartment and allowed it to be photographed for the October 1989 *Architectural Digest*. As of 2008 the Bartlett apartment was still available for purchase at the price of almost $2 million.
11 Priebe, Elmer, interview.
12 Ibid.
13 Ibid.
14 *Tribune*, "Stock Quote," December 3, 1936, 39.
15 Becker, interview, 16.

Chapter Fifteen. Masterpieces for the Gardens

1 Robert Penn Warren, *Promises: Poems 1954-1956* (Random House, 1957), 32.
2 Soruika, interview. At one point in the interview John Gregg stated that Robert first had a site in mind and then sought the sculpture. Later in the interview, he said the opposite.
3 In an August 29, 1977 letter from John Gregg to Walter Keith of the University of Illinois, John wrote that Par Danforth (Allerton Park Director at that time) had visited Madame Bourdelle in Paris in 1952 at #6 Avenue du Maine. During his visit Danforth learned that another casting of the statue had been made for Bourdelle's birthplace of Montuban, France. As indicated by the mark near Bourdelle's signature, the Alexis Rudier Foundry, located in Paris, cast the sculpture.
4 Soruika, interview. Gregg stated that architect David Adler copied the Art Institute's urns for the William Klaus home in Lake Forest, IL. The transcription appears to be in error, the client almost certainly being William E. Clow. A client of David Adler in 1927, Clow was a plumbing manufacturer and author of a 1938 self-published autobiography entitled *My Sixty Years in the Cast Iron Pipe Buisness*. John Gregg said that Robert ordered four urns for himself while they were being cast at Clow's foundry (although, each of the eight pylons supported an urn).
5 Soruika, interview.
6 Young, 37-38.
7 Scheinman, 110.
8 Becker, interview, 7-8. John Holabird bought Milles' *Diana* statue for 540 N. Michigan Avenue in Chicago. It stands today on the west side of the Illini Union building on the University of Illinois Urbana-Champaign campus, a gift of the Class of 1921.
9 Carl Milles (1875-1955), began his career as a decorative woodworker before his art studies in Paris. He came to Cranbrook Educational Community in Bloomfield Hills, Michigan as a sculptor in residence in 1931. Much of his work is exhibited there, throughout the United States, and at his studio, Millesgården, in Lidingö, Sweden.
10 Art Institute of Chicago, news release, June 16, 1945, announcing an exhibition "in celebration of the 70th birthday of Swedish sculptor Carl Milles, showing works lent by Chicago collectors and the artist, featuring *Triton Fountain* donated to AIC in 1930 by A. I. Appleton, V. Bendix, C. E. Carson, E. G. Grundstrom, H. Hedman, A. Lindstrom, C. S. Peterson, J. P. Seeberg, N. Shoan, E. P. Strandberg, F. A. Thulin, and R. Wilson."
11 Becker, interview, 9.
12 Soruika, interview.
13 Ibid.
14 Ibid.
15 Millesgåården website, www.carlmilles.com
16 Scheinman, 130.
17 Ibid., 133.
18 Ibid., 133.
19 Becker, interview, 10.

20 Scheinman, 136.
21 Sasaki Associates and Berg, III-98.
22 Scheinman, 132. The green *Fu Dog* shattered during an attempted theft and then further suffered a poor restoration.
23 Sasaki Associates and Berg, III-16.
24 Mehaffey, 7. *Diana* was later moved to the Seasonal Gardens, and then sent to Robert's estate at Lawai-Kai. The marble *Faun* was later severely damaged.
25 *Tribune*, Cousin Eve, "Mrs. Bradley Didn't Mean to Rattle Skeltons," December 17, 1933, E1. Also, *Tribune*, June Provines, "Front Views and Profiles," January 1, 1935, 31 and *Tribune*, Ruth DeYoung, "Cruise to Call at Lonely Isles in South Atlantic," January 16, 1935, 17.
26 Mehaffey, 5. Francis Brooks was responsible for other woodworking projects at The Farms. He also operated the projector at Monticello's movie house, the Lyric Theater.
27 Allerton Legacy, JGA.

Chapter Sixteen. Death in the Family

1 *LA Times*, "Fall is Fatal to Sportsman," June 9, 1929, B3.
2 *Tribune*, Rosalind Shaffer, "Weird Fatality Mars Lives of Valentino Heirs," June 23, 1929, G1.
3 *LA Times*, "Fall is Fatal to Sportsman," June 9, 1929, B3.
4 Soruika, interview.
5 *LA Times*, "Masons in Charge of Johnstone Funeral," June 12, 1929, 8.
6 Kate donated $2.5 million to Phillips Academy.
7 Johnstone, interview.
8 *NY Times*, "Mrs. J. P. Mitchel Wed to Ex-Broker," January 11, 1931, 7.
9 1900 Census records.
10 Delaney, 153.
11 Ibid., 153.
12 County of Los Angeles, California death certificate.
13 *Tribune*, "Death Notices," January 1, 1938, 15.
14 *Tribune*, "Kate Allerton Leaves $200,000 Trust for Son," March 29, 1938. 12. Cook County of Chicago Circuit Clerk probate court records show that she left land and seven farms in Allerton, Illinois, as well as property in Chicago (932-42 Washington Boulevard, at the northwest corner of Washington and Sangamon Streets).
15 Last Will and Testament of Kate Allerton Johnstone.
16 *LA Times*, "Auction Sales," February 20, 1039, 10.

Chapter Seventeen. The Lawai-Kai Years

1 The manager of the hotel was Clifford Kimball.
2 Typically they occupied a second-floor room in a cottage at the Hotel. Apparently the hotel, like so many in those days, only catered to the "proper clientele." JG to HM, from The Farms to Chicago, May 9, 1939. In preparation for a trip that their bookkeeper anticipated taking to Honolulu, John wrote, "we gave Vanderburg Johnstone as reference the first time and you could do the same plus R.A."
3 At 550 square miles, Kauai is Hawaii's third largest island.
4 Theobald, interview, 18 and 98. The island seemed free from liquor, lacking bars, and the Inn itself did not have a liquor license.
5 JGA Speech.
6 Ibid.
7 Theobald, interview, 33. Further research shows that Robert added to his acreage over time, growing to 180 acres.
8 Ibid., 7.
9 *HBGF Newsletter*, January 1965, Volume II, Number 1.
10 JGA Speech.
11 Theobald, interview, 23.
12 Ibid., 41. Today the banyan tree is gone, replaced by a third generation of four statues. Earlier sets of statues became battering rams, smashing against the house when hurricanes in 1982 and 1992 unleashed their power. The tree itself was damaged by a 1950s hurricane.
13 Ibid., 8.
14 Rent on the Astor Street apartment averaged around $200-275 per month.
15 JG to HM, from Lawai Beach on December 16, 1938.
16 Theobald, interview, 65.
17 Becker, interview, 22. Many of their books, worth thousands of dollars, were swept away by hurricanes. The salvaged ones were placed in freezers, and periodically one page at a time was dried by blow dryer.
18 Theobald, interview, 45.
19 The laborers earned $35 per month, or $515 in 2007 funds.
20 Robert cared for Helen like a cherished family member after her health deteriorated from strokes and other health issues, purchasing a home for her and her husband after they were evicted from their apartment.
21 Theobald, interview, 4.
22 Ibid., 39.
23 JGA Speech.
24 Theobald, interview, 72.
25 Ibid., 64 and 68.
26 Ibid., 52, 67, and 88.
27 Ibid., 16.
28 Hanna, 12.
29 According to a prominent botanist, the island's native species numbered originally just above 900, but there are now approximately 1700 different plants, non-native and native mixed together, growing on Kauai.
30 Theobald, interview, 33.

31 Ibid., 63. The reproductions of the *Cupid* statues may have been created by the Chiurazzi foundry in Naples, Italy.
32 Ibid., 37, the Thanksgiving Pavilion, inspired by a Regency doorway John had glimpsed in London, was first designed as a tea house for the Lost Garden at The Farms in Monticello.
33 Ibid., 63.
34 Ibid., 91.
35 RA to HM, February 12, 1942.
36 Theobald, interview, 63. John Gregg Allerton's inspiration for the *Diana* Pavilion came from a book on lost treasures of New England Architecture.
37 Ibid.
38 According to Artnet Online Auctions in January 2009, the *Mermaid* statues were originally commissioned for and exhibited at the Italian Pavilion of the 1931 Exposition Coloniale Internationale (World's Fair) in Paris. Later they were sold to an Italian cruise ship company for their ballroom.
39 Gelernter, photo page.
40 JG to HM, from The Farms on June 20, 1940: "We expect to keep the Italian mermaids when they come for use some place here at the Farms." Also, Theobald, interview, 49.
41 Theobald, interview, 50.
42 Statement by Adolphe Borie, cousin of John J. Borie III, May, 1933. The Hood Museum, Dartmouth College.
43 JG to HM, from Hawaii on August 12, 1942.
44 Theobald, interview, 75.
45 Ibid., 90.

Chapter Eighteen. Robert's Legacy

1 HM to RA on Kauai, February 19, 1941. ($8,000 is equal to $118,000 in 2007 purchasing power, and $2,600 is equivalent to $38,000 in 2007.)
2 Rubano, 9-10. Auer trained at Munich's Woodcarving Trade School and Decorative Arts School, and at the Academy of Fine Arts (formerly the Royal Academy of Fine Arts where Robert Allerton had studied) from 1927-1930.
3 Frank Henseleit, "Der Bildhauer Bernhard Bleeker (1881-1968), Leben und Werk," (Dissertation, Universität Augsburg, 2005.) Auer was the wife of Fritz Mülhäuser, but Henseleit gives no date for the marriage. (Artwork at auction on the Internet does appear under the name Lili Mülhäuser.)
4 "The Fifty-second Annual Exhibition of American Paintings and Sculpture," (Catalogue, Art Institute of Chicago), 29.
5 Rubano, 10-11.
6 Theobald, interview, 92.
7 RA to GS, September 18, 1946.
8 Theobald, interview, 91.
9 Becker, interview, 22.
10 Theobald, interview, 20.
11 Buckingham, interview. Mrs. Noecker and Mrs. Buckingham would do the cleaning.
12 *Tribune*, Edith Weigle, "Allerton Art Collection is Offered Here," October 24, 1946, 29.
13 Robert donated to the Red Cross of Hawaii and Kauai, and gave $500 each to Piatt County's and Chicago's Red Cross.
14 Laurie Lisle, *Portrait of an Artist*, (New York: Washington Square Press, 1986), 303-305.
15 Phone conversation between author and Rick Hanna of The National Tropical Botanical Garden, August 28, 2008.
16 *Tribune*, "Tea Will Mark Anniversary of Hospital Group," January 22, 1950, S4.
17 RA to GS, October, 18, 1951. The four paintings displayed at The Farms cost Robert about $1,000 (2007 purchasing power of $8,000).
18 JG to HM, September 20, 1944.
19 Buckingham, interview.
20 Two years after it changed its adoption law, Illinois became the first state to repeal its sodomy law (1961).
21 Cook, 78.
22 Ibid., 81.
23 Ibid., 70-71.
24 *Tribune*, "Allerton Dies; Benefactor of Art Institute," December 23, 1964, A6.
25 At the time, the Visiting Nurse Association of Chicago's address was 5 South Wabash Avenue, Chicago, Illinois.
26 *American*, Sybil Lillie, "He's Made an Art out of Giving Away Millions," August 12, 1963, page unknown.
27 Ibid.
28 Circuit Clerk of Piatt County, Illinois, decree 65L10. Records indicate that the name change became final on February 26, 1965.
29 *Tribune*, Eleanor Page, "Art Institute Board Reviews 1970," November 11, 1970, D3.
30 JG to WK, December 23, 1970.
31 Mehaffey, 9.
32 Theobald, interview, 93-94.
33 *Gazette*, Lex Peterson, "Adopted Son Says Park Looking Better," March 30, 1980, A6.
34 *IL Magazine*, David Jeffrey Fletcher, "The Building of Allerton Park," May 1979, 12.

Epilogue. What Would Robert Do?

1 Then Governor Walker, Senators Charles Percy and Adlai Stevenson, Congressman Edward Madigan, and University of Illinois Board of Trustees initially supported the Oakley Dam proposal.
2 *Illinois Issues*, Banton, O. T., "Decatur still needs water, and many think there was a good case for Oakley dam,"

May, 1977, 23.

3 Timothy Doyle, of Indiana's Shannon Stone Co., specializes in Indiana limestone work.

4 *Gazette,* Lex Peterson, "Fixing Old Dogs with New Tricks," June 3, 1983, 8. One *Fu Dog* was recovered from a basement in nearby Champaign, Illinois, one from the closet of a young soldier who had been killed in Vietnam, and another when that thief's girlfriend notified police.

5 Ibid., 9.

6 University of Illinois Archives, Muriel Scheinman Papers, 1874-1999. According to Scheinman's notes, the vandalism may have occurred around 1973.

7 *IlliniWeek,* Andrea Lynn, "Restored Buddhas return to Allerton," August 10, 1989, 1.

8 *Gazette,* Melissa Merli, "Chipping Away at the Ravages of Father Time," April 28, 1995, page number unknown. The grant for $14,339 also covered restoration of Lili Auer's *Girl with a Scarf.*

9 Born in 1904, Lili Auer was also an art restorer. Her date of death is unknown, but if she had been alive in 1993, she may not have been able to accomplish the work.

10 The Institute of Museum Services Collections Assessment Program (IMS-CAP) recommended conservation. The University of Illinois received additional funding from IMS to complete the project.

11 Rubano, 18-20.

12 Tinsley's firm in Chicago is Sculpture Sources.

13 *Herald Review,* Huey Freeman, "Stone carver repairs *The Three Graces* at Allerton Park," July 16, 2008. Page unknown.

INDEX

Page numbers in bold indicate illustrations. Photographs in the color section are indicated by **cs**.

Previous page: *Adam* sculpture. Top: Allerton Mansion.
Bottom left: entrance to Allerton Park and Retreat Center.
Bottom right: *Girl with a Scarf.*

The Death of the Last Centaur at Allerton Park.

Primitive Man at Allerton Park.

Top left: *Chinese Musician.*
Top right: *Fu Dog* Garden.
Below: *The Death of the Last Centaur* statue at Allerton Park.

Top: meadow of wildflowers at Allerton Park.
Bottom left: entrance to the Sunken Garden.
Bottom middle: *Golden Buddha* statue.
Bottom right: *Hari-Hara* statue.

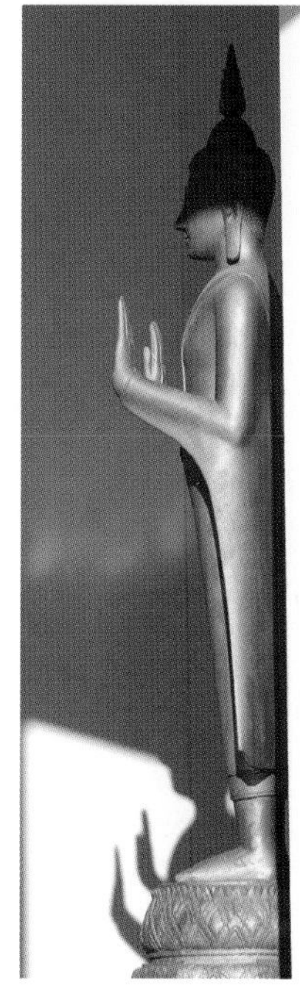

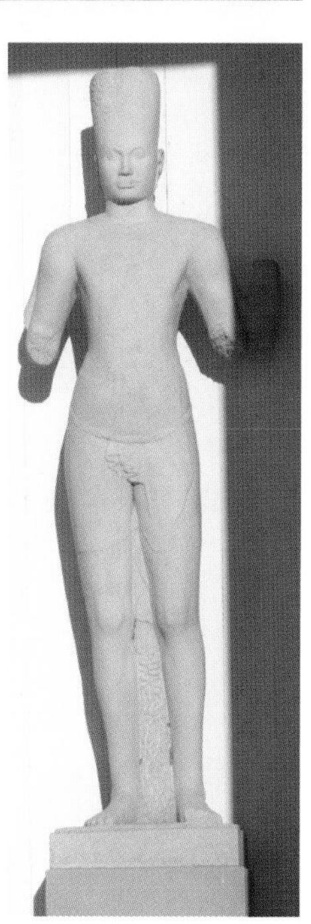

Left: Korean *Fu Dog.*
Below: *The Sun Singer.*

Above: sunset at Lawai-Kai.
Bottom left: *Mermaid* statues and waterway between them.
Bottom right: playful statue in Lawai-Kai *Diana* Pavilion.

Top: Lawai-Kai house with rebuilt Queen Emma's Cottage at far right. Bottom: Buddha statue in bamboo at Lawai-Kai.